D1228510

Guide
to
CHINESE
PHILOSOPHY

The
Asian
Philosophies
and
Religions
Resource
Guides

Guide
to
CHINESE
PHILOSOPHY

CHARLES WEI-HSUN FU
and
WING-TSIT CHAN

G.K.HALL &CO.

70 LINCOLN STREET, BOSTON, MASS.

Copyright © 1978 by Foreign Area Materials Center

Library of Congress Cataloging in Publication Data
Fu, Charles Wei-hsun.
  Guide to Chinese philosophy.

  (An Asian philosophies and religions resource guide)
  Includes index.
  1. Philosophy, Chinese — Bibliography.
I. Chan, Wing-tsit, 1901-   joint author.
II. Title.   III. Series.
Z7129.C5F8   [B126]   016.181'11   78-4670
ISBN 0-8161-7901-8

This publication is printed on permanent/durable acid-free paper
MANUFACTURED IN THE UNITED STATES OF AMERICA

Project on Asian Philosophies and Religions

Sponsoring Organizations

Center for International Programs and Comparative Studies of the New York
State Education Department/University of the State of New York
Council for Intercultural Studies and Programs, Inc.

Steering Committee

Kenneth Morgan	Emeritus, Colgate University
	Chairman
Wing-tsit Chan	Chatham College
	Emeritus, Dartmouth College
David J. Dell	Foreign Area Materials Center
	Columbia University
	Project Manager, 1975-77
Edith Ehrman	Foreign Area Materials Center
	Project Manager, 1971-74
Robert McDermott	Baruch College, City University of New York
Bardwell Smith	Carleton College
H. Daniel Smith	Syracuse University
Frederick J. Streng	Southern Methodist University

Preparation of this series of guides to resources for the study of Asian philosophies and religions was made possible by a grant from the National Endowment for the Humanities, supplemented through the Endowment's matching funds scheme, with additional financial support from the Ada Howe Kent Foundation, C. T. Shen, and the Council on International and Public Affairs, Inc. None of the above bodies is responsible for the content of these guides which is the responsibility of those listed on the title page.

This project has been undertaken by the Foreign Area Materials Center, State Education Department, University of the State of New York, under the auspices of the Council for Intercultural Studies and Program, 60 East 42nd Street, New York, NY 10017.

IN MEMORY OF
EDITH EHRMAN
1932-1974

Straightway I was 'ware
So weeping, how a mystic shape did move
Behind me, and drew me backward by the hair
And a voice said in mastery while I strove, . . .
'Guess now who holds thee? — 'Death', I said, but there
The silver answer rang . . . 'Not Death, but Love.'

Elizabeth Barrett Browning

Contents

Contents

Contents

Contents

Contents

Contents

Contents

Contents

Contents

Contents

Contents

Contents

Contents

Contents

Series Preface

This guide is one of a series of books on resources for the study of Asian philosophies and religions. The series includes volumes on Chinese, Indian, Islamic, and Buddhist philosophies and religions. Since the preparation of the series has been undertaken as a contribution to advancing humanistic learning in America, it is important to place the study of these traditions in that larger context.

Humanistic scholarship and teaching in America has understandably concentrated on Western civilization of which we are a part. Yet Western civilization has historically drawn significantly upon the humanistic accomplishments of other traditions and has interacted with these traditions. Given the increasing mobility of scholars and students in the second half of the twentieth century and the rapidly advancing technological capacity for communicating ideas in the modern world, this interaction is accelerating as we approach the twenty-first century.

Liberal education for American students in the 1970's and 1980's must reflect not only our human heritage in all of its diversity as it has accumulated through past centuries, but also the nature of the future in its intellectual and cultural as well as economic, social and political dimensions. By the year 2000, a logical future reference point for today's college students who will spend most of their adult lives in the next century, four out of five human beings will live in the "Third World" of Asia, Africa, and Latin America about which we study least in our colleges and universities today.

Numerical distribution of humanity is certainly not the only criterion which should determine the content of humanistic learning in our institutions of higher education. But when orders of magnitude achieve the proportions which, according to most demographic projections, will exist in the year 2000, geographical location of humanity is certainly one criterion which will be applied by today's students in assessing the "relevance" of their undergraduate education to the real world of the future.

The argument becomes all the more compelling when the qualitative aspects of civilizations other than our own are considered. Western man can claim no corner on creative accomplishment, as Herbert Muller has rightly recognized in this passage from The Uses of the Past.

> Stick to Asia, and we get another elementary lesson in humility. Objectively its history looks more important than the history of Europe....It has produced more civilizations, involving a much greater proportion of mankind, over a longer period of time, on a higher level of continuity. As for cultural achievement, we have no universal yardstick; but by one standard on which Western Christendom has prided itself, Asia has been far more creative. It has bred all the higher religions, including Christianity.*

There is little doubt that the rapid growth of student interest in the study of these traditions is the result in part of their search for new value systems in contemporary society. But this interest is also a recognition of other civilizations as being intrinsically worthy of our attention.

Origins of the Project on Asian Philosophies and Religions

The project was initiated in response to this growth of student interest, which began in the 1960's and has persisted in the 1970's, notwithstanding a current general decline in the exponential growth rates in American colleges and universities. Faculty members with specialized training in Asian philosophical and religious traditions, however, are still limited in number and most courses in these subjects are being taught by non-specialists. While the proportion of those with specialized training has certainly increased in recent years, the situation is unlikely to improve greatly due to the ceilings on faculty size which many institutions have imposed because of financial stringency.

The need for a series of authoritative guides to literature in these fields for use in both undergraduate and beginning graduate study of Asian philosophies and religions, which first prompted us to seek support from the National Endowment for the Humanities for the project in 1971, remains just as compelling as the project draws to a close.

Organization of the Project

The project on Asian philosophies and religions was conceived from the beginning as a cooperative venture involving scholars and teachers of these subjects. The key element in the organization of the project

---

*The Uses of the Past, New York: New American Library, 1954, p. 314.

has been the project team or working group, a deliberately informal structure with its own leader, working autonomously but within a general conceptual framework developed early in the project by all of those who were involved in the project at that time.

The individual working groups have been linked together by a project steering committee, which has been concerned with the overall organization and implementation of the project. The members of the project steering committee, working group leaders, and other key project personnel are as follows:

Kenneth Morgan, Emeritus, Colgate University (Chairman of the Project Steering Committee)

Wing-tsit Chan, Chatham College and Emeritus, Dartmouth College (Member, Project Steering Committee; Leader of Working Group on Chinese Philosophy and Religion)

Bardwell Smith, Carleton College (Member, Project Steering Committee and Working Group on Buddhist Religion)

H. Daniel Smith, Syracuse University (Member, Project Steering Committee and Working Group on Hinduism)

Robert McDermott, Baruch College, City University of New York (Member, Project Steering Committee and the Working Group on Hinduism)

Thomas Hopkins, Franklin and Marshall College (Leader of the Working Group of Hinduism)

David Ede, Western Michigan University and McGill University (Leader of the Working Group on Islamic Religion)

Karl Potter, University of Washington (Leader of the Working Group on Indian Philosophy)

Frank Reynolds, University of Chicago (Leader of the Working Group on Buddhist Religion)

Kenneth Inada, State University of New York at Buffalo (Leader of the Working Group on Buddhist Philosophy)

Frederick J. Streng, Southern Methodist University (Member, Project Steering Committee and Working Groups on Buddhist Religion and Philosophy)

David Dell (Project Manager, 1975-77 and a Member of the Working Group on Hinduism)

Two characteristics of the project's organization merit mention. One has been the widespread use of other scholars and teachers, in addition to the members of the project steering committee and working groups, in the critical review of preliminary versions of the guides. Reviewers were asked to comment on both commissions and omissions, and their comments were used by the compilers in making revisions. A far more extensive exercise than the customary scholarly review of manuscripts, this process involved well over 200 individuals who contributed immeasurably to improving the quality of the end product.

A similar effort to enlarge participation in the project has been made through discussions at professional meetings about the project among interested scholars and teachers while it was in progress. Over the past four years a dozen such sessions, involving over 300 participants, have been held at both national and regional meetings of the American Academy of Religion and the Association for Asian Studies.

The Classification Scheme and Criteria of Selection for the Guide

Early in the project a conference of most of the key project personnel mentioned above, as well as other members of the project working groups, was held in New York City in June 1972 to develop a common classification scheme and criteria for inclusion of materials in the resource guides.

This task generated lively and intense debate because underlying any classification scheme are the most fundamental issues of conceptualization and periodization in the study of religious and philosophical traditions. The classification schemes for guides in religion and in philosophy have generally been followed by each working group, although there have been inevitable variations. Each of the traditions included in the project has distinctive qualities and characteristics which make it difficult to fit all aspects of all traditions into the same set of categories.

The objective of developing a common set of categories was to facilitate examination of parallel phenomena across traditions. We believe this objective has been at least partially achieved through this series, although we recognize the need for continued refinement before a common set of categories compatible with all the traditions being covered can be evolved.

If developing categories to span diverse religious and philosophical traditions has been difficult, definition and reasonably uniform application of criteria for inclusion of material in the guides has been no easier. The project's basic objective, as originally elaborated at the June 1972 working conference, has been to provide an authoritative guide to the literature, both texts in translation and commentary and analysis, for teachers and advanced undergraduate and beginning graduate students who are not specialized scholars with access to primary texts in their original languages. Because of the limited number of teachers in American colleges and universities who have the necessary language skills, particularly outside their own primary field of scholarly interest, it was expected that the guides would be useful to those teaching in the field who, even though they might have a high level of scholarly specialization on one tradition, would often find it necessary to deal with other traditions in their teaching.

We also sought to achieve some consistency in annotations of entries in the guides. The objective has been to provide short, crisp, critical annotations which would help the user of the guide in identifying material pertinent to his or her interest or most authoritative in its coverage of a particular topic. We recognize, of course, that we have not achieved this objective throughout the entire series of guides encompassing more than 12,000 individual entries.

Because of the difficulties in applying a common set of categories and subcategories to the diverse traditions being covered by the guides, not all categories have been covered in each guide, and in some cases, they have been grouped together as seemed appropriate to the characteristics of a particular tradition. Extensive cross-referencing has been provided to guide the user to related entries in other categories.

The Problem of Availability of Resources in the Guide and the Microform Resource Bank

We realized from the beginning that a series of guides of this character would have little value if the users could not acquire materials listed in the guides. We therefore sought the cooperation of the Institute for the Advanced Studies of World Religions, which is engaged in a major effort to develop a collection of resources for the study of world religions in microform, and through the Institute, have established a microform resource bank of material in the guides not readily available from other sources.

Subject to the availability of the material for microfilming and depending upon its copyright status, the Institute is prepared to provide in microform any item included in any of the guides out-of-print or otherwise not readily available, in accordance with its usual schedule of charges. Where an item is already included in the Institute's microform collection, those charges are quite modest, and an effort is being made by the Institute to increase its holding of materials in the guides. Material can also be provided in hard xerographic copy suitable for reproduction for multiple classroom use at an additional charge.

Under the terms of a project agreement with the Institute, the Institute is undertaking the microfilming of some 30,000 pages of material included in these guides. In addition, the Institute already has in its microform collection a substantial number of titles in the fields of Buddhist and Chinese philosophy and religion.

The Institute will from time to time issue lists of material in microform from the guides available in its collections, but as its microform collections are continually being expanded, users are urged to contact the Institute directly to see if a particular title in which they are interested is available:

> Institute for Advanced Studies of World Religions
> Melville Memorial Library
> State University of New York
> Stony Brook, New York 11794

Acknowledgments

An undertaking of this scope and magnitude, involving such wide-spread participation, is bound to accumulate a long list of those who have contributed in one way or another to the project. It would be impossible to identify by name all of those who have contributed, and it is hoped that those who are not so identified will nonetheless recognize themselves in the categories which follow and understand that their help, interest, and support are also appreciated.

To begin with, primary thanks must be extended to the members of the project steering committee, the leaders of the various project working groups, and the members of each of the groups. Those responsible for each guide in the series are separately listed on the title page of that volume.

Thanks should also be expressed to the large number of scholars and teachers who served as critical reviewers of preliminary versions of the guides and the many who participated in sessions at regional and national meetings where the guides were subject to further scrutiny and where many constructive suggestions for their improvement were made.

We wish to acknowledge with grateful thanks the generous financial support of the National Endowment for the Humanities, and through its matching fund scheme, additional support from the Ada Howe Kent Foundation, C.T. Shen, and Council for International and Public Affairs, Inc. The patience and understanding of the Endowment's Education Division during the long and protracted period of completion of this project has been particularly noteworthy.

Many institutions have provided support to the project indirectly by making possible participation of their faculty in the various project working groups. In addition, both the South Asia Center at Columbia University and the Institute for Advanced Studies of World Religions have provided special assistance.

Series Preface

The project has been undertaken under the auspices of the Council for Intercultural Studies and Programs by the Foreign Area Materials Center, a project office of the Center for International Programs and Comparative Studies, State Education Department, University of the State of New York. The last-named institution, acting as the agent of the Council for Intercultural Studies and Programs, has been responsible for administering the National Endowment for Humanities grant and other financial support received for the project and has contributed extensively out of its own resources throughout the project, particularly in the concluding months, to assure its proper completion. Without the interest and support of key officials in the Center for International Programs and the New York State Education Department, the project could not have been completed.

A particular word of appreciation is in order for Norman Abramowitz of the Center, who succeeded me as Project Director after my resignation from the directorship of the Center in October, 1976 and to whom fell the unenviable task of overcoming administrative and financial obstacles in the final months of the project. Appreciation should also be expressed to G.K. Hall and Company, the publishers of this series, and to Barbara Garrey, the editor. Their forebearance, as the manuscripts have been completed over a far longer time than we anticipated, has been exemplary.

Last but certainly not least are the project managers who have carried responsibility from day to day for implementing the project. Perhaps the most difficult and demanding role has been played by David J. Dell who came into the project at mid-stream and who has been struggling ever since to assure its orderly completion, including final preparation of the series of guides for publication.

Different, but in many ways no less difficult, was the task confronting the interim project director, Josephine Case, whose services were kindly made available to the project by the New York Public Library in 1974 and 1975. She responded with dignity and sensitivity to the demands of this task.

But in many ways the most important figure in the project is one who is no longer with us. Edith Ehrman was the Manager of the Foreign Area Materials Center from its inception in 1963, a key figure in the conceptualization of this project, and its manager from the beginning until her untimely death in November, 1974. She was the moving spirit behind the project during its first three years. It is to her memory that this series of guides is dedicated by all those involved in the project who witnessed the extraordinary display of courage borne of her love of life during her last difficult illness.

Ward Morehouse, President
Council for Intercultural Studies
and Programs

Preface

Guide to Chinese Philosophy is one of the series of Guides to
Resources for the Study of Asian Philosophies and Religions prepared
as part of the Asian Philosophies and Religions Project of the Council
for Intercultural Studies and Programs, undertaken by the Foreign
Area Materials Center, University of the State of New York/State
Education Department.

Prior to our actual work we were advised by the Steering Committee
that our bibliographical guide was to serve as a teaching and research
aid to college instructors and students in philosophy and/or religion,
although it was also our hope that sinological scholars and students
might find our Guide useful. It was also understood that our bibliographical work was to limit its sources chiefly to the English
language. Where appropriate, however, we have added some important
French and German language material.

According to the Asian Philosophies and Religions Project categories, which were set up as basic guidelines for all the bibliographical projects concerned, there are nineteen categories for
philosophy. We have followed these guidelines with only one excep-
tion: the category "Paths of Liberation" is missing in our Guide,
since we feel that this category does not apply properly to Chinese
Philosophy. We have also found that while some categories, such as
"Theory of Human Nature" or "Ethics," are extremely important in
studies of Chinese Philosophy, other categories like "Philosophy of
Science" are less significant. This judgment has, of course, affected
our decision on the matter of the number of entries to be included
under each category.

Under Professor Chan's supervision, I have taken the primary
responsibility for the topical classification in Chinese philosophy
under each philosophical category. We make no claim that our
topical classification is complete or perfect, and we certainly wel-
come suggestions or comments from users for any future revision.
We acknowledge for example, that under the category "Comparisons,"
there is no real justification for the exclusion of topics such as
"T'ien-t'ai and Hua-yen" or "Comparison with Indian Philosophy,"

while at the same time including topics like "Hua-yen, Zen and Neo-Confucian Philosophy," and "Comparison with Western Philosophy." Another example is the nonexistence of the topics concerning the development of Neo-Confucian Philosophy during the Yuan period. One important explanation is that these topics have not yet been studied or explored systematically, and it is, therefore, very difficult to find English publications dealing with such "cold" topics at the present time. In this respect at least, our Guide is like a sinological mirror reflecting to a great extent current sinological scholarship as well as current scholarly contributions in Chinese philosophy in the English-speaking world. In this sense our Guide can be considered a good "negative teacher," to quote Mao's term.

Current availability of publications in the areas concerned has also affected our decision regarding inclusion. For example, despite the fact that the category "Authoritative Texts and Their Philosophical Significances" is one of the most important subjects in Confucian Philosophy, we found very few English publications dealing with this subject. We would hope that the task of systematic translation of the Chinese works on this subject can be undertaken in the near future.

The Guide to Chinese Philosophy clearly indicates that we need more sinological and philosophical works in many areas of Chinese philosophy. One conspicuous example is that the Neo-Confucian philosophy of Wang Fu-chih (1619-1692), which is philosophically as rich and deep as Chu Hsi's, has not yet been studied systematically nor understood well in the West. Another interesting example is that no complete works on Chuang Tzu or the Neo-Taoist philosophy of Wang Pi and Kuo Hsiang have been published in the English language, in spite of the Western interest in and familiarity with both Taoism and Neo-Taoism. It is only after we, in the English-speaking world, are able to explore Chinese philosophy and its historical development as fully as we have studied Western philosophy, that we can expect a genuine breakthrough in the current comparative studies of Chinese and Western philosophy. As this Guide has tried to show, we are presently on the way to such a creative philosophical dialogue between Chinese and Western thinkers.

Our Guide is not meant to be a comprehensive or exhaustive one; we owe, nonetheless, an apology to those authors whose books or articles in the field of Chinese philosophy are not mentioned--sometimes inadvertently--in this Guide. In particular, it was too late for us to include newest publications, such as Francis H. Cook's Hua-yen Buddhism: The Jewel Net of Indra (Pennsylvania State University Press, 1977), Paul J. Lin's A Translation of Lao Tzu's Tao Te Ching and Wang Pi's Commentary (Center for Chinese Studies, University of Michigan, 1977), or Ariane Rump's translation, in collaboration with Wing-tsit Chan, of Wang Pi's Commentary on the Lao Tzu (Society for Asian and Comparative Philosophy monograph, forthcoming). We sincerely hope that many more entries will be added and annotated in the second edition of the Guide. In this connection, we would like to suggest to the readers that they also make use of Guide to Chinese Religion and Guide to Buddhist Philosophy, both to be published by G. K. Hall, for the simple reason that Chinese philosophy and Chinese religion are often inseparable and that Buddhist philosophy covers Chinese (Mahayana) Buddhist philosophy.

In addition to his supervisory work, Professor Wing-tsit Chan's contribution toward the completion of this Guide has equalled mine. Professor Chan has requested, however, that the alphabetic order be ignored and that my name appear before his. He also insisted that I write this preface to the Guide. I take this opportunity to express my heartful thanks for the human-kindness (jen) of Professor Chan, my mentor in Chinese philosophy.

Both Professor Chan and I would like to extend our sincere thanks to Far Eastern Publications, Yale University, for permission to adapt approximately 100 annotations from Professor Wing-tsit Chan's An Outline and an Annotated Bibliography of Chinese Philosophy, which was published in 1969. We should also express our deep appreciation to Barbara Garrey and her staff of G. K. Hall & Co., for their meticulous and patient work on the preliminary and final manuscripts of our Guide to Chinese Philosophy.

Charles Wei-hsun Fu

Temple University
Philadelphia

1. History of Chinese Philosophy

1.1 GENERAL OVERVIEWS

CHAN, WING-TSIT. "Chinese Philosophy," in The New Encyclopaedia
Britannica (Macropaedia). 15th ed. 1975. Vol. 4, pp. 415-421.
A comprehensive account of the historical development of Chinese
philosophy, including classical philosophical schools, Confucianism,
Neo-Confucianism, Marxism in Mao's China, etc.

CHENG, CHUNG-YING. "Chinese Philosophy: A Characterization," in
Inquiry, 14 (1971): 113-137.
This article attempts a synthetic characterization of Chinese
philosophy based on an analytical reconstruction of its main traditions and thinking. Four characteristics of Chinese philosophy are
presented: intrinsic humanism, concrete rationalism, organic
naturalism, and a pragmatism of self-cultivation.

FU, CHARLES WEI-HSUN. "Confucianism and Taoism," in Historical Atlas
of the Religions of the World. Ed. by Ismáil Rāgī al Fārūqī. New
York: Macmillan, 1974. Pp. 109-125.
A philosophical account of the distinction between "the Great
Tradition" and "the Little Tradition," of the historical development
of both Confucian and Taoist philosophy, as well as of Taoist
religion.

KOLLER, JOHN M. Oriental Philosophies. New York: Scribner, 1970.
303 pp., esp. pp. 197-278.
An interesting elementary survey of Chinese philosophy. Topics
include basic characteristics of Chinese philosophies, historical
perspectives, Confucianism, Taoism, Neo-Confucianism, and Mao
Tse-tung.

MOORE, CHARLES A., ed. The Chinese Mind: Essentials of Chinese
Philosophy and Culture. Honolulu: East-West Center Press and
University of Hawaii Press, 1967. P. 402.
Seven essays on Chinese philosophy include: Wing-tsit Chan's
"Chinese Theory and Practice, with Special Reference to Humanism,"
Hu Shih's "The Scientific Spirit and Method in Chinese Philosophy,"

Hsieh Yu-wei's "Filial Piety and Chinese Society," John Wu's
"Chinese Legal and Political Philosophy," and T'ang Chun-i's "The
Development of Ideas of Spiritual Value in Chinese Philosophy."
There are also five essays on the individual.

1.2 PRE-CONFUCIAN AND TRADITIONAL ELEMENTS

1.2.1 Historical Factors

CHAN, WING-TSIT, tr. and comp. A Source Book in Chinese
Philosophy. New Jersey: Princeton University Press, 1963.
856 pp.
  Chapter 1 is a philosophical treatment of the growth of
humanism in the pre-Confucian.

CREEL, HERRLEE G. Chinese Thought from Confucius to Mao
Tse-tung. Chicago: University of Chicago Press, 1953.
293 pp.
  Chapter 2 deals with social and political conditions, the
role of aristocrats, and the concept of Mandate of Heaven
before Confucius.

de BARY, WM. THEODORE, WING-TSIT CHAN, and BURTON WATSON,
comps. Sources of Chinese Tradition. New York: Columbia
University Press, 1960. 967 pp.
  Well chosen and newly translated selections on various
phases of Chinese civilization. Chapter 1 deals with the
Chinese tradition in antiquity.

DUBS, HOMER H. "The Archaic Royal Jou Religion," in T'oung
Pao, 46 (1959): 218-259. Revised slightly as "Theism and
Naturalism in Ancient Chinese Philosophy," in Philosophy
East and West, 9 (1959-1960): 163-172.
  Traces the development of the concepts of Shang-ti (Lord
on High) and T'ien (Heaven) in the early Chou Dynasty and
Confucius' belief in heaven and spiritual beings.

FUNG YU-LAN. A History of Chinese Philosophy. Tr. by Derk
Bodde. Princeton, New Jersey: Princeton University Press
1952-53. 2 vols. Vol. 1, 455 pp. Vol. 2, 783 pp.
  Thus far the best treatment of the subject in the English
language. Chapter 3 of Vol. 1 gives a good discussion of
the philosophical and religious thought prior to Confucius
in terms of divine beings, divination and magic, heaven and
God, beginnings of enlightenment, and the rise of
rationalism.

LIU, SHU-HSIEN. "The Religious Import of Confucian Philosophy: Its Traditional Outlook and Contemporary Significance," in Philosophy East and West, 21 (1971): 157-175.
Liu traces the development of the Confucian religious attitude and points out its general characteristics, as well as discussing its contemporary significance with reference to the current development of theology and religious philosophy in the West.

MOTE, FREDERICK W. Intellectual Foundations of China. New York: Knopf, 1971. 135 pp.
Aside from special chapters on early Confucianism, early Taoism, and Mo Tzu, the chapters on the beginning of a world view, chiefly the Book of Changes, and the problem of knowledge involving various ancient philosophers are well-organized and informative.

THOMPSON, LAURENCE G. Chinese Religion: An Introduction. Belmont, Cal: Dickenson Publishing Co., 1969. 119 pp.
A clear and readable account of Chinese religious history. Chapter 2 deals with proto-science and animistic religion, and chapter 3 deals with ancient Chinese conceptions of the family (kindred and ancestors). Both chapters are useful for the preliminary understanding of the pre-Confucian elements in historical perspective.

YANG, C.K. Religion in Chinese Society: A Study of Contemporary Social Functions of Religion and Some of Their Historical Factors. Berkeley: University of California Press, 1961. 473 pp.
Probably the best work on Chinese popular religions in almost all respects from the sociological point of view, based on highly reliable sources, primary or secondary. The historical factors of the pre-Confucian cult are discussed in various places in the book.

1.2.2 Early Beliefs and Concepts

BODDE, DERK. "Harmony and Conflict in Chinese Philosophy," in Studies in Chinese Thought. Ed. by Arthur F. Wright. Chicago: University of Chicago Press, 1953. Pp. 19-80.
Highly recommended for a general view of Chinese ideas on cosmic pattern, history, social harmony, the sage, etc.

CREEL, HERRLEE G. "The Origin of the Deity T'ien," in his The Origins of Statecraft in China, I: The Western Chou Empire. Chicago: University of Chicago Press, 1970. Pp. 493-506.

3

Creel believes that from a consideration of Chinese characters in the oracle bones it can be argued that T'ien was
not a deity of the Shang (1751-1112 B.C.) people, but was of
Chou (1111-249 B.C.) origin, and that the meaning of t'ien
evolved from that of man to important man to king to lord
and finally to a deity.

FUNG YU-LAN. A History of Chinese Philosophy. Cross
reference: 1.2.1.

MEI, Y.P. "The Basis of Social, Ethical, and Spiritual Values
in Chinese Philosophy," in Essays in East-West Philosophy.
Ed. by Charles A. Moore. Honolulu: University of Hawaii
Press, 1951. Pp. 301-316. Reprinted in Moore, ed. The
Chinese Mind. Honolulu: University of Hawaii Press, 1967.
Pp. 149-166.
A general survey of the teachings on moral and spiritual
values in Confucius, Mencius, Mo Tzu, Lao Tzu, Chuang Tzu,
and some Neo-Confucianists.

MUNRO, DONALD J. The Concept of Man in Early China.
Stanford: Stanford University Press, 1969. 256 pp.
A good account of the subject from the standpoint of comparative philosophy. Weak in less reliance on primary
sources. The basic beliefs and concepts in the pre-Confucian
period are treated in the light of the development of the
concept of man in early Confucianism and Taoism.

SHIH, JOSEPH. "The Notions of God in the Ancient Chinese
Religion," in Numen, 16 (1969): 13-16.
A short but interesting account of various notions of God
in ancient China.

SMITH, D.H. Chinese Religions. New York: Holt, Rinehart and
Winston, 1968. 222 pp.
An introductory work on Chinese religions. Chapters 1 and
2 deal with both the historical factors and the basic beliefs and concepts of the pre-Confucian cult such as ming
(mandate, fate), Shang-ti (Lord-on-High), T'ien (Heaven),
dragon, filial piety, tsu (ancestor), shamanism, etc.

T'ANG CHUN-I. "Cosmologies in Ancient Chinese Philosophy,"
in Chinese Studies in Philosophy, 5 (1973): 4-47.
The subject is discussed under 8 headings: (1) cosmologies
in Western philosophy and science; (2) Chinese cosmologies:
law as immanent rather than transcendent; (3) the life
principle; (4) the nothingness and substantiveness principle;
(5) space and time; (6) unity and inseparability of principle,

form, and number; (7) value as immanent in Nature; (8) a
comparison of Confucianism, Taoism, Legalism, and the Yin
Yang school in cosmology. Unquestionably the most comprehensive and authoritative article on the subject.

_____. "The Development of the Chinese Humanistic Spirit,"
in Chinese Studies in Philosophy, 4 (1974): 39-71.
    Section headings are: (a) Humanistic, Nonhumanistic, Super-
humanistic, Subhumanistic, and Antihumanistic Concepts;
(b) The Origin of Chinese Humanism; (c) The Humanism of Confucius and Mencius, the Subhumanism of Mo Tzu, the Super-
humanism of Chuang Tzu, and the Antihumanism of the Legalists; (d) The Han People's Historical Spirit of Understanding
Changes in the Past and Present; (e) The Natural Display of
Feelings Valued by the Wei and Chin Dynasties; (f) The Rise
of the Superhumanistic Thought of Buddhism; (g) The Spirit
of Establishing the Human Ultimate in Sung-Ming Neo-
Confucianism; (h) The Accentuation of the Culture of the
Ch'ing Dynasty on Cultural Relics, Philological Studies, and
the Meeting of Cultural and Natural Realms; (i) The Reason
Why Contemporary Antihumanistic Marxism-Leninism Conquered
the Chinese Mainland; (j) The Future Development that
Chinese Humanism Should Undergo.

_____. "The T'ien-ming (Heavenly Ordinance) in Pre-Ch'in
China," in Philosophy East and West, 11 (1962): 195-218 and
12 (1962): 29-49.
    A thorough and scholarly investigation of the notion of
Heavenly Ordinance in the ancient classics as well as in the
teachings of early Confucianism, Taoism, and Moism.

YANG, C.K. Religion in Chinese Society. Cross reference:
    1.2.1.

1.3 EARLY CONFUCIANISM

FU, CHARLES WEI-HSUN. "Fingarette and Munro on Early Confucianism: A
    Methodological Examination." Philosophy East and West, 28, no. 2
    (April 1978): 181-198.
    Critically examines the two recent American interpretations of
early Confucianism in Fingarette's Confucius (1972) and Munro's
The Concept of Man in Early China (1969), by focusing on three
interrelated topics: (1) the essential nature and philosophical
implications of the moral way founded by Confucius, (2) the Confucian controversy over human nature in relation to everyday socio-
moral practice, and (3) the problem of apostolic succession to
Confucian orthodoxy.

LIU, SHU-HSIEN. "The Religious Import of Confucian Philosophy: Its
  Traditional Outlook and Contemporary Significance." Cross
  reference: 1.2.1.

MEI, Y.P. "Confucianism," in The New Encyclopaedia Britannica
  (Macropaedia). 15th ed. 1975. Vol. 4, pp. 1091-1099.
    A general survey of Confucianism under three headings: Patterns
  of Confucian thought, Basic concepts of Confucianism, and Influence
  of Confucianism.

PULLEYBLANK, EDWIN G. "History of Confucianism," in The New Encyclopaedia Britannica (Macropaedia). 15th ed. 1975. Vol. 4,
  pp. 1099-1103.
    This article presents the history of Confucianism, the character-
  istic philosophy and ethical teaching of China, from its archaic
  prelude up to the present time.

1.3.1 Confucius (551-479 B.C.)

See also 3.3, 15.1, 15.14.

The Analects of Confucius. Tr. by Arthur Waley. London:
    Allen and Unwin, 1938. 268 pp.
      A complete translation of the Analects with an introduc-
    tory essay, footnotes, interpretations, biographical dates,
    and additional notes. The translation demonstrates the
    author's solid scholarship in Chinese classics. His sensi-
    tivity to various nuances of the Chinese original is much
    appreciated.

CHAN, WING-TSIT. A Source Book in Chinese Philosophy. Cross
    reference: 1.1.1, chapter 2.

"Confucian Analects." Tr. by James Legge in The Chinese
    Classics. Oxford, Eng.: Clarendon Press, 1893. Vol. 1,
    pp. 137-354.
      A pioneer and solid translation, though a little dated,
    of the complete Analects, with a scholarly interpretation
    heavily relying on that of Chu Hsi, the Neo-Confucian
    synthesizer. Legge's lifelong sinological work, as exhibited
    in this translation, is indeed a great milestone in the
    history of the English translation and interpretation of
    Chinese classics.

CREEL, HERRLEE G. Chinese Thought. (See 1.2.1), pp. 10-24.
      Explains how Confucius departed from traditional patterns
    and offered innovative ideas on the gentleman, education,
    religious sacrifice, the nature of man, etc. There is also

1. History of Chinese Philosophy

a good discussion of Confucius' position in religion and whether Confucian political doctrines are democratic. Very brief on Buddhism and Neo-Confucianism.

_____. Confucius, the Man and the Myth. New York: John Day, 1949. 363 pp. Also published as Confucius and the Chinese Way. New York: Harper Torchbooks.
An excellent work on what is real and what is mythical (legendary) about Confucius, based on authentic sources.

FINGARETTE, HERBERT. Confucius--the Secular as Sacred. New York: Harper & Row, 1972. 84 pp.
A very insightful approach to Confucius and his teachings in the Analects, with a special view to exploring its application and meaning to our own time.

FUNG YU-LAN. A History of Chinese Philosophy. (See 1.2.1), Vol. 1.
Chapter 4 gives a very comprehensive and philosophical account of almost all aspects of Confucius' teachings. The unique position of Confucius in the history of Chinese philosophy is particularly stressed. Highly recommended for a good understanding of Confucius and the rise of early Confucianism.

_____. A Short History of Chinese Philosophy. Ed. by Derk Bodde. New York: Macmillan, 1948. 368 pp.
Chapter 4 discusses Confucius, the first teacher, and his ethical humanism in a clear outline.

HU SHIH. "Der Ursprung der Ju und ihre Beziehung zu Konfuzius und Lao-dsi." Tr. by von Wolfgang Franke in Sinica Sonder-ausgabe, 1935, pp. 141-171 and 1936, pp. 10-24.
On the basis of strong historical and documentary evidence, Dr. Hu argues that Confucius, originally a ju, "the weak," transformed his school and made it the ju of the strong. Hu also argues vigorously and with much historical support that Confucius was a contemporary of Lao Tzu.

HUGHES, E.R. Chinese Philosophy in Classic Times. London: J.M. Dent & Sons, 1942. 356 pp.
Aside from various aspects of Confucius and his teachings, there is a long discussion on Confucius' discovery of the self-conscious moral individual and his preoccupation with and careful study of this individual on pp. 12-20.

KAIZUKA, SHIGEKI. Confucius. Tr. from the Japanese by Geoffrey Bowns. New York: Macmillan, 1956. 193 pp.

A fairly accurate and readable account of the life and times of Confucius under the headings of (a) the age of Confucius, (b) the early days of Confucius, (c) Confucius and his predecessors, (d) the views of Confucius, and (e) Confucius the statesman.

KUAN FENG and LIN YÜ-SHIH. "Third Discussion on Confucius," in Chinese Studies in Philosophy, 2 (1971): 246-263.
   Discussions are under the topics of "Opposition to the Usurpation of Chou Rites by the Grandees," "Rites and Music Emanate from the Son of Heaven," "Using the Duke of Chou's (d. 1094 B.C.) Code to Oppose the Chi Family's Land Tax," "Using the Chou Rites to Oppose Ch'in's Casting of Vessels Inscribed with the Penal Law," and "Rites do not Extend Down to the Common People." The authors conclude that Confucius' doctrine of rules of propriety meant that rites were not really applicable to all.

LIN YUTANG. The Wisdom of Confucius. New York: Random House, 1942. 290 pp.
   A good, if not always philosophically accurate, translation of the Analects of Confucius, as well as the Doctrine of the Mean and the Great Learning, selected and arranged in accordance with (a) central harmony, (b) ethics and politics, (c) aphorisms of Confucius, (d) education, (e) music, (f) social order, and (g) the Six Classics. Some translations of the Book of Mencius are also included, and Ssu-ma Ch'ien's (145-86 B.C.?) famous biography of Confucius is also translated in chapter 2.

LIU, WU-CHI. Confucius: His Life and Time. New York: Philosophical Library, 1956. 189 pp.
   By using stories and anecdotes, the author describes the life and times of Confucius. A good reading for beginning students.

RUBIN, VITALY A. Individual and State in Ancient China: Essays on Four Chinese Philosophers. New York: Columbia University Press, 1976. 149 pp.
   Confucius is presented in terms of tradition and human personality, Mo Tzu as attacker of culture and advocate of the supremacy of the state, Shang Yang as the founder and the most important representative of Legalism, and Chuang Tzu as the key figure in Taoism with quotations from Lao Tzu only incidentally.

WU, JOHN. "The Real Confucius," in T'ien Hsia Monthly, 1 (1935): 11-20, 180-189.

Confucius is described as an essentially human being, filially pious to his mother, humorous, struggling hard throughout life, etc.

1.3.2 Mencius (372–289 B.C.?)

See also 2.1, 2.5.1, 15.3.

FUNG YU-LAN. A History of Chinese Philosophy. (See 1.2.1), Vol. 1, chapter 6.
   A more elaborate, though earlier than the below-mentioned, treatment of Mencius and his school. Mencius' Confucian mission as well as his position in the history of Chinese philosophy is clearly pointed out. See chapter 6.

_____. A Short History of Chinese Philosophy. (See 1.3.1).
   Chapter 7 deals with Mencius' idealistic teachings in terms of the goodness of human nature, fundamental differences between Confucianism and Moism, political philosophy, and mysticism. Very philosophical and well written.

GRAHAM, A.C. "The Background of the Mencian Theory of Human Nature," in Tsing Hua Journal of Chinese Studies, n.s., 6, 1–2 (1967): 215–274.
   The chief points made here are that before Mencius hsing (nature) was understood in the sense of life and not human nature and that the focus of discussion was not whether human nature is good or evil but how to nourish the nature and preserve life, thus suggesting that the usual interpretation of Mencius' theory of original goodness of human nature may not be truthful.

LAU, D.C. "On Mencius's Use of the Method of Analogy in Argument," in Asia Major, n.s., 10 (1963): 133–194.
   On the basis of Mencius' own words (4A:17 and 6A:1–5), Lau demonstrates how skillfully Mencius employed analogy to sharpen the philosophical issues, such as human nature and social behavior, on which he was attacking his opponents. See also Lau's comparison of Mencius with Hsün Tzu (1.3.3).

Mencius. Tr. by W.A.C.H. Dobson. Toronto: University of Toronto Press, 1963. 215 pp.
   A complete and generally accurate translation under seven headings and annotated for the general reader.

_____. Tr. by D.C. Lau. Baltimore: Penguin Books, 1970. 280 pp.
   A generally scholarly and reliable translation with commentary.

SHIH, VINCENT Y.C. "Metaphysical Tendencies of Mencius," in
Philosophy East and West, 12 (1963): 319-341.
On Mencius' various doctrines on Heaven, human nature,
moral cultivation, sagehood, etc., from the metaphysical
point of view.

SIH, PAUL T.C. "The Natural Law Philosophy of Mencius," in
New Scholasticism, 31 (1957): 317-337.
According to this essay, there is the idea of a "universal
law" pervading Nature and present in all phases of human
life and social order--a law proceeding from a supreme
Reason evident in all existence.

WALEY, ARTHUR. Three Ways of Thought in Ancient China.
London: Allen and Unwin, 1939. 275 pp. Also in Doubleday
Anchor paperbacks, 1956. 216 pp.
Selected translation of the works of Mencius, as well as
of Chuang Tzu and of Han Fei Tzu, with the author's own
interpretations. Of exquisite style and much human interest,
though a little dated in philosophical scholarship.

The Works of Mencius. Tr. by James Legge. Oxford: Clarendon
Press, 1893-1895. 402 pp. (The Chinese Classics, 2).
Still one of the standard translations of the Book of
Mencius, with scholarly notes and commentaries. The original
Chinese text is also given for useful reference.

WU, JOHN. "Mencius' Philosophy of Human Nature and Natural
Law," in Chinese Culture, 1, no. 1 (1957): 10-19.
A specialist on the Chinese legal tradition analyzes
Mencius' doctrine of human nature in relation to the will of
God and emphasizes the similarity between Mencius' concept
of Natural Law and the classical Natural Law tradition of
the West.

1.3.3 Hsün Tzu (313-238 B.C.?)

See also 2.1, 2.5.1, 15.3.

DUBS, HOMER H. Hsüntze, the Moulder of Ancient Confucianism.
London: Probsthain, 1927. 308 pp. Reprinted in New York:
Paragon.
Thus far the most comprehensive and authoritative work on
the philosophy of Hsün Tzu by one of the foremost sinolo-
gists in the West. Essentially correct in interpretation,
some parts of the book need to be re-examined in the light
of new, critical scholarship.

_____. "Mencius and Sun-dz on Human Nature," in <u>Philosophy East and West</u>, 6 (1956): 213-222.
Hsün Tzu's doctrine of human nature is understood to be intended to support Confucius' authoritatianism. Dubs suggests that Chu Hsi was closer to Hsün Tzu than Mencius.

FUNG YU-LAN. <u>A History of Chinese Philosophy</u>. (<u>See</u> 1.2.1).
Chapter 12 of Vol. 1 deals with Hsün Tzu in terms of his attitudes toward Confucius, Mencius, and the Chou institutions, heaven and human nature, system of psychology, the rectification of names and other philosophical doctrines of Hsün Tzu. More elaborate, though earlier than the below-mentioned.

_____. <u>A Short History of Chinese Philosophy</u>. (<u>See</u> 1.3.1).
Chapter 13 deals with Hsün Tzu, representing the realistic wing of Confucianism. Topics such as Hsün Tzu's position, theory of human nature, origin of morality, theory of rites and music, logical theories, and fallacies of other schools are all well discussed.

<u>Hsün Tzu: Basic Writings</u>. Tr. by Burton Watson. New York: Columbia University Press, 1963. 177 pp. Also in combined edition of <u>Basic Writings of Mo Tzu, Hsün Tzu, and Han Fei Tzu</u>, 1967.
Generally accurate and lucid translation of chapters 1, 2, 9, 15, 17, 19-23. Unfortunately, chapters 6 and 8 appraising and criticizing various schools are not included.

LAU, D.C. "Theories of Human Nature on Mencius and Shyuntzyy," in <u>Bulletin of the School of Oriental and African Studies</u>, 15 (1953): 541-565.
The opposing theories of the two Confucian followers on human nature are carefully examined with the conclusion that they were not really as much opposed as in their theories of morality. Hsün Tzu is looked upon as inferior to Mencius in inspiring people to great deeds.

LIANG CH'I-HSIUNG. "A Descriptive Review of Hsün Tzu's thought," in <u>Chinese Studies in Philosophy</u>, 6, no. 1 (1974): 4-60.
Epistemology, the view of the Way of Heaven, the doctrine of human nature, the theory of rectification of names, political doctrines with rule by propriety as fundamental and rule by law as supplementary, and the doctrine of learning. Hsün Tzu is here explained as a materialist.

MACHLE, EDWARD J. "Hsün Tzu as a Religious Philosopher," in
Philosophy East and West, 26 (1976): 443-461.
     Argues that the biased view of Hsün Tzu as nonreligious or
antireligious is due to his rejection of superstition and
his appearance of demythologizing Heaven, but he was actually
trying to protect the religious substance of Confucianism
from the superstitious, from the Moists who appeal to heavenly
reward and punishment, from the Taoists who downgrade all
rites, and even from the followers of Mencius who threaten
the Confucian discipline.

MEI, Y.P. "Hsün Tzu's Theory of Education, with an English
Translation of the Hsün Tzu, Chapter 1, An Exhortation to
Learning," in Tsing Hua Journal of Chinese Studies, n.s., 2,
no. 2 (1961): 361-377.
     Hsün Tzu's philosophy of education, why he was a Confucian-
ist, and how he differed from Mencius. The translation runs
side by side with the Chinese text.

ROSEMONT, HENRY. "Hsün-tzu," in The New Encyclopaedia
Britannica (Macropaedia). 15th ed. 1975. Vol. 8,
pp. 1127-1128.
     A brief discussion of Hsün Tzu's doctrine of man's evil
nature, his stress on value of ritual practices, as well as
his social and ethical philosophy.

_____. "State and Society in the Hsün Tzu: A Philosophical
Commentary," in Monumenta Serica, 29 (1970-71): 38-78.
     On Hsün Tzu's idea of geography, population, economy,
political institutions, and social structure in an ideal
state: rites and education as the basic stuff to build the
ideal state, and whether the ideal state is a closed society,
rational, and moral.

SHIH, VINCENT Y.C. "Hsüntzu's Positivism," in Tsing Hua
Journal of Chinese Studies, n.s., 4, no. 2 (1966): 162-173.
     Hsün Tzu's concept of T'ien (Nature) is here analyzed in
its various senses, namely, as the source of existence, the
precondition of all things, Nature, Heaven, destiny, ultimate political authority, etc.

The Works of Hsüntze. Tr. by Homer H. Dubs. London:
Probsthain, 1928. 336 pp. Reprinted in Taipei: Chinese
Materials and Research Aids Service Center.
     The standard, if not complete, translation of the writings
of Hsün Tzu, including all key chapters. Some revisions
need to be done in the light of recent research.

1.3.4 *The Great Learning*

CHAN, WING-TSIT. A Source Book in Chinese Philosophy. (See 1.2.1).
    A complete translation of the text, with an introduction, as well as Chu Hsi's remarks which are very important for the understanding of Chu's unique interpretation in contrast to Wang Yang-ming's.

FUNG YU-LAN. A History of Chinese Philosophy. (See 1.2.1).
    In chapter 14 of Vol. 1, a very good account of the text is given. One interesting point by Fung from the standpoint of textual criticism is that the text is regarded as the product of Ch'in-Han Confucianism.

The Great Learning and The Mean-in-Action. Tr. by E.R. Hughes. New York: Dutton, 1943. 176 pp.
    Basically a philosophical translation and interpretation of the Great Learning as well as of the Doctrine of the Mean, much more improved than Legge's translation, though not always accurate. The older text in the Thirteen Classics, not rearranged by Chu Hsi, is used.

1.3.5 *The Doctrine of the Mean*

See also 3.17, 3.18, 6.7.

CHAN, WING-TSIT. A Source Book in Chinese Philosophy. (See 1.2.1).
    Chapter 5 contains a translation of the complete text, with an introduction, footnotes, comments, as well as Chu Hsi's remarks, which are extremely important and helpful for comparison between Chu's interpretation of the text and Wang Yang-ming's.

The Conduct of Life. Tr. by Ku Hung-ming. London: John Murray, 1906. 60 pp., included in Lin Yutang, ed., The Wisdom of Confucius (See 1.3.1), pp. 104-134.
    As the English title shows, this is the author's free and original rendering of the text with some personal insight, revealing his understanding of the true meaning of the classic to the Chinese.

"The Doctrine of the Mean," tr. by James Legge in The Chinese Classics. (See 1.2.1). Vol. 1, pp. 382-434.
    Still a reliable translation, with the Chinese text. Chu Hsi's rearranged text is used.

FUNG YU-LAN. A History of Chinese Philosophy. (See 1.2.1).
   In chapter 14 of Vol. 1 (pp. 369-377), Fung discusses the
fundamental notions of the text, such as equilibrium, normal-
ity, the timely mean, absolute sincerity, and nature. As in
the case of his treatment of the Great Learning, Fung regards
the text as one of the Confucian products in the Ch'in-Han
period.

HSU, L.S. The Political Philosophy of Confucianism: An Interpretation of the Social and Political Ideas of Confucius,
His Forerunners, and His Early Disciples. London: Routledge,
1932. 258 pp.
   In chapter 10, the author discusses the Doctrine of the
Mean under the headings of (a) the definition of chung-yung,
(b) the nature of chung-yung, (c) the practical principles
of chung-yung, and (d) ch'eng (sincerity) as the fundamental
of good government. Emphasis on the political significance
of the Doctrine of the Mean.

LIU, SHU-HSIEN. "The Confucian Approach to the Problem of
Transcendence and Immanence," in Philosophy East and West,
22 (1972): 45-52.
   A fresh exploration of the philosophical meaning of the
Doctrine of the Mean in terms of transcendence and immanence,
thereby suggesting that "If one sees the world and human
life from the Confucian perspective, then the dichotomy
between the transcendent and the immanent becomes no longer
necessary" (p. 51).

TU WEI-MING. Centrality and Commonality: An Essay on Chung-
yung. Honolulu: The University Press of Hawaii, 1976.
168 pp.
   Combining objective analysis and personal appreciation,
the monograph focuses on the profound person, the fiduciary
community, and the moral metaphysics as three interconnected
ways of expounding the basic insight of the Doctrine of the
Mean. As a true leader of humanity, the profound person can
set in motion a process of moral transformation, thus creating a realm of value which is metaphysically significant.

1.3.6 Other Confucian Classics

Book of Changes (See 7.19.1, 7.19.2).

Book of Rites (See 3.3, 10.12).

Classic of Filial Piety (See 3.1.3).

1.4 TAOIST PHILOSOPHY

See also 3.6, 7.3.

1.4.1 Origin

CREEL, HERRLEE G. What is Taoism? and Other Studies in Chinese
  Cultural History. Chicago: University of Chicago Press,
  1970. 192 pp.
    Includes eight scholarly essays, four of which deal exclu-
  sively with early Taoism. "On Two Aspects in Early Taoism"
  distinguishes the "purposive" and the "contemplative" as the
  two aspects of ancient Taoism. "On the Origin of Wu-wei"
  focuses on the concept of wu-wei (nonaction) and throws some
  light also on the origin of the Taoist school. The chapter
  on "The Great Clod" is among the best and clearest from the
  philosophical point of view.

FUNG YU-LAN. A History of Chinese Philosophy. (See 1.2.1).
    Chapter 8 of Vol. 1 deals with Lao Tzu and his school of
  Taoism, but little discussion is made of the origin of
  Taoism.

_____. A Short History of Chinese Philosophy. (See 1.3.1).
    In this short work, Fung discusses more on the origin of
  Taoism by regarding Yang Chu as one of the earliest Taoists
  (the first phase of Taoism), whereas Lao Tzu is put in the
  second phase of Taoism. See chapters 6 and 9 for an interesting treatment of the subject.

LAO TZU. The Way and Its Power. Tr. by Arthur Waley. London:
  Allen and Unwin, 1935. 262 pp.; also in Evergreen paperbacks, New York: Grove Press.
    Some discussion is made of the origin of the Taoist school
  in this work, which is primarily a translation of the Lao Tzu.

1.4.2 Lao Tzu (6th-4th century B.C.?)

See also 7.16.1, 11.7.5, 11.7.6, 15.1, 15.2, 15.10.

CHEN, CHUNG-HWAN. "What Does Lao-tzu Mean by the Term 'Tao'?"
  in Tsing Hua Journal of Chinese Studies, n.s., 4, no. 2
  (1964): 150-160.
    Tao is variously understood as the source of things, the
  storehouse of things, the ultimate model in its static
  aspect, and various processes in its dynamic aspect.

CHEN, ELLEN MARIE. "Is There a Doctrine of Physical Immortality in the Tao Te Ching?" in History of Religions, 12 (1973):
231-249.
   After a lengthy discussion of the Taoist attitude toward
the body and death, the conclusion is drawn that the Taoist
ideal is to accept both life and death cheerfully, and at
the end of this life, when the Taoist loses his body, he
remains unending, because he now returns to his root and
joins the Universal Life of Tao itself.

_____. "The Meaning of Te in the Tao Te Ching: An Examination
of the Concept of Nature in Chinese Taoism," in Philosophy
East and West, 23 (1973): 457-470.
   Concludes that te stands for the initial state of nature,
when nature, having emerged from Tao, returns to and abides
by Tao, and when man, as a child of nature, keeps close to
and abides by nature.

DUBS, HOMER H. "The Date and Circumstances of the Philosopher
Lao-dz," in Journal of the American Oriental Society, 61
(1941): 215-221. Further discussions with Bodde, ibid., 62
(1942): 8-13, 300-304, 64 (1944): 24-27.
   An inconclusive debate between Dubs who ingeniously
theorized that Lao Tzu was the father of a viscount in the
third century B.C., and Bodde who raised ojections.

FU, CHARLES WEI-HSUN. "Lao Tzu's Conception of Tao," in
Inquiry, 16 (July, 1973): 367-394.
   Uses a combined method of philosophical and linguistic
analyses to reconstruct Lao Tzu's conception of Tao in terms
of six inseparable dimensions or perspectives, i.e., Tao as
reality, Tao as origin, Tao as principle, Tao as function,
Tao as virtue, and Tao as technique.

FUNG YU-LAN. A History of Chinese Philosophy. (See 1.2.1),
Vol. 1.
   Chapter 8 gives a philosophical interpretation of Lao
Tzu's metaphysical thinking, theory of knowledge, as well as
politico-social philosophy.

_____. A Short History of Chinese Philosophy. (See 1.3.1).
   Contains an excellent discussion of the philosophical
doctrines of Lao Tzu, such as Tao the unnamable, the invari-
able law of nature, human conduct, and political philosophy.

HU SHIH. "A Criticism of Some Recent Methods Used in Dating
Lao Tzu," in Harvard Journal of Asiatic Studies, 2 (1937):
373-397.
   Shatters much wishful thinking on the subject.

KALTENMARK, MAX. "Lao Tzu," in The New Encyclopaedia Britannica
(Macropaedia). 15th ed. 1975. Vol. 10, pp. 679-680.
A short description of the little-known life of Lao Tzu.

_____. Lao Tzu and Taoism. Stanford: Stanford University
Press, 1969. 158 pp.
An interesting account of Lao Tzu, the man and his teach-
ing, with emphasis on his influence on the development of
Taoist philosophy and religion.

KIMURA, EIICHI. "A New Study of Laotzu," in Philosophical
Studies of Japan, 1 (1959): 85-104.
The author's important book by the same title is here sum-
marized. The concept of Tao is discussed at length. Lao
Tzu is regarded as a myth and the Lao Tzu as an anthology of
sayings from the 4th to the 2nd century B.C.

KUAN FENG and LIN YÜ-SHIH. "Third Discussion of Lao Tzu's
Philosophy," in Chinese Studies in Philosophy, 2 (1971):
158-186.
The authors argue that Lao Tzu's dialectics did not produce any revolutionary conclusions and his philosophy was no
threat to the slave-owning class, and that Lao Tzu's system
remains fundamentally idealistic despite some materialistic
tendencies and naive dialectical method in his philosophy.

Lao Tzu. Tr. by John C.H. Wu. New York: St. John's University Press, 1961. 115 pp.
A charming translation with the Chinese text. The author's
keen insight into the naturalistic meaning of the text is
fully expressed in the translation, though the last sentence
of the 4th chapter is misleadingly translated as "It seems
to be the common ancestor of all, the father of things."

Lao Tzu. Tao Te Ching, The Book of The Way and Its Virtue.
Tr. by J.J.L. Duyvendak. London: John Murray, 1954.
172 pp.
The translation is generally correct and scholarly but the
arrangement of the text lacks textual or historical
justification.

_____. The Way and Its Power. Tr. by Arthur Waley. (See
1.4.1).
One of the pioneer works on the Lao Tzu. A very good
translation, particularly from the standpoint of literary
style, though too much quietism is read into the text. The
long introductory essay discussing linguistic questions,
cross-currents of thought, date and authorship, etc., is
extremely helpful.

Tao Te Ching. Tr. by Gia-fu Feng and Jane English. New York:
  Knopf, 1972. 170 pp.
    A fresh translation of the Lao Tzu with the original text
  and many beautiful photographs to illustrate the natural
  way of Lao Tzu in a modern sense. No note or comment added.

The Way of Lao Tzu. Tr. by Wing-tsit Chan. Indianapolis:
  Bobbs-Merrill, 1963. 285 pp.
    A translation of the Lao Tzu with philosophical comments,
  notes, bibliography, as well as a long introductory essay
  discussing the philosophy of Tao, Lao Tzu the man and the
  book.

The Wisdom of Laotse. Tr. by Lin Yutang. New York: The
  Modern Library, 1948. 326 pp.
    Another highly recommended translation of the Lao Tzu,
  with selections from the Chuang Tzu to serve as elaborate
  Taoist commentaries on the text.

1.4.3 Chuang Tzu (b. 369 B.C.?)

See also 6.13, 12.2, 12.3, 15.2.

CHAN, WING-TSIT. A Source Book in Chinese Philosophy. (See
  1.1.1).
    Chapter 8 introduces the mystical way of Chuang Tzu, with
  a complete translation of two important chapters (chapters
  2 and 6) and selected translations from the text arranged
  under the topics of (a) the nature and reality of Tao,
  (b) Tao everywhere, (c) constant flux, (d) evolution, (e) Tao
  as transformation and one, (f) nature vs. man, (g) calmness
  of mind, (h) sageliness and kingliness, (i) the equality of
  life and death, (j) subjectivity, and (k) the inner spirit.

CHUANG TZU. A New Selected Translation with an Exposition of
  the Philosophy of Kuo Hsiang. Tr. by Fung Yu-lan. Shanghai:
  Commercial Press, 1933. 164 pp. Reprinted in New York:
  Paragon.
    Philosophically most accurate, this translation only con-
  tains the seven "inner" chapters of the Chuang Tzu, with
  selected translations from the Neo-Taoist work of Kuo Hsiang
  (d. 312) on the text. The introduction deals with the basic
  ideas of Chuang Tzu, such as Tao, Virtue, "letting alone,"
  equality of things and opinions, and absolute freedom. The
  appendix includes Fung's essays on the characteristics of
  the Neo-Taoist philosophy of Kuo Hsiang.

The Complete Works of Chuang Tzu. Tr. by Burton Watson. New
York: Columbia University Press, 1968. 397 pp.
  The most reliable translation of the writings of Chuang
Tzu, complete, generally accurate, and lucid. The introductory essay sums up the central theme of the Chuang Tzu in a
single word: freedom. The translator also pays some, if not
full, attention to the problem of textual criticism.

CREEL, HERRLEE G. What is Taoism? (See 1.4.1).
  The third essay, "On Two Aspects in Early Taoism," gives a
very interesting interpretation, with substantial evidence,
of Chuang Tzu as primarily representing the "contemplative
aspect," while Lao Tzu is said to represent the "purposive
aspect."

FUNG YU-LAN. A History of Chinese Philosophy. (See 1.2.1),
Vol. 1.
  Chapter 10 discusses the philosophy of Chuang Tzu by
focusing on the way, the power, nature, change, happiness,
liberty, equality, immortality, absolute freedom, as well as
Chuang Tzu's pure experience. Clearly written, with many
quotations from the text to substantiate the author's
interpretation.

_____. A Short History of Chinese Philosophy. (See 1.3.1).
  Chapter 10 deals with Chuang Tzu as the philosopher in the
third phase of Taoism. This is probably Fung's latest interpretation of Chuang Tzu before he became a Marxist philosopher. His comparison of "the finite point of view" and "the
higher point of view" is particularly interesting.

_____. The Spirit of Chinese Philosophy. Tr. by E.R. Hughes.
London: Kegan Paul, 1947. 224 pp. Also in Beacon paperbacks.
  The unique characteristic of the work consists in Fung's
use of Chuang Tzu's term "inner sagehood and outer kingliness" as the basic criterion for his personal evaluation of
different schools of Chinese philosophy in its historical
perspective. Fung praises Chuang Tzu's philosophy highly
for its bringing up Chinese philosophy to the transcendent
level. See especially chapter 4.

GRAHAM, A.C. "Chuang-tzu's Essay on Seeing Things as Equal,"
in History of Religions, 9 (1969): 137-159.
  A very scholarly translation of the most philosophical
chapter of the Chuang Tzu, with the translator's introductory essay.

KUAN FENG. "Critique of the Philosophy of Chuang Tzu," in
Chinese Studies in History of Philosophy, 1 (1967): 36-94.
A prominent writer on Chinese philosophy in the People's
Republic of China strongly attacks Chuang Tzu's "subjective
idealism" as reactionary, pessimistic, and representing the
viewpoint of slave-owners. Philosophically, the stress is
put on Chuang Tzu's inquiring into the origin of the universe
and the contrast between the relative and the absolute.

MAJOR, JOHN S. "The Efficacy of Uselessness: A Chuang-tzu
motif," in Philosophy East and West, 25 (1975): 265-279.
An interesting analysis of the Chuang-tzu motif in the
short parables and anecdotes fitting one or the other of the
two patterns Major has found in the Chuang Tzu.

MERTON, THOMAS. The Way of Chuang Tzu. New York: New Direc-
tions, 1965. 159 pp.
Passages are selected from existing translations and
arranged in verse form and given a warm and poetic interpretation (sometimes somewhat inaccurate).

RUBIN, VITALY A. Individual and State in Ancient China.
Cross reference: 1.3.1.

THIEL, P. JOS. "Das Erkenntnisproblem bei Chuang-tzu," in
Sinologica, 11 (1970): 11-89.
The development of the concept of Tao, Chuang Tzu the man,
the problem of knowledge in late Chou (notably in Mo Tzu),
Hsün Tzu, the dialecticians, the Tao-te ching, and Mencius,
the concepts of the pure or perfect man in Taoism and the
method of achieving perfection, the concepts of self-
transformation and the Absolute Tao.

WALEY, ARTHUR. Three Ways of Thought in Ancient China. (See
1.3.2), pp. 17-112.
Extracts, with comments and discussions, of stories of
Hui Shih, Lao Tzu, Confucius, and Chuang Tzu himself, and on
the ancients, the sage, death, yoga, nurturing life, the
Taoist and Tao, etc.

WALTHAM, CLAE, ed. Chuang Tzu, Genius of the Absurd. New
York: Ace Books, 1971. 398 pp.
James Legge's translation plus introduction and outline
by the editor. New romanization of Legge's original one.

1.4.4   Yang Chu (440-360 B.C.?)

See also 3.6.

CHAN, WING-TSIT. A Source Book in Chinese Philosophy. (See
    1.2.1), pp. 70-73, 80.
       Mencius' moral criticism of Yang Chu (and Mo Ti) is found,
    as Chan says on p. 51, in three places in the Book of
    Mencius (3A:5, 3B:9, and 7A:26), all of which are trans-
    lated by Chan.

CHANG, ALOYSIUS. "A Comparative Study of Yang Chu and the
    Chapter on Yang Chu (Part One)," in Chinese Culture, 12,
    no. 4 (December, 1971): 49-60. Part 2, ibid., 13, no. 1
    (March, 1972): 44-84.
       A detailed study of Yang Chu's life, his relation with
    Chuang Tzu and Tang Tzu-chu, his teachings, their sources,
    and Yang's position in the history of Chinese thought. The
    second part is devoted to the "Yang Chu" chapter in the
    Lieh Tzu, particularly the authors of various concepts
    expressed in the chapter. Very useful.

FUNG YU-LAN. A Short History of Chinese Philosophy. (See
    1.3.1).
       Chapter 20 deals with Neo-Taoism of the Sentimentalists,
    in which Fung says that the "Yang Chu" chapter of the Lieh
    Tzu cannot represent the view of the genuine Yang Chu of
    ancient times. The Lieh Tzu, with no exception of the "Yang
    Chu" chapter, is considered to be a work of the third
    century A.D.

_____. The Spirit of Chinese Philosophy. (See 1.4.3).
       In chapter 2, Fung discusses the philosophers Yang Chu and
    Mo Ti, and regards Yang Chu's school as an early form of
    Taoism. Yang Chu's line of reasoning is said to consist in
    that of "despising things and valuing life." Fung also says
    in the same way in the 6th chapter of A Short History of
    Chinese Philosophy that Yang Chu is considered as the repre-
    sentative of the first phase of Taoism.

"Yang Chu." Tr. by L.A. Lyall in T'ien Hsia Monthly, 9
    (1939): 189-204.
       A smooth and generally accurate translation of the seventh
    chapter of the Lieh Tzu, the representative work of Chinese
    hedonism.

1.5 MOISM

1.5.1 Mo Tzu (468-376 B.C.?)

See also 3.5, 6.14, 6.15, 10.15, 10.16, 10.17.

The Ethical and Political Works of Motse. Tr. by Y.P. Mei.
London: Probsthain, 1929. 275 pp.
  A fluent and mostly accurate translation of the greater
part of the Mo Tzu, with the omission of all the Neo-Moist
(logical) chapters. The best Chinese commentary is used,
though consultation with several more commentaries is
desirable.

FUNG YU-LAN. A History of Chinese Philosophy. (See 1.2.1),
Vol. 1.
  In chapter 5 a clear exposition is made of Mo Tzu and the
early Moist school. All important teachings of Mo Tzu are
treated in much detail, such as utilitarianism, universal
love, religious and political sanctions.

_____. A Short History of Chinese Philosophy. (See 1.3.1).
  Chapter 5 treats Mo Tzu's thought in terms of all-embracing
love, the will of God and existence of spirits, origin of
the state, and stresses Mo's criticism of Confucianism. Indeed, Mo Tzu is regarded by Fung as the first opponent of
Confucius.

MEI, Y.P. Motse, The Neglected Rival of Confucius. London:
Probsthain, 1934. 222 pp.
  A systematic presentation of Mo Tzu's ethical, political,
economic, and religious views. A pioneer work on Mo Tzu's
thought, though a little dated.

Mo Tzu: Basic Writings. Tr. by Burton Watson. New York:
Columbia University Press, 1963. 140 pp.
  Reliable and lucid translation of the eleven most important sections of the Mo Tzu with an introductory essay and
notes.

RUBIN, VITALY A. Individual and State in Ancient China.
Cross reference: 1.3.1.

SHIH, VINCENT Y.C. "A Critique of Motzu's Religious Views and
Related Concepts," in Symposium on Chinese Studies Commemorating the Golden Jubilee of the University of Hong Kong,
1911-1961. Department of Chinese, University of Hong Kong,
1968. Vol. 3, pp. 1-17.

A general examination of Mo Tzu's basic doctrines, such as
the anthropomorphic Heaven, universal love, benefit for the
people, criticism of Confucianists, attack on belief in fate,
wasteful festivals, warfare, etc.

1.5.2 The Moist Followers

CHMIELEWSKI, JANUSZ. "Linguistic Structure and Two-Valued
  Logic: The Case of Chinese," in To Honor Roman Jakobson:
  Essays on the Occasion of His Seventieth Birthday. The
  Hague: Mouton, 1967. Pp. 475-482.
  Having observed that the linguistic structure of Chinese
has a strong tendency toward two-valued logic, the author
maintains that at an early date the Chinese arrived at a
fairly sophisticated formulation of the principle of non-
contradiction and that the dialectical procedure of the
Moists was based on the laws of non-contradiction and of
the excluded middle.

_____. "Notes on Early Chinese Logic." Cross reference:
  1.6.2.

FUNG YU-LAN. A History of Chinese Philosophy. (See 1.2.1),
  Vol. 1.
  Chapter 11 presents in detail the philosophy and logical
thinking of the later Moist school, or the Neo-Moist school.
All major teachings of Neo-Moism, such as utilitarianism in
the "Moist Canon," theory of knowledge, dialectics, "similarity and difference," "hard and white," discussion on other
problems of the dialecticians, arguments for universal love,
and arguments with other philosophical schools are systematically treated.

_____. A Short History of Chinese Philosophy. (See 1.3.1).
  Chapter 11 gives a good account of the philosophy and
logical thinking of the later Moists in terms of knowledge
and names, dialectics, as well as clarification of all-
embracing love.

GRAHAM, A.C. "Later Mohist Treatise on Ethics and Logic
  Reconstructed from the Ta-ch'u chapter of Mo Tzu," in Asia
  Major, 17 (1971): 137-189.
  Part 1 contains an introduction, reconstruction of frag-
ments, and discussion on syntactic problems and dating.
Parts 2 and 3 are devoted to translation, section by section,
with ample notes. The logical aspect involves names and
objects.

GRAHAM, A.C. "The Logic of the Mohist <u>Hsiao-ch'u</u>," in <u>T'oung Pao</u>, 51 (1964): 1-54.
   Translation and discussion of chapter 45 of the <u>Mo Tzu</u> in terms of Moist logic and the Chinese language, interpreting the phrase in the chapter, "to kill a robber is not to kill a <u>jen</u>" to mean "not to kill the robber as a person."

HU SHIH. <u>The Development of the Logical Method in Ancient China</u>. 3rd ed. Shanghai: Oriental Book Co., 1928. 187 pp. Reprinted in New York: Paragon.
   An outstanding work, the first to treat ancient Chinese thought as genuine philosophy, to present Lao Tzu, Confucius, Chuang Tzu, and others in an entirely new light, to view Chinese thought in ancient China as a logical development. In particular, the author makes the corrupted texts of the Neo-Moists quite intelligible. A great contribution indeed.

LAU, D.C. "Some Logical Problems in Ancient China," in <u>Proceedings of the Aristotelian Society</u>, n.s., 53 (1953): 189-204.
   The methods of analogy, parallel, precedent, and extension in chapter 45 (<u>Hsiao-ch'ü</u>) of the <u>Mo Tzu</u> are examined for their efficacy in overcoming the opponent. It is contended that the Chinese language handicapped ancient logicians.

1.6   THE LOGICIANS

CHMIELEWSKI, JANUSZ. "Linguistic Structure and Two-Valued Logic: The Case of Chinese." Cross reference: 1.5.2.

_____. "Notes on Early Chinese Logic." Cross reference: 1.6.2.

1.6.1   <u>Hui Shih (380-305 B.C.?)</u>

CHAN, WING-TSIT. <u>A Source Book in Chinese Philosophy</u>. (<u>See</u> 1.2.1), pp. 233-235.
   In chapter 10 there is a translation of some sections in the <u>Chuang Tzu</u>, chapter 33; with comments and notes concerning the paradoxes of Hui Shih and the debaters.

FUNG YU-LAN. <u>A History of Chinese Philosophy</u>. (<u>See</u> 1.2.1), Vol. 1.
   In chapter 7, Fung discusses the relations between Hui Shih and Chuang Tzu, Hui's ten paradoxes, and particularly points out the philosophical differences between Hui Shih and Chuang Tzu in order to clarify the basic positions of the logicians and the Taoists.

NEEDHAM, JOSEPH. Science and Civilisation in China.
  Cambridge, England: Cambridge University Press, 1954-1962.
  4 vols. Vol. 2, History of Scientific Thought (1956):
  696 pp.
    A truly monumental work, with an incredible amount of
  scholarship and original thought. On pp. 189-197 Needham
  gives a careful analysis of the paradoxes of Hui Shih by
  consulting the original texts of Chuang Tzu, Hsün Tzu, Mo
  Tzu, and Kung-sun Lung. The analysis focuses on relativity
  and the all-pervadingness of change, space, and time, infi-
  nity and the problem related to atomism, universals and
  classification, epistemology, potentiality and actuality,
  and natural wonders seemingly paradoxical.

SOLOMON, BENARD S. "The Assumptions of Hui-Tzu," in Monumenta
  Serica, 28 (1969): 1-40.
    The point of departure of this essay on Hui Shih's ten
  paradoxes is that they conceal no new knowledge of the
  physical world or new insights into it. Their technique
  reveals itself as they are kept empty of such knowledge or
  insight. There is also an attempt to understand three
  dialogues in the Chuang Tzu in the light of what the assumptions disclose.

1.6.2 Kung-sun Lung (b. 380 B.C.?)

See also 9.4.

CHENG, CHUNG-YING. "Logic and Ontology in the 'Chih-wu-lun'
  of Kung-sun Lung-tzu," in Philosophy East and West, 20
  (1970): 137-154.
    A new attempt at the reconstruction of the logic and
  ontology in the "Chih-wu lun" by utilizing modern methodology and technique of symbolic logic.

CHMIELEWSKI, JANUSZ. "Notes on Early Chinese Logic," in
  Rocnik Orientalistyczny, 26, no. 1 (1962): 2-21; no. 2
  (1963): 91-105; 27, no. 1 (1963): 103-121; 28, no. 2 (1965):
  87-111; 30, no. 1 (1966): 31-52.
    An attempt is made to find in the Kung-sun Lung Tzu the
  general laws in ancient Chinese logic by applying modern
  symbolic logic in terms of the theory of classes. (See 9).

FUNG YU-LAN. A History of Chinese Philosophy. (See 1.2.1),
  Vol. 1.
    In chapter 7, a systematic presentation is made of Kung-
  sun Lung's "Discourse on the White Horse," "Discourse on

Hard and White," "Discourse on <u>Chih</u> (universals) and Things,"
"Discourse on the Explanation of Change," as well as of Kung-
sun's conception of the <u>chih</u> as such. A good account.

GRAHAM, A.C. "Kung-Sun Lung's Essay on Meanings and Things,"
in <u>Journal of Oriental Studies</u>, 2 (1955): 282-301.
    A scholarly attempt at reexamination of a hopelessly cor-
rupt text. The article should be evaluated in the light of
new research by (e.g.) Chung-ying Cheng's essay as mentioned
above. (For Graham on the <u>Kung-sun Lung Tzu</u>, <u>see</u> 18.5).

MEI, Y.P. "The <u>Kung-sun Lung Tzu</u>, with a Translation into
English," in <u>Harvard Journal of Asiatic Studies</u>, 16 (1953):
404-437.
    A helpful though not exhaustive study and a good transla-
tion, with the Chinese text.

NEEDHAM, JOSEPH. <u>Science and Civilisation in China</u>. (See
1.6.1), Vol. 2, <u>History of Scientific Thought</u>, pp. 185-189.
    A short but careful discussion of the philosophy and
logical thinking of Kung-sun Lung.

1.6.3 <u>Other Logicians</u>

FUNG YU-LAN. <u>A History of Chinese Philosophy</u>. (See 1.2.1),
Vol. 1.
    A short but clear discussion is made in chapter 10 of the
general tendencies in the dialecticians' doctrines, along with
the discussion of both Kung-sun Lung and Hui Shih.

_____. <u>The Spirit of Chinese Philosophy</u>. (See 1.4.3).
    In chapter 3 on the dialecticians and the logicians, Fung
evaluates their philosophical contributions in terms of
abstract thinking, and points out why and how the Taoists
transcend "names" (concepts) in order to establish the metaphysics of Tao.

GRAHAM, A.C. "The 'Hard' and 'White' disputation of the
Chinese Sophists," in <u>Bulletin of the School of Oriental and
African Studies</u>, 30, part 2 (1967): 358-368.
    Graham contends that <u>chien-pai</u> to the Chinese Sophists
and Kung-sun Lung did not mean a paradox of hard and white
but the relation between space and time, interpreting <u>chien-
pai</u> not to mean "hard and white" but "as hard is to white."

HU SHIH. <u>The Development of the Logical Method in Ancient
China</u>. (See 1.5.2).

Thus far the most comprehensive and systematic treatment
of all the logical theories of Kung-sun Lung and other
logicians and dialecticians in ancient China in the context
of historical development. See chapters 5 and 6.

1.7   THE YIN YANG SCHOOL AND TSOU YEN (305-240 B.C.?)

See also 2.16, 7.17, 11.3, 11.7.5.

CHAN, WING-TSIT. A Source Book in Chinese Philosophy. (See 1.2.1),
   chapter 11.
   A translation of some ancient texts in which are found valuable
sources about Tsou Yen's life and thought, with an introductory
essay and comments.

FORKE, ALFRED. The World-Conception of the Chinese. London:
   Probsthain, 1925. 300 pp.
   A fairly complete collection of information on Chinese astronomy,
Chinese concepts of physical space and time, heaven and earth, yin
and yang, as well as of the Five Elements or Five Agents.

FUNG YU-LAN. A History of Chinese Philosophy. (See 1.2.1), Vol. 1.
   In chapter 7 on the "Hundred Schools," Fung cites accounts in
the Historical Records, the Lü-shih ch'un-ch'iu, the "Grand Norm"
of the Book of History, the Kuan Tzu, and other ancient sources to
trace the origin of the Yin Yang school before Tsou Yen. Generally
reliable.

_____. A Short History of Chinese Philosophy. (See 1.3.1), Vol. 1.
   A very good and readable account is given of the Yin Yang School
and early Chinese cosmology under the topics of the Six Classics of
occult arts, the Five Elements as described in the "Grand Norm,"
the "Monthly Commands," the Yin and Yang principles (as described
in the "Appendices" of the Book of Changes), etc.

HUGHES, E.R. Chinese Philosophy in Classic Times. (See 1.3.1),
   pp. 215-225.
   Selections from the Kuan Tzu, the Lü-shih ch'un-ch'iu, the Book
of Rites, and the Book of History to show the influence exercised
by Tsou Yen's way of thinking.

IKEDA, SUETOSHI. "The Origin and Development of the Wu-hsing (five
   elements) Idea: A Preliminary Essay," in Philosophy East and West,
   16 (1966): 297-309.
   A historical study of the five-element idea by stressing the
social and religious conditions of the fourth and third centuries
B.C.

NEEDHAM, JOSEPH. Science and Civilisation in China. (See 1.6.1),
  Vol. 2, History of Scientific Thought.
    On p. 252 ff., a very careful discussion, substantiated by many
  reliable sources, is made of the origin and development of the Five
  Element theory leading to Tsou Yen's systematization of the theory
  into that of Yin Yang. Needham thinks that in this school are found
  the seminal ideas of Chinese science.

1.8 THE LEGALIST SCHOOL

See also 10.18, 10.19.

CREEL, HERRLEE G. "The Fa-chia: 'Legalists' or 'Administrators'?" in
  Bulletin of the Institute of History and Philology, Academia Sinica,
  extra Vol. 4 (1961): 607-636.
    The Legalist school is said to stem from two schools of thinkers,
  one founded by Shang Yang (d. 338 B.C.) stressing penal law and the
  other by Shen Pu-hai (d. 337 B.C.) concerned with the ruler's role
  and control of the bureaucracy.

FUNG YU-LAN. A History of Chinese Philosophy. (See 1.2.1), Vol. 1.
    Chapter 13 deals with Han Fei Tzu and the other Legalists in much
  more detail than in the below-mentioned work. Topics include the
  Legalist doctrines and the social, political and economic tendencies
  of their time, the Legalist concept of history, rectification of
  names and actualities, the evilness of human nature, non-activity,
  Han Fei Tzu and three groups in the Legalist school, and others.
  A very scholarly account.

_____. A Short History of Chinese Philosophy. (See 1.3.1).
    Chapter 14 deals with Han Fei Tzu and the Legalist school under
  the headings of (a) social background of the Legalists, (b) Han Fei
  Tzu, the synthesizer of the Legalist school, (c) Legalist philosophy
  of history, (d) way of government, (e) Legalism and Taoism, and
  (f) Legalism and Confucianism. A very clear account.

HSIAO, KUNG-CH'UAN. "Legalism and Autocracy in Traditional China," in
  Tsing Hua Journal of Chinese Studies, n.s., 4, no. 2 (1964):
  108-121.
    It is contended that although China has been a Confucian state,
  the Confucian autocracy has been largely supported by Legalist
  theories and practices, so that the Legalist element in Chinese
  history has been much more prominent than it is generally realized.

HUGHES, E.R. "Political Idealists and Realists of China of the
  Fourth and Third Centuries B.C.," in Journal of the North China
  Branch of the Royal Asiatic Society, 63 (1932): 46-64.
    A short but generally good account of Mo Tzu, Hsün Tzu, and the
  Legalists in particular.

LEE, K.K. "The Legalist School and Legal Positivism," in Journal
of Chinese Philosophy, 3 (1975): 23-56.
   The essay draws mainly from the Book of Lord Shang and the Complete Works of Han Fei Tzu, with major emphasis on Shang Yang, who
is viewed as merely concerned with establishing the supremacy of
positive law at the expense of customary and natural law. The law
of the Legalist is contrasted with the Confucian li (rites) and also
with Western concepts of law.

LIANG CH'I-CH'AO. History of Chinese Political Thought during the
Early Tsin Period. Tr. by L.T. Ch'en. London: Kegan Paul, 1930.
210 pp.
   A celebrated work in China by an eminent scholar. Liang's discussion of the Legalist school in the pre-Ch'in (221-206 B.C.)
period is basically sound. See pp. 113-138.

RUBIN, VITALY A. Individual and State in Ancient China. Cross
reference: 1.3.1.

WALEY, ARTHUR. Three Ways of Thought in Ancient China. (See 1.3.2),
pp. 199-247.
   Calling the Legalists Realists, Waley covers their affinities
with the Taoists and Confucianists, their conception of law, their
doctrines of agriculture and war, their attitude toward the past,
their emphasis on the rule and power, and their attack on social
classes.

1.8.1   The Early Thinkers

The Book of Lord Shang. Tr. by J.J.L. Duyvendak. London:
Probsthain, 1928. 346 pp. Also published in Chicago:
University of Chicago Press, 1963. 346 pp.
   The only available English translation of this important,
though probably spurious, ancient text in the Legalist
school. The introduction is a good study of Shang Yang as
well as of the text.

CREEL, HERRLEE G. Shen Pu-hai, A Chinese Political Philosopher
of the Fourth Century B.C. Chicago: University of Chicago
Press, 1974. ix, 341 pp.
   A critical approach to traditional accounts of Shen Pu-hai
and his relation with the Legalists and the Taoists, and his
influence on later thinkers. Product of meticulous scholarship and well-documented. Creel argues that Shen should not
have been called a Legalist since he emphasized technique.
Cf. Ignatius J.H. Ts'ao's review of the book in Journal of
Asian Studies, 36 (1976): 123-124.

CREEL, HERRLEE G. "Shen Pu-hai: A Secular Philosopher of
Administration," in Journal of Chinese Philosophy, 1 (1974):
119-136.
     Creel argues that the traditional Chinese state was derived
from the "administrative philosophy" founded by Shen Pu-hai,
who exerted a strong influence on the traditional system of
government.

HALOUN, G. "Legalist Fragments," in Asia Major, n.s., 2
(1952): 85-120.
     A translation of the Kuan Tzu, chapter 55 and related texts
with many notes and textual references, for the specialist.

KUAN FENG and LIN YÜ-SHIH. "On Kuan Chung's System of Thought,"
in Chinese Studies in Philosophy, 1 (1970): 252-321.
     A lengthy and systematic discussion on Kuan Chung's (4th
century B.C.) political thought in terms of his naive materialist view of Heaven, of material force, of natural laws,
of Tao and its concrete character, of his dialectic method
and theory of knowledge, and of his naive materialist political theory. All this ended up in advocating freeing the
slaves, developing a feudal mode of production, establishing
a unified and centralized state with the rule of law and
esteem for virtuous officials.

Kuantzu, a Repository of Early Chinese Thought. Tr. by W.
Allyn Rickett. Hong Kong: Hong Kong University Press, 1965.
269 pp.
     Translation of twelve of eighty-six chapters on law, gov-
ernment, military strategy, etc., presumably by Kuan Chung.

LI, YU-NING, ed. Shang Yang's Reforms and State Control in
China. New York: M.E. Sharpe, 1977. 392 pp.
     Explores the increasingly intense relationship between
historiography and politics in contemporary China. Includes
a complete translation of Yang K'uan's Shang Yang's Reforms
and a variety of pre-modern and modern interpretations of
Shang Yang.

RUBIN, VITALY. "Shen Tao and Fa-chia," in Journal of the
American Oriental Society, 94 (1974): 337-346.
     The aim of the article is to distinguish Shen Tao's (350-
275 B.C.) genuine ideas from those attributed to him, to
determine that he was not the author of the only text which
links his name with the concept of shih as power, and to
show that shih in Shen Tao means force or circumstance, for
he opposed circumstance, position, or condition to personal
efforts.

1.8.2 Han Fei Tzu (d. 233 B.C.)

CHEN, ELLEN MARIE. "The Dialectic of Chih (Reason) and Tao
   (Nature) in the Han Fei Tzu," in Journal of Chinese Philosophy, 3 (1975): 1-21.
      Discussion is under the headings of "the solitude of the
   ruler," "law as the antithesis of selfishness," "reason and
   morality," "love through punishment," and "the unresolved
   tension between reason and nature." It is held that in Han
   Fei's theory of law there is no concrete universal, there can
   be no reconciliation between the private and public interests,
   and the individual and state are each imprisoned in its abstract negation.

The Complete Works of Han Fei Tzu. Tr. by W.K. Liao. London:
   Probsthain. Vol. 1 (1939): 310 pp. Vol. 2 (1959): 338 pp.
      The only available complete translation of the most impor-
   tant work of the Legalist school in ancient China, generally
   smooth and accurate.

Han Fei Tzu: Basic Writings. Tr. by Burton Watson. New York:
   Columbia University Press, 1964. 134 pp.
      Reliable and lucid translations of sections 5-10, 12, 13,
   17, 18, and 49, all important political treatises, and section 50, a critique of Confucianism, but not sections 20-21,
   the first philosophical and exceedingly important commentary
   on passages from the Lao Tzu.

LANDERS, JAMES RUSSELL. The Political Thoughts of Han Fei.
   Indiana University Ph.D. thesis, 1972. 192 pp.
      Each of the 55 chapters of the Han Fei Tzu is briefly re-
   viewed. The main body of the thesis is occupied with the
   four basic premises of Han Fei, namely, the concept of
   historical progression, correspondence of name and form,
   selfishness as the primary motivation, and strength as the
   national goal, and with the three pillars of law, statecraft,
   and position.

SAH, MONG-WU. "The Import of Hanfeiism on the Early Han Cen-
   sorial System," in Chinese Culture, 1, no. 1 (1957): 75-111.
      An objective and well-documented study of the subject.

1.9 HAN (B.C. 206-220 A.D.) THOUGHT IN GENERAL

de BARY, WM. THEODORE, WING-TSIT CHAN, and BURTON WATSON, comps.
   Sources of Chinese Tradition. (See 1.2.1).
      Chapters 7 and 8 deal with the eclectic tendency of Han philos-
   ophy and religion under the headings of theory of portents, the

dynastic mandates, the intellectual synthesis, the creation, structure, and working of the universe, the Five Agents (elements), the
concept and marking of time, heaven, earth, man, etc. A very good
introduction to Han eclecticism, with selected readings translated
from the original texts during the Han period.

FUNG YU-LAN. A History of Chinese Philosophy. (See 1.2.1), Vol. 1.
    A more elaborate and detailed treatment of Han eclecticism. All
important topics of Han philosophy are discussed carefully and
clearly under the headings of (a) the Confucians of the Ch'in and
Han dynasties, (b) the appendices of the Book of Changes and the
cosmology of the Huai-nan Tzu, (c) Confucian discussions on the Six
Disciplines, (d) the period of classical learning, (e) Tung Chung-
shu and the New Text school, (f) prognostication texts, apocrypha,
and numerology during the Han dynasty, (g) the Old Text school, and
Yang Hsiung and Wang Ch'ung. Probably the best secondary source in
the English language.

_____. The Spirit of Chinese Philosophy. (See 1.4.3).
    Chapter 6 describes Han eclecticism in terms of cosmology, meta-
physics, the Five-Element theory, Yin Yang philosophy, etc., and
evaluates the pro's and con's of the philosophy of Tung Chung-shu
as well as other representative systems of thought during the Han
dynasty.

LIU, WU-CHI. A Short History of Confucian Philosophy. Baltimore:
    Penguin Books, 1955. 229 pp.
    On pp. 112-129 is given a very good account of the revival of
learning in the Han, the institution of eruditi of the Five
Classics, the civil service examination system, the growth of the
"science of catastrophes and anomalies," the two imperial conferences on political and ethical issues, the conflict between the
Old Script and Modern Script schools, the growth of rationalism,
and the canonization of Confucius.

    1.9.1 Various Han Thinkers

    BUSCH, HEINRICH. "Hsün Yüeh, ein Denker am Hofe des letzten
        Hankaisers," in Monumenta Serica, 10 (1945): 58-59.
        Hsün Yüeh's (148-209 A.D.) ideas on the Classics, the
    universe, and life are systematically outlined with the sup-
    port of extensive quotations in translation and in Chinese
    characters.

    CHEN, CHI-YUN. Hsün Yüeh, The Life and Reflections of an Early
        Medieval Confucian. Cambridge University, 1974. 242 pp.
        On the life and thoughts of Hsün Yüeh the Han Confucian
    scholar-official. A case study of the intellectual and

political preoccupations of the later Han cultural elite and
a detailed analysis of the cross-currents and triangular
struggle of the Confucianists, Taoists, and Legalists at the
end of the Han and in the immediate post-Han era.

HUAN T'AN. Hsin-lun (new treatise) and other writings by Huan
T'an. Tr. by Timoteus Pokora. Ann Arbor, Michigan: Center
for Chinese Studies, The University of Michigan, 1975.
414 pp.
   Translation of over 200 fragments, found in sixty-four
sources, of the New Treatise by Huan T'an (B.C. 24-56 A.D.),
a minor Han dynasty scholar, whose unconventional, creative,
and independent ideas on literature, music, natural and
strange phenomena, etc., formed a significant link between
early and later Han thought. Previous translations of even
partial fragments have been noted. With substantial footnotes and a forty-page bibliography.

POKORA, TIMOTEUS. "The Life of Huan T'an," in Archiv Orientalni, 31 (1963): 1-79, 521-576.
   A very scholarly and thorough study of the life of this
Han dynasty scholar who is virtually unknown in the west.
Also an examination into the basis of his materialistic and
rationalistic standpoint and his criticism of Yang Hsiung
and others.

YÜ, YING-SHIH. "Life and Immortality in the Mind of Han
Chinese," in Harvard Journal of Asiatic Studies, 25 (1965):
80-122.
   A section of the author's doctoral dissertation, View of
Life and Death in Later Han China, A.D. 25-220, Harvard
University Ph.D. thesis, 1962, 201 pp. An extensively docu-
mented and excellent study of the theories of cultivation of
life, destiny, death, the soul, and immortality, chiefly in
Han times. Some light is thrown, in this connection, on the
nature of Han eclecticism.

1.9.2 Tung Chung-shu (179-104 B.C.)

See also 11.3.

CHAI, CH'U and WINBERG CHAI, eds. The Humanist Way in Ancient
China: Essential Works of Confucianism. New York: Bantam
Books, 1965. 373 pp.
   Chapter 8 introduces Tung's thought with selected readings
translated from the Ch'un-ch'iu fan-lu (luxuriant gems of
the Spring and Autumn Annals). Generally good.

CHAN, WING-TSIT. <u>A Source Book in Chinese Philosophy</u>. (<u>See</u> 1.2.1).

Chapter 14 introduces the Yin Yang Confucianism of Tung, with selected translations from the original text of Tung's major work, <u>Luxuriant Gems of the Spring and Autumn Annals</u>. Additional selections are also made and rearranged under the subjects of (a) the Origin (yüan), (b) humanity and righteousness, (c) humanity and wisdom, (d) historical cycles. With comments.

FUNG YU-LAN. <u>A History of Chinese Philosophy</u>. (<u>See</u> 1.2.1), Vol. 2.

In chapter 2 on Tung Chung-shu and the New Text school, Fung gives an extensive discussion of the various aspects of the subject, such as the cosmological system of the Yin Yang school, the Origin, Heaven, the Five Elements, the four seasons, the correlation of man with the numerical categories of heaven, human nature and feelings, individual and social ethics, political and social philosophy, philosophy of history, and significance of the <u>Spring and Autumn Annals</u>.

_____. <u>A Short History of Chinese Philosophy</u>. (<u>See</u> 1.3.1).

In chapter 17, Tung is considered the Confucian theorizer of the Han empire. The eclectic Confucianism of Tung is discussed in a clear outline.

NEEDHAM, JOSEPH. <u>Science and Civilisation in China</u>. (<u>See</u> 1.6.1), Vol. 2, <u>History of Scientific Thought</u>.

An excellent analysis of the philosophy of Tung Chung-shu under the three headings of (a) roots of the philosophy of organism, (b) element theories and experimental science in China and Europe, and (c) macrocosm and microcosm. Needham clarifies the scientific as well as the pseudo-scientific aspect of Tung's philosophy of organism.

POKORA, TIMOTEUS. "Notes on New Studies on Tung Chung-shu," in <u>Archiv Orientalni</u>, 33 (1965): 256-271.

One of the best books written in contemporary China by Chou Fu-ch'eng in 1962 is here summarized along with a list of translations of Tung's works as well as a very extensive bibliography in Chinese, Japanese, and Western languages on Tung.

TAIN, TZEY-YUEH. <u>Tung Chung-shu's System of Thought: Its Sources and Its Influence on Han Scholars</u>. University of California, Los Angeles, Ph.D. thesis, 1974. 301 pp.

Aside from a long bibliography of Tung, Tung's system of thought and its sources form the major portion of the thesis.

The former includes the philosophy of the One and the Many, man and his destiny, the state, history, and the Spring and Autumn Annals. The latter includes sources of Tung's cosmological thought of material force, the One, Origin, his ethical, political and economic theories, and his theory of history. Tung's extensive influence on Han dynasty scholars is shown. With ample textual support, but the Moist influence on Tung is highly questionable.

YAO, SHAN-YU. "The Cosmological and Anthropological Philosophy of Tung Chung-shu," in Journal of the North China Branch of the Royal Asiatic Society, 73 (1948): 40-68.
An informative essay on Tung's philosophy in terms of the cosmic order, the state, and the individual man.

1.9.3 Huai-nan Tzu (d. 122 B.C.)

FUNG YU-LAN. A History of Chinese Philosophy. (See 1.2.1), Vol. 1.
In chapter 15 the cosmology of the Huai-nan Tzu is briefly introduced with some explanations of the terms such as ch'i (the fluid), yüan-ch'i (the primal fluid), and t'ai-shih (the Great Beginning).

NEEDHAM, JOSEPH. Science and Civilisation in China. (See 1.6.1), Vol. 2 History of Scientific Thought.
Needham treats the philosophy of the Huai-nan Tzu at least in two places (pp. 71-79, pp. 121-127), where he tries to find some scientific empiricist tendency in the text. Short but scholarly.

Tao, ·The Great Luminant. Tr. by Evan Morgan. London: K. Paul, Trench, Trubner & Co., 1935. 287 pp. Reprinted in Taipei: Chinese Materials and Research Aids Service Center.
Poor and unreliable.

WALLACKER, BENJAMIN E. The Huai-nan Tzu, Book Eleven: Behavior, Culture, and the Cosmos. New Haven: American Oriental Society, 1962. 88 pp.
Translation of a chapter not included in the above-mentioned work, with a long, good discussion on the text and its commentaries and a summary of the chapter.

1.9.4 Yang Hsiung (53 B.C.-18 A.D.)

CHAN, WING-TSIT. A Source Book in Chinese Philosophy. (See 1.2.1).

Chapter 15 introduces the Taoistic Confucianism of Yang
Hsiung with short, selected translation from the text, with
footnotes and comments.

DOERINGER, FRANKLIN MELVIN. Yang Hsiung and His Formulation
of a Classicism. Columbia University Ph.D. thesis, 1971.
    Traces Yang's classicism against his life and intellectual
development and shows how he used the Taoist concept of a
mystical order underlying the universe as a basis of revival
of Confucianism in his Fa-yen (model sayings) to combine
Taoist cosmology and Confucian ethics to restore Confucian
thought. According to Yang, only the sage can grasp ultimate
truth and beauty and make them available to the people.
Hence the importance of the Classics.

FORKE, A. Geschichte der mittelalterlichen chinesischen
Philosophie. Hamburg: Friederichsen, de Gruyter and Co.,
1934. 410 pp.
    Brief sketches of Yang Hsiung's life and work, Chinese
literature on Yang Hsiung, and the contents of his two works,
including his doctrines on human nature, Tao and virtue, im-
mortals, and critique of other philosophers.

FUNG YU-LAN. A History of Chinese Philosophy. (See 1.2.1),
Vol. 2.
    In chapter 4, a very good discussion is given of Yang's
eclectic philosophy. A good analysis of the main contents
of two major works, the Great Mystery Classic and the Model
Sayings. See pp. 136-150.

YANG HSIUNG. Le catechisme philosophique de Yang-Hiong-tse.
Tr. by B. Belpaire. Brussels: Edition de L'Occident, 1960.
113 pp.
    A translation of Yang Hsiung's Fa-yen. The thirteen chap-
ters deal with moral cultivation, study, filial piety,
spiritual beings, longevity, the sage, prophecy, the superior man, etc.

1.9.5 Wang Ch'ung (27-100?)

FUNG YU-LAN. A History of Chinese Philosophy. (See 1.2.1),
Vol. 2, pp. 150-167.
    An excellent treatment of Wang Ch'ung's philosophy, by
focusing on the following points: (a) naturalism; (b) criticism of contemporary beliefs; (c) view of history; (d) methodology; (e) theory of human nature; and (f) view of fate.

LI, SHI-YI. "Wang Ch'ung," in T'ien Hsia Monthly, 5 (1937):
162-184, 209-307.
   On Wang's methodology, view of history, criticism of contemporary beliefs, human nature, education, as well as on
the background of Wang's philosophy, the discussion of which
is particularly good.

Lun-Heng. Tr. by Alfred Forke. London: Luzac, 1907-1911.
   Vol. 1, 577 pp. Vol. 2, 531 pp.; reprinted in New York:
Paragon.
   This translation of the Lun-heng (balanced inquiry) and
critical essays of Wang Ch'ung is indeed an excellent one,
highly scholarly and meticulous, with very good notes on the
ideas of the Five Agents, cycles, and other important
subjects.

NEEDHAM, JOSEPH. Science and Civilisation in China. (See
1.6.1), Vol. 2, History of Scientific Thought, pp. 371-386.
   A very keen analysis, with reference to science, of Wang
Ch'ung's philosophy under three subjects: (a) centrifugal
cosmology, (b) Wang Ch'ung's denial of anthropocentrism, the
phenomenalists and Wang's struggle against them, and (c) Wang
and human destiny.

POKORA, TIMOTEUS. "The Necessity of a More Thorough Study of
Philosopher Wang Ch'ung and His Predecessors," in Archiv
Orientalni, 30 (1962): 231-257.
   Works by contemporary Chinese writers on Wang Ch'ung are
reviewed. According to Pokora, the materialism in Wang
Ch'ung was not a sudden development but a gradual unfolding
from the thoughts of his predecessors, like Yang Hsiung and
Huan T'an.

T'IEN CH'ANG-WU. "Methodological Problems in the Study of the
History of Philosophy from an Evaluation of Wang Ch'ung," in
Chinese Studies in Philosophy, 4 (1972-73): 70-99.
   The main points of the article are that Wang Ch'ung represented by Tung Chung-shu which is feudalistic, that his overall analysis in the perspective of his time is still
subjective, and that his relationship to the class struggle
and the function of that struggle must be carefully explored.

_____. "Wang Ch'ung: An Ancient Chinese Militant Materialist,"
in Chinese Studies in Philosophy, 7 (1975-76): 4-197.
   Selected translations from T'ien's book in Chinese,
arranged under the headings of "materialistic naturalism,"
"militant atheism," "sociohistorical viewpoints," and "criticism of the way of Confucius and Mencius and of other

writers." T'ien's aim is not to show that Wang Ch'ung has
given China Marxism, but to apply Marxism in making a scientific recapitulation of Wang Ch'ung's work (the Lun-heng)
to expedite China's socialist revolution.

1.10 NEO-TAOISM

See also 15.4.

1.10.1 Historical Factors and the Intellectual Climate

CHAN, WING-TSIT. A Source Book in Chinese Philosophy. (See
  1.2.1).
    Chapter 19 contains an introductory essay on both the
historical factors and the intellectual climate, with
selected translations from the major writings of Wang Pi,
Ho Yen, Kuo Hsiang. With comments.

CHEN CHI-YUN. Hsün Yüeh, The Life and Reflections of an Early
  Medieval Confucian. Cross reference: 1.9.1.

FUNG YU-LAN. A History of Chinese Philosophy. (See 1.2.1),
  Vol. 2.
    Chapters 5 and 6 give a clear and detailed account of the
Neo-Taoist movement. The historical factors, the intellectual climate, along with individual Neo-Taoist thoughts, are
all discussed well.

MATHER, RICHARD B. "The Controversy Over Conformity and
  Naturalness During the Six Dynasties," in History of Religions, 9 (1969/1970): 160-180.
    A very interesting discussion of the two modes of thought
during the Six Dynasties (222-589), viz. the Teaching of
Names (ming-chiao) advocated by the activists and the principle of naturalness (tzu-jan) upheld by the quietists.

SIU, RALPH GUN HOY. Ch'i: A Neo-Taoist Approach to Life.
  Cambridge: MIT Press, 1974. 351 pp.
    Explores the "time-light-life continuum" via a synthesis
of philosophical and scientific ideas. In the ancient
Chinese style a synoptic text of some 80 short expositions
is followed by extended commentaries keyed to each one.

1.10.2 Lieh Tzu (Date Uncertain)

See also 16.5.

The Book of Lieh Tzu. Tr. by A.C. Graham. London: John
  Murray, 1960. 183 pp.
    A reliable translation with many useful notes. Many quo-
  tations from earlier works, such as the Chuang Tzu, have been
  located.

FUNG YU-LAN. A History of Chinese Philosophy. (See 1.2.1),
  Vol. 2, pp. 190-204.
    The philosophy of Lieh Tzu is regarded as a kind of Taoist
  materialism and mechanism, with a more elaborate discussion
  of hedonism in the "Yang Chu" chapter.

GRAHAM, A.C. "The Date and Composition of Liehtzyy," in Asia
  Major, n.s., 8 (1961): 139-198.
    Concludes on the basis of certain passages shared by it
  and certain other texts and its use of certain terms and ex-
  pressions that the Lieh Tzu was written in the fourth century
  A.D., likely within the family of its commentator, Chang
  Chan (fl. 310).

Taoist Teachings from the Book of Lieh Tzu. Tr. by Lionel
  Giles. London: John Murray, 1912. 121 pp.
    A fairly good translation with some of the most important
  passages omitted. The text, generally considered a product
  of the 3rd century A.D., is here presented as older than the
  Chuang Tzu.

1.10.3 The "Light Conversation" Movement

CHEN CHI-YUN. Hsün Yüeh, The Life and Reflections of an Early
  Medieval Confucian. Cross reference: 1.9.1.

FUNG YU-LAN. A Short History of Chinese Philosophy. (See
  1.3.1).
    Chapter 20 deals with Neo-Taoism of the sentimentalists in
  the "light-conversation" movement. Quotations are cited
  from the Shih-shuo hsin-yü (new accounts of the talks of the
  time) for a very interesting and humorous discussion of the
  feng-liu ("wing and stream") tradition, the romanticist
  teaching of loving according to impulse, etc. An enjoyable
  reading.

MATHER, RICHARD B. "The Controversy Over Conformity and
  Naturalness During the Six Dynasties." Cross reference:
  1.10.1.

1.10.4 Ho Yen (190-249)

CHAN, WING-TSIT. A Source Book in Chinese Philosophy. (See
    1.2.1).
    In chapter 19 on Neo-Taoism, there is a translation of Ho's
very short Treatise on Tao with some comment.

1.10.5 Juan Chi (210-263)

1.10.6 Hsi K'ang (223-262)

de BARY, WM. THEODORE, WING-TSIT CHAN, and BURTON WATSON, comps.
    Sources of Chinese Tradition. (See 1.2.1).
    In chapter 11 on Neo-Taoism, there is a translation of
Hsi's writings on partiality and on the nourishment of life.
A useful material, though too short.

HOLZMAN, DONALD. La vie et la pensée de Hi K'ang (223-262
    APJ-C). Leiden: Brill, 1957. 186 pp.
    This is the only work on this Neo-Taoist thinker in a
Western language. Hsi's background, life, and thought are
given on pp. 3-79, and his treatises are translated on
pp. 83-130.

1.10.7 Wang Pi (226-249)

BERGERON, MARIE-INA. Wang Pi, philosophe du "Non-avoir."
    Étude de la philosophie de Wang Pi à partir du Tcheou Yi
    lio-li. University of Paris Ph.D. thesis, 1971. 225 pp.
    A translation of Wang Pi's "General Introduction to the
Book of Changes" with the aid of Wang Pi's commentaries on
the Book of Changes and on the Tao-te-ching, with emphasis
on the philosophy of non-being.

CHAN, WING-TSIT. A Source Book in Chinese Philosophy. (See
    1.2.1), pp. 318-324.
    A translation of selections from Wang's Simple Exemplifi-
cations of the Principles of the Book of Changes, Commentary
on the Book of Changes, as well as of Commentary on the Lao
Tzu, with comments.

FUNG YU-LAN. A History of Chinese Philosophy. (See 1.2.1),
    Vol. 2, pp. 179-189.
    In chapter 5, Fung gives a careful philosophical analysis
of Wang Pi's ideas of non-being, sagely emotions, concepts
and principles, with many quotations from Wang's writings.

T'ANG YUNG-T'UNG. "Wang Pi's New Interpretation of the <u>I ching</u> and <u>Lun-yü</u>." Tr. by Walter Liebenthal in <u>Harvard Journal of Asiatic Studies</u>, 10 (1947): 124-161.
    This study of Wang's interpretation of the <u>Book of Changes</u> and the <u>Analects</u> sheds new light on Wang Pi as a unique philosopher in the history of Chinese philosophy.

WRIGHT, ARTHUR F. "Review of A.A. Petrov's Wang Pi (226-249): His Place in the History of Chinese Philosophy," in <u>Harvard Journal of Asiatic Studies</u>, 10 (1947): 75-88.
    A good summary of Petrov's work, which is a highly scholarly study of Wang's philosophy.

1.10.8 <u>Hsiang Hsiu (fl. 250) and Kuo Hsiang (d. 312)</u>

See also 11.7.7.

CHAN, WING-TSIT. "The Evolution of the Neo-Confucian Concept Li as Principle," in <u>Tsing Hua Journal of Chinese Studies</u>, n.s., 4, no. 2 (1964): 123-149.
    An account and analysis of the cardinal Chinese philosophical concept, its development in ancient schools, its interpretations in Han times, Neo-Taoist and Buddhist contributions to its evolution, its development in Neo-Confucianism, etc. Note in particular the discussion of the philosophical contributions by Kuo Hsiang as well as by Wang Pi in terms of the concept <u>Li</u>.

_____. <u>A Source Book in Chinese Philosophy</u>. (<u>See</u> 1.2.1), pp. 326-335.
    A translation of Kuo Hsiang's <u>Commentary on the Chuang Tzu</u>, rearranged with comments.

<u>Chuang Tzu, a New Selected Translation with an Exposition of the Philosophy of Kuo Hsiang</u>. Tr. by Fung Yu-lan. Cross reference: 1.4.3.

FUNG YU-LAN. <u>A History of Chinese Philosophy</u>. (<u>See</u> 1.2.1), Vol. 2.
    A very good account of the Neo-Taoist philosophy of Hsiang Hsiu and Kuo Hsiang under the headings of (a) the relationships of things in the universe, (b) self-transformation, (c) natural and social change, (d) non-activity, (e) sage wisdom, (f) "the happy excursion," (g) "the equality of things," and (h) the perfect man.

_____. <u>A Short History of Chinese Philosophy</u>. (<u>See</u> 1.3.1), pp. 220-230.

A very good account of Hsiang Hsiu's and Kuo Hsiang's Neo-
Taoism, by focusing on their ideas of the self-transformation
of things, institution and morals, wu-wei (nonaction) and
yu-wei (having action), knowledge and imitation, equality of
things, as well as on absolute freedom and absolute happiness.

_____. The Spirit of Chinese Philosophy. (See 1.4.3),
pp. 135-146.
    In chapter 7 on the Mythical school, Fung gives his own
evaluation of both Kuo Hsiang and Wang Pi by using the criterion of "inner sagehood and outer kingliness."

1.11 BUDDHIST PHILOSOPHY IN CHINA

See also 3.6, 15.14.

CH'EN, KENNETH. The Chinese Transformation of Buddhism. Princeton,
N.J.: Princeton University Press, 1973. 345 pp.
    A comprehensive account of the Sinicization of Buddhism under the
headings of ethical life, political life, economic life, literary
life, educational and social life. The Chinese transformation of
Buddhist philosophical doctrines is not touched upon.

FU, CHARLES WEI-HSUN. "Mahāyāna Buddhism (China)," in Historical
Atlas of the Religions of the World. Ed. by Ismáil Rāgí al Farūqí.
New York: Macmillan Publishing Co., 1974. Pp. 185-194.
    A philosophical account of the historical and doctrinal develop-
ment of Chinese Mahayana Buddhism.

1.11.1 Introduction and Response

See also 15.4.

BALAZS, STEFAN. "Der Philosoph Fan Tschen und sein Traktat
gegen den Buddhismus," in Sinica, 7 (1932): 220-234.
   One of the most important treatises concerning Chinese
response to Buddhism. Here Fan (fl. 502) argues that the
spirit is merely the function of the body, like sharpness in
a knife, and does not survive the body. Balazs has given
valuable information about Fan.

CHANG, ALOYSIOUS. "Fan Chen and His 'Treatise on the Destruction of the Soul,'" in Chinese Culture, 14, no. 4 (1975):
1-8.
   Fan Chen's famous essay is here translated. Fan held that
when the body is destroyed, the soul is also destroyed, and
that the popular belief in heaven and hell is imaginary.

CH'EN, KENNETH. <u>Buddhism in China: A Historical Survey</u>.
Princeton, N.J.: Princeton University Press, 1964. 560 pp.
   In the Introduction, a very good account is given of the
background, importation, and early development of Buddhism
in the Han dynasty. Further, in the first part on growth
and domestication of Buddhism, the author gives a smooth
narrative of Buddhist contact with the indigenous traditions
of China.

       . <u>The Chinese Transformation of Buddhism</u>. Cross
reference: 1.11.

de BARY, WM. THEODORE, et al., eds. <u>The Buddhist Tradition in
India, China, and Japan</u>. New York: The Modern Library, 1969.
417 pp.
   Chapter 5, "The Coming of Buddhism to China," contains
source material on Chinese reactions to such questions as
Buddhism and the body, marriage, worldly pleasure, Indian
influence, immorality, etc.

DEMIÉVILLE, PAUL. "La Pénétration du Bouddhisme dans la Tra-
dition Philosophique Chinoise," in <u>Cahiers d'Histoire
Mondiale</u>, 1 (1956): 19-38.
   Shows conclusively that Monk Chih Tun (314-366) interpreted
Buddhist Thusness, the Absolute, in terms of Neo-Taoist <u>li</u>,
or principle, thereby turning Neo-Taoist naturalism into
Buddhist transcendentalism. There are also illuminating dis-
cussions on sudden and gradual enlightenment.

FANG, LI-T'IEN. "A Tentative Treatise on the Buddhist Philosophical Thought of Hui-yüan," in <u>Chinese Studies in Philos-
ophy</u>, 4 (1973): 36-76.
   A survey of Hui-yüan's (334-416) life and times, his tran-
sition from idealist "original non-being" philosophy to
mysterious transcendentalism, his propagation of the theory
of retribution, his idealist theory of spirit and body, and
his effort to harmonize the contradiction between Buddhism
and Chinese traditional morals and institutions. The author
thinks that his doctrines are vulgar, his theology absurd
and ridiculous, and his philosophy but a tool to fool the
people.

HU SHIH. "The Indianization of China: A Case Study of Cultural
Borrowing," in <u>Independence, Convergence, and Borrowing in
Institutions, Thought and Art</u>. Cambridge, Mass.: Harvard
University Press, 1937. Pp. 239-246.
   A general survey on Buddhist influence on Neo-Confucian
thought with special emphasis on the clear Neo-Confucian

distinction between Principle of Nature and human desires
and the new religious character of the Confucian doctrine of
reverence.

HURVITZ, LEON. "'Render Unto Caesar,' in Early Chinese
Buddhism: Hui-yüan's Treatise on the Exemption of the
Buddhist Clergy from the Requirement of Civil Etiquette,"
in Sino-Indian Studies, 5, parts 3 and 4 (1957): 80-114.
    Hui-yüan's treatise explains why monks should not prostrate
before emperors, why they live on a different spiritual level
of life, and why they attempt to seek the source of truth.

LIEBENTHAL, WALTER. "Shih Hui Yüan's Buddhism as Set Forth in
his Writings," in Journal of the American Oriental Society,
70 (1950): 243-259.
    Selected translations from the monk's works on karma,
meditation, transmigration, abandonment of secular life, etc.

MAKITA, TAIRYO. "Hui-yüan--His Life and Times," in Zinbum,
Memoirs of the Research Institute for Humanistic Studies.
Kyoto University, 6 (1962): 1-28.
    An excellent study of the life and ideas of this crucial
monk who shaped the development of Buddhism in China. The
article concentrates on the key issues on which Hui-yüan
defended Buddhism against Chinese criticisms, namely, retribution and why monks do not prostrate before the emperor.

T'ANG YUNG-T'UNG. "Professor Tang Yong-tong's 'Various Traditions Concerning the Entry of Buddhism into China.'" Tr. by
Authur E. Link in Phi Theta Annual, 4 (1953).
    The most eminent and authoritative writer on the history
of Chinese Buddhism utilized obscure sources in a most meticulous and fully documented deliberation on a subject sur-
rounded by controversy.

YU, DAVID C. "Skill-in-means and the Buddhism of Tao-sheng:
A Study of a Chinese Reaction to Mahāyāna of the Fifth Century," in Philosophy East and West, 24 (1974): 413-428.
    The article attempts to investigate two doctrines: skill-
in-means as embodied in the Lotus Scripture and sudden
enlightenment as expounded by Tao-sheng (d. 434). Skill-in-
means is understood as power of the Supreme Buddha, as
provincial truth, and as power of the celestial bodhisattvas.
In formulating his doctrine of sudden enlightenment, Tao-
sheng adopted only the meaning of skill-in-means as provincial truth from India.

ZURCHER, E. "Buddhism in China," in <u>The Legacy of China</u>. Ed.
  by R. Dawson. London: Oxford University Press, 1964. 392 pp.
    A good historical essay, outlining well the historical
  development of Buddhism in China since its importation from
  India.

_____. <u>The Buddhist Conquest of China</u>. Leiden: Brill, 1959.
  2 vols. 468 pp.
    The best study of Chinese Buddhism from the first through
  the fifth century, with abundant and scholarly notes and
  evidences.

1.11.2 <u>Early Buddhist Schools</u>

  1.11.2.1 *The Seven Schools of Original Non-being, etc.*

    CHAN, WING-TSIT. <u>A Source Book in Chinese Philosophy</u>.
      (<u>See</u> 1.2.1).
        Chapter 20 introduces the seven early Buddhist
      schools with selected translations from the major
      writings of Chi-tsang, the greatest Mādhyamika (Middle
      Doctrine school) monk, synthesizing the previous teach-
      ings in early schools.

    de BARY, WM. THEODORE, et al., eds. <u>The Buddhist Tra-
      dition in India, China and Japan</u>. (<u>See</u> 1.11.1),
      pp. 139-143.
        A brief account is here given of the early Buddhist
      schools in China.

    ZURCHER, E. <u>The Buddhist Conquest of China</u>. (<u>See</u>
      1.11.1).
        The most comprehensive and profound analysis of the
      formation and basic doctrines of the early Buddhist
      schools. Undoubtedly the best on the subject thus
      far produced in the English language.

  1.11.2.2 *Seng-chao (384-414)*

    CHAN, WING-TSIT. <u>A Source Book in Chinese Philosophy</u>.
      (<u>See</u> 1.2.1).
        Chapter 21 contains an introductory essay on Seng-
      chao's doctrine of reality, with a translation of the
      two most important chapters (1 and 2) of Seng-chao's
      <u>Treatises</u>. Comments added.

    <u>Chao Lun: The Treatises of Seng-chao</u>. Tr. by Walter
      Liebenthal. Hong Kong: Hong Kong University Press,
      1968. 152 pp.

Thus far the most authoritative translation and
interpretation of the most important work in the early
Buddhist schools. Complete and scholarly translation
of the Chao-lun, with excellent historical notes on
the situation in Ch'ang-an, the life and language of
Seng-chao, and on the extent of his learning, as well
as with careful notes and comments on Seng-chao's
philosophy.

FUNG YU-LAN. A History of Chinese Philosophy. (See
1.2.1), Vol. 2, pp. 258-270.
   A philosophical analysis of Seng-chao's ideas of the
immutability of things, emptiness of the unreal, as
well as of "prajñā is not knowledge," with many quotations cited from the original text.

ROBINSON, RICHARD H. Early Mādhyamika in India and
China. Madison: University of Wisconsin Press, 1967.
347 pp.
   A scholarly treatment of the subject. Chapter 6
discusses the life and writings of Seng-chao, with a
philosophical reconstruction of the basic terms, concepts, and logical structure of Seng-chao's work.
Robinson gives his own translation of the three most
important chapters of the Chao-lun. See Documents 8,
9, and 10 of the Appendix.

_____. "Mysticism and Logic in Seng-Chao's Thought,"
in Philosophy East and West, 8 (1958-59): 99-120.
   Seng-chao's mysticism is seen from his understanding
of samādhi (calmness) and vijñana (wisdom). This is
followed by an examination of Seng-chao's discussion
of the relation between language and facts and the
problem of talking about the unimaginable. Then
Seng-chao's paradoxes and syllogisms are evaluated.
In all cases, ample citation from documents is given
as support.

SENG-CHAO. "Nirvana is Nameless," tr. by Chung-yuan
Chang in Journal of Chinese Philosophy, 1 (1973-1974):
247-276.
   A fresh translation of one of the four important
essays of Buddhist philosophy which comprises the
Chao-lun, with the translator's introduction.

1.11.3 The Three-Treatise School of Chi-tsang (549-623)

CH'EN, KENNETH. Buddhism in China. (See 1.11.1), pp. 131-134.
    A very brief account of the San-lun (three-treatises)
    school.

de BARY, WM. THEODORE, et al., eds. The Buddhist Tradition in
    India, China, and Japan. (See 1.11.1), pp. 143-150.
    Given here is the translation of selected passages from
    Chi-tsang's work on Twofold Truth.

FUNG YU-LAN. A History of Chinese Philosophy. (See 1.2.1),
    Vol. 2.
    In the first section of chapter 8, Fung gives a philo-
    sophical interpretation of Chi-tsang's theory of double
    truth, the central theme of the Chinese Mādhyamika repre-
    sented by Chi-tsang.

JAN YÜN-HUA. "Nāgārjuna, One or More? A New Interpretation
    of Buddhist Hagiography," in History of Religions, 10
    (1970): 139-155.
    Based on extensive consultation of Indian, Chinese, Japan-
    ese, and European sources, and with well-supported arguments,
    the author concludes that there is very little authenticity
    about the claim of the historicity of a "Tantric Nāgārjuna"
    or a "Later Nāgārjuna." There was only one Nāgārjuna (c.
    100-200), founder of the Three-Treatise school, to whom the
    later Buddhist hagiographers attributed many strange stories.

TAKAKUSU, J. The Essentials of Buddhist Philosophy. 3rd ed.
    Honolulu: Office Appliance Co., 1956. 221 pp.
    Chapter 7 deals with the Three-Treatise school in both the
    historical and philosophical perspectives. A very good in-
    troduction to this school.

1.11.4 The Consciousness-Only School of Hsüan-tsang (590-664)

CHAN, WING-TSIT. A Source Book of Chinese Philosophy. (See
    1.2.1).
    Chapter 23 contains an introduction to the Buddhist ideal-
    ism of Hsüan-tsang as well as a selected translation from
    The Treatise on the Establishment of the Doctrine of
    Consciousness-Only with Hsüan-tsang's commentary and Chan's
    comments, arranged under eight headings.

FUNG YU-LAN. A History of Chinese Philosophy. (See 1.2.1),
    Vol. 2, pp. 299-338.

A careful and philosophical treatment in detail of Hsüan-
tsang's as well as K'uei-chi's (632-682) completion of the
doctrine of "mere ideation" (Consciousness-Only) under the
headings of (a) the mere ideation theory of equally avoiding
being and non-being, (b) the four functional divisions of
consciousness, (c) the eighth or ālaya consciousness, (d) the
seventh or <u>manas</u> consciousness and the six other consciousnesses, and (e) the transformation of consciousness into
wisdom.

HSÜAN-TSANG. <u>Ch'eng wei-shih lun--Doctrine of Mere-Conscious-</u>
<u>ness</u>. Tr. by Wei Tat. Hong Kong: The Ch'eng wei-shih lun
Publication Committee, 1973. 818 pp.
    A complete translation of one of the most important works
in Consciousness-Only idealism, with the original Chinese
text and the translator's long introductory essay.

_____. <u>Vijñaptimātratāsiddhi, le siddhi de Hiuan-Tsang</u>. Tr.
by Louis de la Vallée Poussin. Paris: Geuthner, 1928-29.
2 vols. 820 pp.
    An authoritative translation of Hsüan-tsang's <u>Treatise on</u>
<u>the Establishment of the Doctrine of Consciousness-Only</u>.
The treatise synthesizes various Indian Buddhist idealist
theories and represents Hsüan-tsang's own doctrine which
forms the basis of the philosophy of the Consciousness-Only
school.

TAKAKUSU, J. <u>The Essentials of Buddhist Philosophy</u>. (See
1.11.3).
    Chapter 6 deals with the "Mere-Ideation" (Consciousness-
Only) school in both historical and philosophical perspectives. A good analysis of all important concepts and
doctrines of the school represented by Hsüan-tsang and his
disciple K'uei-chi, with a complete list of the one hundred
<u>dharmas</u> (elements of existence).

VASUBANDHU. <u>Vimsatikā</u>. <u>Wei Shin Er Shih Lun or the Treatise</u>
<u>on Twenty Stanzas on Representation-Only</u>. Tr. by Charles H.
Hamilton. New Haven: American Oriental Society, 1938.
82 pp.
    Careful translation of Vasubandhu's (c. 420-c. 500) work.
A basic philosophical text of the Consciousness-Only school
of Buddhism, the philosophical assumptions of which are
neatly summed up in verses.

VERDU, ALFONSO. <u>Dialectical Aspects in Buddhist Thought:</u>
<u>Studies in Sino-Japanese Mahāyāna Idealism</u>. New York:
Paragon Book Gallery, 1974. 273 pp.

An extremely sophisticated philosophical analysis of the
Ālayavijñāna concept, the Ālayavijñāna scheme of Tsung-mi,
the five degrees dialectic of the Soto-Zen School, and so on.

1.11.5 The T'ien-t'ai School of Chih-i (538-595) and Hui-wen
        (550-577)

See also 7.5, 7.6, 16.2.1.

de BARY, WM. THEODORE, et al., eds. The Buddhist Tradition in
   India, China, and Japan. (See 1.11.1).
      The section entitled "The Lotus School," pp. 155-166, con-
   tains an introduction on T'ien-t'ai (heavenly terrace)
   syncretism and translations on Buddha-nature in all, the
   method of concentration and insight, emptiness, temporari-
   ness, and the Mean, and the One Mind comprising all dharmas.

FUNG YU-LAN. A History of Chinese Philosophy. (See 1.2.1),
   Vol. 2, pp. 360-386.
      A comprehensive and philosophical treatment of the T'ien-
   t'ai school's Mahāyāna method of cessation and contemplation
   under the headings of (a) the Bhūtatathatā (Thusness) and
   Tathāgatagarbha (Storehouse of the Thus-Come), (b) the three
   characters, (c) universal and non-universal consciousness,
   (d) the integration of all things, (e) cessation and contemplation, (f) the impure natures of the Buddhas, (g) enlightenment and unenlightenment, etc. Some comparison with other
   schools is also made.

HURVITZ, LEON. Chih-i (538-597). An Introduction to the Life
   and Ideas of a Chinese Buddhist Monk. Bruges: Imprimerie
   Sainte-Catherine, 1963. 372 pp.
      A systematic and comprehensive presentation of the five-
   fold classication of Buddhist schools and the four basic doctrines of the school represented by Chih-i. The only available secondary source in book form on Chih-i.

1.11.6 The Hua-yen School of Fa-tsang (643-712) and Tsung-mi
        (780-841)

See also 7.6, 7.7.1, 7.7.2, 7.7.3, 15.13, 16.2.2.

CHANG, GARMA C.C. The Buddhist Teaching of Totality: The
   Philosophy of Hwa Yen Buddhism. University Park: Pennsylvania State University Press, 1971. 270 pp.
      Divided into three parts: (a) the realm of totality;
   (b) the philosophical foundations of Hua-yen (flowery splen-
   dor) Buddhism; and (c) a selection of Hua-yen readings and

the biographies of the patriarchs from various sources, including the writings of Fa-tsang, Tu-shun (557-640), and
others. A scholarly work.

COOK, FRANCIS H. "The Meaning of Vairocana in Hua-yen Buddhism," in Philosophy East and West, 22, no. 4 (October,
1972): 403-415.
    A philosophical exploration of the meaning of Vairocana
mainly through Fa-tsang's commentaries. The author directly
answers (p. 413) the question of who Vairocana was "by giving
an equation such as Fa-tsang is so fond of: emptiness=
interdependence=Vairocana."

de BARY, WM. THEODORE, et al., eds. The Buddhist Tradition in
India, China, and Japan. (See 1.11.1), pp. 166-196.
    A good account of Fa-tsang's Treatise on the Golden Lion,
Buddhist vows, and a complete translation of Tsung-mi's On
the Original Nature of Man.

FORKE, ALFRED. Geschichte der mittelalterlichen chinesischen
Philosophie. Hamburg: Friederichsen, de Gruyter and Co.,
1934. 410 pp. Reprinted in New York: Paragon.
    Still a very valuable history of the middle period. See
pp. 366-371 for Tsung-mi's analysis and criticism of Ch'an
and synthesis of Buddhist philosophy.

FUNG YU-LAN. A History of Chinese Philosophy. (See 1.2.1),
Vol. 2, pp. 339-359.
    A careful and detailed analysis of Fa-tsang's "Essay on the
Golden Lion" under the headings of (a) understanding of
arising through causation, (b) discriminating the emptiness
of matter, (c) summarizing the Three Characters, (d) revela-
tion of the qualityless, (e) explaining non-generation,
(f) discussing the first teachings, (g) mastering the Ten
Mysteries, (h) embracing the Six Qualities, (i) achievement
of bodhi, (j) entry into Nirvāna, and (k) subjective and
objective idealism.

JAN YÜN-HUA. "Tsung-mi, His Analysis of Ch'an Buddhism," in
T'oung Pao, 58 (1972): 1-53.
    A most scholarly treatise on Tsung-mi as a young scholar,
as a mature scholar, his socio-political environment, his
religious attitude, his analyses of Ch'an Buddhism, and his
significance for the development of Buddhism in China. In
the most important section, Tsung-mi analyzed Ch'an sects
into three groups, namely "Esoteric teaching on the Characters as based on their Nature," "Esoteric teaching of revealing Nature itself by negation of the Characters," and the

"Exoteric teaching revealing that the True Mind itself is
the (Buddha) Nature." Three important documents are translated, and there is a table of Ch'an sects in the 8th and
9th centuries.

TAKAKUSU, J. The Essentials of Buddhist Philosophy. (See
1.11.3), chapter 8.
A very good summary of the school in both historical and
philosophical perspectives. Almost all aspects of the teachings of this school are presented.

1.11.7 The Ch'an (Zen) School

See also 7.5, 8.4, 8.8, 15.13.

BREAR, A.D. "The Nature and Status of Moral Behavior in Zen
Buddhist Tradition," in Philosophy East and West, 24 (1974):
429-442.
The thesis of the essay is that Zen (meditation) is part
of the Mahāyāna tradition, sharing its definite approach to
moral behavior. Certain intellectual and moral precondi-
tions may be required before enlightenment can be obtained.
Thus the Zen life consists of the practice of usual Mahāyāna
virtues. This practice is consistently enjoined within the
tradition and is not affected by the absolute statements on
the irrelevance of good and evil.

CHANG, CHEN-CHI. "The Nature of Ch'an (Zen) Buddhism," in
Philosophy East and West, 6 (1957): 333-355.
Answers four questions: (1) Is Ch'an altogether incompre-
hensible and completely beyond the reach of human understanding? (2) What is "enlightenment" or wu (nothingness)
as understood by Ch'an? (3) How does the teaching of Ch'an
compare with the two main schools of Mahāyāna, namely
Yogācāra and Mādyhamika? (4) Is there a system, or order,
or category that we can follow to make Ch'an more intelligible? Very substantial and instructive.

DUMOULIN, HEINRICH VON. The Development of Chinese Zen after
the Sixth Patriarch in the Light of Mumonkan. Tr. from the
German by Ruth Fuller Sasaki. New York: The First Zen
Institute of America, 1953. 146 pp.
Translation of the 48 famous Zen questions and answers
collected in the "Gates of Monk No-Gate." The development
of the use of the question and answer technique is also
traced.

HU SHIH. "Ch'an (Zen) Buddhism in China: Its History and
Method," in Philosophy East and West, 3 (1953): 3-24.
   Strongly argues that the development of Ch'an in China
depended on historical factors, was part of the general
stream of Chinese thought, and involved the use of rational
methods. The main attempt is to strip the mystical and
mythical character of Chinese Ch'an Buddhism. The essay is
a result of penetrating research by the eminent scholar.

_____. "Development of Zen Buddhism in China," in Chinese
Social and Political Science Review, 15 (1931-32): 475-505.
Reprinted in Sino-Indian Studies, 3 (1949): 99-126.
   After intensive investigation, Dr. Hu offers the theory,
with strong historical and exhaustive textual support, that
Chinese Ch'an is not an unfolding of Indian yoga or dhyāna
(meditation), but a revolt against it. The distinctly
Chinese elements in Ch'an are clearly brought out.

SUZUKI, DAISETZ TEITARO. Essays in Zen Buddhism. London:
Luzac, 1927: 423 pp., 1st series. In paperback in New York:
Grove Press, 1933, 326 pp. (Evergreen). 2nd series, 1933,
326 pp. 3rd series, 1934, 392 pp.
   The celebrated authority on Zen Buddhism presents a series
of essays on Chinese interpretation of Enlightenment, practical methods of Zen instruction, the meditation hall and
ideals of Zen life, kōan exercises, karma, sin, prayer,
passivism, etc., with ample sources from Chinese Zen masters.
Series 3 deals chiefly with basic texts and philosophical
concepts and also Zen contributions to Japanese culture.

_____. Manual of Zen Buddhism. Kyoto: The Eastern Buddhist
Society, 1935. 232 pp.
   Translations of hymns, prayers, scriptures and treatises
by Chinese and Japanese Zen Masters, with a discussion of
Buddhist statues and pictures in a Zen monastery. A tre-
mendous amount of source material.

_____. "Zen: A Reply to Hu Shih," in Philosophy East and West,
3 (1955): 25-46. Reprinted in his Studies in Zen. New York:
Dell Publications, 1955. Pp. 129-164.
   Vigorously attacks Hu Shih's interpretation of Zen as a
historical and rational development and insists that no one
can understand Zen and its history without first comprehend-
ing it in itself and doing so intuitively.

ZEUSCHNER, ROBERT B. "A Selected Bibliography on Ch'an
Buddhism in China," in Journal of Chinese Philosophy, 3
(1976): 299-311.

A simple listing, without comment or evaluation, of works
in Western languages and in Japanese, but not in Chinese.

1.11.7.1 *Hui-neng (638-713)*

HUI-NENG. The Platform Scripture. Tr. by Wing-tsit
Chan. New York: St. John's University Press, 1963.
193 pp.
   A translation of the text with an introductory
essay dealing with the historical background, the
problem of textual criticism, as well as with Hui-
neng's unique position in the history of Chinese Ch'an.

_____. The Platform Sūtra of the Six Patriarchs. Tr.
by Philip B. Yampolsky. New York: Columbia University
Press, 1967. 216 pp.
   A translation with an excellent introductory essay
describing Ch'an in the eighth century under the headings of (a) the formation of the legend, the Lankāvatāra school, Shen-hui, (b) the birth of a patriarch:
biography of Hui-neng, (c) the making of a book: the
Platform Sūtra, and (d) content analysis.

SUZUKI, DAISETZ TEITARO. The Zen Doctrine of No-Mind.
London: Rider, 1949. 155 pp.
   A very unique interpretation of Hui-neng's Zen
teachings under the headings of Hui-neng's attack
upon quietism, doctrine of mindlessness, the nature
of mondo (questions-answers) illustrating the no-mind,
as well as the nature of Zen "unconscious," etc.
Throws some new light on Hui-neng's dynamic approach
to Zen.

WU, JOHN. The Golden Age of Zen. Taipei: National War
College, 1967. 332 pp.
   An outstanding account of the history of Zen in
China. Chapter 3 deals with Hui-neng's life and time,
and chapter 4 analyzes his fundamental insights into
Zen.

1.11.7.2 *Shen-hsiu (605?-706)*

See 1.11.7.1 for passages contrasting the Zen teachings
of Hui-neng ("sudden enlightenment") and Shen-hsiu
("gradual enlightenment").

1.11.7.3 *Shen-hui (670-760)*

CHAN, WING-TSIT. A Source Book in Chinese Philosophy.
(See 1.2.1), pp. 440-444.
   Selected passages from the Recorded Conversations
of Shen-hui are translated, with comments and footnotes.

DUMOULIN, HEINRICH VON. A History of Zen Buddhism. Tr.
from the German by Paul Peachey. Boston: Beacon
Press, 1969. 335 pp. Pp. 83-87.
   A brief but clear account of Shen-hui's teachings
and activities as the key bearer of Hui-neng's school
of sudden awakening.

LIEBENTHAL, WALTER. "Shen Hui's Sermon on Sudden Awakening," in Asia Major, n.s., 3 (1953): 132-155.
   This is necessary reading for those interested in
technical Ch'an philosophy. Besides the scholarly
translation, there are surveys of early Buddhist
philosophical schools and various doctrines on
Enlightenment.

SHEN-HUI. "Entretiens du Maître de Dhyāna Chen-houei
du Ho-tsö." Tr. by Jacques Gernet in Publications de
L'École Francaise d'Extrème-Orient, 31 (1949): 1-126.
   French translation of the writings and sayings of
Shen-hui which have been collected by Hu Shih. Fundamental Ch'an concepts are formulated and deliber-
ated on in this work. The Neo-Taoist influence is
evident.

ZEUSCHNER, ROBERT B. "The Hsien Tsung Chi (An Early
Ch'an [Zen] Buddhist Text)," in Journal of Chinese
Philosophy, 3 (1976): 253-266.
   Translation of a short treatise by Shen-hui (670-
762), a famous disciple of the Sixth Patriarch of
Ch'an Buddhism, who contributed much to the development of its Southern School. In this treatise Shen-
hui's important ideas of intuitive wisdom, emptiness,
suchness, "seeing", etc. are expressed.

1.11.7.4 *The Lin-chi School*

CHAN, WING-TSIT. A Source Book in Chinese Philosophy.
(See 1.2.1).
   In chapter 26 some important passages from the
Recorded Conversations of Ch'an Master I-hsüan

(d. 867) are selected and translated, with useful
comments and footnotes.

CHANG, CHUNG-YUAN. Original Teachings of Ch'an
Buddhism. New York: Pantheon Books, 1969. 333 pp.
    A good translation of I-hsüan's sayings from the
Transmission of the Lamp, with some notes. But these
notes are not as helpful as those in the Charles Luk
work (see below).

de BARY, WM. THEODORE, et al., eds. The Buddhist Tradition in India, China, and Japan. (See 1.11.1),
pp. 225-231.
    Selected passages from the recorded sermon by I-
hsüan translated under the title "Seeing into One's
Nature."

I-HSÜAN (d. 867). Entretiens de Lin-tsi. Tr. by Paul
Demiéville. Paris: Fayard, 1972. 256 pp.
    A most scholarly and authoritative translation of
the Lin-chi yü-lu (recorded sayings of I-hsüan). One
of the basic works of Ch'an, by an outstanding scholar
of Buddhism. Excellent comments and numerous notes.

LUK, CHARLES. Ch'an and Zen Teaching. London: Rider,
1960. 254 pp. Second series, reprinted as paperback, Berkeley: Shambala Publications, 1971.
    In chapter 3 of part 2, a very reliable translation
of I-hsüan's sayings, from The Five Lamps Meeting at
the Source, is given, with excellent and detailed
notes showing the author's insightful interpretation
of I-hsüan.

WU, JOHN. The Golden Age of Zen. (See 1.11.7.1).
    Chapter 11 discusses I-hsüan as the founder of the
Lin-chi school. A very good and interesting account.

1.11.7.5 *The Ts'ao-tung School*

CHANG, CHUNG-YUAN. Original Teachings of Ch'an Buddhism.
(See 1.11.7.4).
    Part 2 introduces the school as that of interfusion
of universality and particularity, with a good translation of the sayings of Tung-shan Liang-chieh (807-
869) and Ta'so-shan Pen-chi (840-901) from the Transmission of the Lamp. Notes are added, but not as
useful as those in the below-mentioned work.

LUK, CHARLES. Ch'an and Zen Teaching (Second series). (See 1.11.7.4).
    Chapter 5 of part 2 gives a good translation of the sayings by Ts'ao-shan Pen-chi, the second patriarch of the school, from The Five Lamps Meeting at the Source. Excellent notes added.

WU, JOHN. The Golden Age of Zen. (See 1.11.7.1).
    Chapter 10 deals with Tung-shan Liang-chieh, the founder of the Ts'ao-tung school. Clear and interesting.

1.11.7.6 *The Yün-men School*

CHANG, CHUNG-YUAN. Original Teachings of Ch'an Buddhism. (See 1.11.7.4).
    Part 7 introduces the school as that of "the swiftness and steepness"--a forceful means to enlightenment, with a good translation of the Ch'an sayings by Hsüeh-feng I-ts'un (822-908), Yün-men Wen-yen (d. 949), etc., from the Transmission of the Lamp. With notes, though not very useful.

LUK, CHARLES. Ch'an and Zen Teaching (Second series). (See 1.11.7.4).
    Chapter 6 of part 2 contains a reliable translation of the Ch'an sayings of Yün-men Wen-yen from The Five Lamps Meeting at the Source, with excellent and detailed notes.

WU, JOHN. The Golden Age of Zen. (See 1.11.7.1).
    A detailed discussion of Yün-men Wen-yen's Ch'an teaching, the founder of the school.

1.11.7.7 *The Kuei-shan School*

CHANG, CHUNG-YUAN. Original Teachings of Ch'an Buddhism. (See 1.11.7.4).
    Part 5 introduces the school as that of inner experience illustrated in three-way interplay, with a good translation of the sayings of Kuei-shan Ling-yu (771-853), Yang-shan Hui-chi (814-890), etc., from the Transmission of the Lamp. Notes are brief and not very helpful.

LUK, CHARLES. Ch'an and Zen Teaching (Second series). (See 1.11.7.4).

Chapter 2 of part 2 contains a reliable translation
of the Ch'an sayings of Yang-shan Hui-chi of the
school, from the Transmission of the Lamp. Excellent
and detailed notes added.

WU, JOHN. The Golden Age of Zen. (See 1.11.7.1).
    Chapter 9 discusses the Zen teaching of Kuei-shan
Ling-yu, the founder of the school. Good and
interesting.

1.11.7.8 *The Fa-yen School*

CHANG, CHUNG-YUAN. Original Teachings of Ch'an Buddhism.
(See 1.11.7.4).
    Part 6 introduces the school as that of the six
phenomena and the Void, with a good translation of the
sayings of Fa-yen Wei-i and Yung-ming Yen-shou (904-
975), from the Transmission of the Lamp. Notes are
brief and not very useful.

LUK, CHARLES. Ch'an and Zen Teaching (second series).
(See 1.11.7.4).
    Chapter 7 of part 2 contains a reliable translation
of Fa-yen Wen-i's Ch'an sayings from the Transmission
of the Lamp, with helpful notes.

WU, JOHN. The Golden Age of Zen. (See 1.11.7.1).
    Chapter 13 provides an interesting discussion of
Fa-yen Wen-i, the founder of the school.

1.12 T'ANG (618-907) THINKERS: HAN YÜ (768-824), LI AO (FL. 798),
AND LIU TSUNG-YÜAN (773-819)

CHAN, WING-TSIT. A Source Book in Chinese Philosophy. (See 1.2.1).
    Chapter 27 contains a short introductory essay describing the
historical significance of Han Yü and Li Ao as the two forerunners
of Neo-Confucian movement, with a translation of two important
writings by Han Yü ("An Inquiry on the Way") as well as of Li Ao's
"The Recovery of Nature" (part 2).

CHANG, CARSUN. The Development of Neo-Confucian Thought. (See
1.13.1), Vol. 1.
    A very good account of the life, time, and philosophy of both Han
Yü and Li Ao is given in chapters 4 and 5.

HOU WAI-LU. "Liu Tsung-yüan's Materialist Thought and Social Thought,"
in Chinese Studies in Philosophy, 4 (1973): 4-72.

A full exposition of Liu's Theory of Heaven in which he debated with Liu Yü-hsi (772-842) on the questions of the nature of Heaven and the relation between Heaven and man. Liu Tsung-yüan's viewpoint is that of materialism and atheism, rejecting the theological theory of the Mandate of Heaven but affirming man's struggle with nature and the concrete progress of history.

LAMONT, H.G., tr. "An Early Ninth-Century Debate on Heaven: Liu Tsung-yüan's T'ien-shuo and Liu Yü-hsi's T'ien-lun," in Asia Major, 18, part 2 (1973): 181-208.
    The debate was not so much on the nature of Heaven as on its rela-tion to man. The term t'ien is used variously to mean Nature, Heaven as the supreme power, and physical heaven, but the basic issue is whether man's actions are controlled and rewarded or punished by Heaven.

LIU, WU-CHI. A Short History of Confucian Philosophy. Baltimore: Penguin Books, 1955. 229 pp.
    A generally accurate historical account of Confucian philosophy. See pp. 138-145 for a brief discussion of the positions of the two forerunners of Neo-Confucianism.

PULLEYBLANK, EDWIN G. "Neo-Confucianism and Neo-Legalism in T'ang Intellectual Life," in Confucian Persuasion. Ed. by Arthur F. Wright. Stanford: Stanford University Press, 1960. Pp. 77-114.
    On the Ancient Script school, new criticism of the Spring and Autumn Annals, and T'ien-t'ai Buddhism.

1.13 NEO-CONFUCIANISM

See also 3.2, 7.9.1, 7.9.2, 15.5, 15.13.

    1.13.1 Neo-Confucianism in General

    CHAI, CH'U. "Neo-Confucianism of the Sung-Ming Periods," in Social Research, 18 (1951): 370-392.
        On the relation between Neo-Confucianism and Buddhism and on certain characteristics of Neo-Confucianism. The latter include li (principle, order, reason), ch'i (material force), human nature, mind, and the interpretation of the Great Learning. The presentation is rather general, but instructive.

    CHAN, WING-TSIT. "The Evolution of the Neo-Confucian Concept of Li as Principle," in Tsing Hua Journal of Chinese Studies, n.s., 4, no. 2 (1964): 123-149. Reprinted in Chan, Neo-Confucianism, Etc. (See below), pp. 45-87.

A comprehensive account and analysis of the cardinal
Chinese philosophical concept, its development in ancient
schools, its interpretation in Han times, Neo-Taoist and
Buddhist contributions to its evolution, its Neo-Confucian
elaboration, its culmination in Chu Hsi, and its influence
in subsequent centuries.

_____. "The Neo-Confucian Solution of the Problem of Evil,"
in Studies Presented to Hu Shih on His Sixty-fifth Birthday,
Bulletin of the Institute of History and Philology, Academia
Sinica, 28 (1957): 773-791. Reprinted in Chan, Neo-
Confucianism, Etc. (See below), pp. 88-116.
After surveying the doctrines of good and evil among
ancient and medieval Chinese philosophers, the author goes
into detail on how Chang Tsai, for the first time in Chinese
history, offers transforming one's physical nature as the
solution to the problem of evil, and how Ch'eng Hao and
Ch'eng I developed the doctrine of jen as seed, that is,
life-giving.

_____. "Neo-Confucianism and Chinese Scientific Thought," in
Philosophy East and West, 6 (1957): 309-332. Reprinted in
Chan, Neo-Confucianism, Etc. (See above), pp. 186-226.
On the compatibility or incompatibility of Chinese philos-
ophy from ancient Confucianism and Taoism to Neo-Confucianism
with modern scientific thought, with special reference to
Joseph Needham's discussions on Chinese scientific thought.
(See 1.13.8).

_____. "Neo-Confucianism as an Integrative Force in Chinese
Thought," in Studia Asiatica: Essays in Asian Studies in
Felicitation of the Seventy-fifth Anniversary of Professor
Ch'en Shou-yi. Ed. by Laurence G. Thompson. San Francisco:
Chinese Materials Center, Inc., 1975. Pp. 315-336.
Contends that the comprehensiveness, syncretism and char-
acter of adherence to the Mean of Neo-Confucianism makes it
an integrative force.

_____. Neo-Confucianism, Etc. Essays by Wing-tsit Chan. Ed.
by Charles K.H. Chen. Hanover, N.H.: Oriental Society, 1969:
516 pp. (the English section) and 129 pp. (the Chinese
section).
A collection of 14 essays dealing with the Neo-Confucian
concepts of jen, man, Buddhism, li, evil, scientific thought,
Wang Yang-ming, K'ang Yu-wei, Hu Shih, Taoism, etc. The
Chinese section contains nine essays on similar subjects.

CHAN, WING-TSIT. "Neo-Confucianism: New Ideas in Old Termin-
ology," in Philosophy East and West, 12 (1967): 15-35.
Explains how Neo-Confucian philosophers gave traditional
philosophical terms and concepts a new interpretation, thus
developing Chinese philosophy to a higher level and making
Confucianism new. The terms and concepts discussed are: li,
hsing (nature), ts'ai (capacity, natural endowment), Tao,
t'i-yung (substance and function), ch'i (concrete things,
utensil), and jen.

CHANG, CARSUN. The Development of Neo-Confucian Thought.
New York: Bookman Associates, 1962. Vol. 1. 376 pp.
The best introduction to the historical factors of Neo-
Confucian movement, clear, accurate, and detailed. Chapters
1, 2, 3, and 6 are particularly important for the subject
under the different headings of (a) Confucianism in Chinese
history and a comparison with Western philosophy, (b) fundamental principles of the philosophy of reason, (c) institutions according to the school of the philosophy of reason,
and (d) Buddhism as a stimulus to Neo-Confucianism.

de BARY, WM. THEODORE. "A Reappraisal of Neo-Confucianism,"
in Studies in Chinese Thought. Ed. by Arthur F. Wright.
Chicago: University of Chicago Press, 1953. Pp. 81-111.
A fair appraisal, showing how the Neo-Confucianists followed tradition and yet departed, in some cases radically,
from their predecessors.

_____. "Some Common Tendencies in Neo-Confucianism," in
Confucianism in Action. Ed. by David S. Nivison and Arthur
F. Wright. Stanford: Stanford University Press, 1959.
Pp. 25-49.
The tendencies discussed are fundamentalism, humanism,
rationalism, and historical mindedness in both China and
Japan.

FORKE, ALFRED. Geschichte der neueren chinesischen Philosophie.
Hamburg: Friederichsen, de Gruyter and Co., 1938. 693 pp.
Reprinted in New York: Paragon.
About 100 thinkers are included, some at length and some
only very briefly. Many minor figures are covered here but
not elsewhere in the West. Instead of a systematic digest
of doctrines, the book is rather a collection of biographical
material and scattered sayings. The selections are from
standard Chinese sources and quotations of full paragraphs in
Chinese are most helpful.

FU, CHARLES WEI-HSUN. "Morality or Beyond: The Neo-Confucian
confrontation with Mahāyāna Buddhism," in Philosophy East
and West, 3 (July, 1973): 375-396.
    Philosophical discussion of Mahāyāna Buddhist influences on
Neo-Confucian thought as well as the orthodox Neo-Confucian
confrontation with Mahāyāna Buddhism, especially Ch'an.

FUNG YU-LAN. A History of Chinese Philosophy. (See 1.2.1),
Vol. 2.
    Chapter 10 discusses the rise of Neo-Confucianism and its
borrowings from Buddhism and Taoism under the headings of
(a) Han Yü, (b) Li Ao, (c) Neo-Confucianism and Buddhism,
one stream of thought in religious Taoism, and (d) the scientific spirit of religious Taoism. A very scholarly analysis
of the Mahāyāna Buddhist and Taoist influences on the formation of Neo-Confucian thought.

KUSUMOTO, MASATSUGU. "Conflict between the Thought of the
Sung Dynasty and the Ming Dynasty," in Philosophical Studies
of Japan, 5 (1964): 39-68.
    Preferring to see the similarities between Chu Hsi and Lu
Hsiang-shan in the Sung Dynasty and between Wang Yang-ming
and others in the Ming Dynasty, the writer contends that
Sung thought emphasizes Nature which is universal, whereas
Ming thought emphasizes the human element, a distinction that
is definitely too sharp.

LIU, SHU-HSIEN. "The Religious Import of Confucian Philosophy:
Its Traditional Outlook and Contemporary Significance."
Cross reference: 1.2.1.

SCHIROKAUER, CONRAD. "Neo-Confucians under Attack: The Condemnation of Wei-hsüeh," in Crisis and Prosperity in Sung
China. Ed. by John Winthrop Haeger. Tucson: University of
Arizona Press, 1975. Pp. 163-198.
    A virtually exhaustive account of how the tao-hsüeh (doc-
trine of the true way) was turned into the so-called wei-
hsüeh (false learning) by politicians at court in the latter
part of the twelfth century, which was primarily an attack
on Chu Hsi and his followers. The role of the emperors, the
activities of national university students in support of the
tao-hsüeh, the arguments directed at the so-called wei-hsüeh,
the lists of victims, etc., are all carefully discussed and
documented.

T'ANG CHUN-I. "The Spirit and Development of Neo-Confucianism,"
in Inquiry, 14 (1971): 56-83. Reprinted in Arne Naess and

Alastaire Hannay, eds., Invitation to Chinese Philosophy.
Oslo: Universitetsfordget, 1972. Pp. 56-83.
   The author outlines the views of successive Neo-Confucianists and their versions of the "way," seeing their teachings
as developments towards the doctrine presented by Wang Yang-
ming, whose thought can be seen in particular as a synthesis
of the views of Chu Hsi and Lu Hsiang-shan.

1.13.2 Sung (960-1279) Neo-Confucianism

CHU HSI. Djin-si lu. Tr. by Olaf Graf. Cross reference:
   1.13.8.

_____. Reflections on Things at Hand. Tr. by Wing-tsit Chan.
Cross reference: 1.13.8.

GRAF, OLAF. Tao und Jen, Sein und Sollen im sungchinesischen
   Monismus. Wiesbaden: Otto Harrassowitz, 1970. 429 pp.
   A broad view with deep insight into Neo-Confucian concepts
of the Great Ultimate, principle, material force, Heaven,
destiny, jen, the four virtues of benevolence, righteousness,
property, and wisdom, equilibrium and harmony, the way of
man, investigation of things, mind and the will, the mind of
Heaven and Earth, criticism of Buddhism, etc., centering on
Chu Hsi. Chapters are divided into natural philosophy,
ethics, the way of man, the Confucian Classics, and comparison with western philosophy, especially Thomas Aquinas
(1225?-1274?), etc.

1.13.3 Chou Tun-i (1017-1073)

CHAN, WING-TSIT. A Source Book in Chinese Philosophy. (See
   1.2.1).
   Chapter 28 contains an introductory essay describing the
unique position of Chou Tun-i as the first philosopher of
Neo-Confucianism, with a translation of Chou's Explanation
of the Diagram of the Great Ultimate (Supreme Ultimate),
as well as of his T'ung-shu (penetrating the Book of Changes)
completely translated.

CHANG, CARSUN. The Development of Neo-Confucian Thought.
   (See 1.13.1), Vol. 1, chapter 7.
   Scholarly discussion of the cosmological speculations of
Chou Tun-i by focusing on Chou's Explanation of the Diagram
of the Supreme Ultimate. See chapter 7.

CHU HSI. Reflections on Things at Hand. Tr. by Wing-tsit
   Chan. Cross reference: 1.13.8.

EICHORN, WERNER. "Chou Tun-i, ein chinesisches Gelehrtenleben aus dem 11. Jahrhundert," in <u>Abhandlungen für die Kunde des Morgenlandes</u>, 21 (1936): 1-58.
  Primarily a long biography.

FUNG YU-LAN. <u>A History of Chinese Philosophy</u>. (<u>See</u> 1.2.1), Vol. 2.
  The first section of chapter 11 discusses the philosophy of Chou by focusing on the origin of the <u>Diagram of the Supreme Ultimate</u>, as well as on the philosophical meanings of the two major writings of Chou's as mentioned above. (See under Wing-tsit Chan).

1.13.4 <u>Shao Yung (1011-1077)</u>

CHAN, WING-TSIT. <u>A Source Book in Chinese Philosophy</u>. (<u>See</u> 1.2.1).
  Chapter 29 contains an introduction to the numerical and objective tendencies in Shao Yung, with the translation of selections from his <u>Huang-chi ching-shih</u> (supreme principles governing the world), the most important of his writings.

CHANG, CARSUN. <u>The Development of Neo-Confucian Thought</u>. (<u>See</u> 1.13.1), Vol. 1, pp. 159-169.
  The first section of chapter 8 deals with the cosmological speculations of Shao Yung.

FUNG YU-LAN. <u>A History of Chinese Philosophy</u>. (<u>See</u> 1.2.1), Vol. 2.
  The second section of chapter 11 gives a philosophical exposition of Shao's numerical metaphysics under the headings of (a) the Supreme Ultimate and the eight trigrams, (b) "Diagram of What Antedates Heaven" and other diagrams, (c) creation of individual things, (d) men and the sage, (e) cosmological chronology, and (f) political philosophy.

1.13.5 <u>Chang Tsai (1020-1077)</u>

CHAN, WING-TSIT. <u>A Source Book in Chinese Philosophy</u>. (<u>See</u> 1.2.1).
  Chapter 30 contains an introduction to Chang Tsai's philosophy of material force, with the translation of the complete text of the <u>Hsi-ming</u> (western inscription) with a long comment, as well as of <u>Cheng-meng</u> (correcting youthful ignorance) selected with comments.

CHANG, CARSUN. <u>The Development of Neo-Confucian Thought</u>. (<u>See</u> 1.13.1), Vol. 1.

The second half of chapter 8 discusses Chang's life, time, works, as well as his philosophical teachings. Clear, though not in detail.

CHU HSI. <u>Reflections on Things at Hand</u>. Tr. by Wing-tsit Chan. Cross reference: 1.13.8.

EICHORN, WERNER. "Die Westinschrift des Chang Tsai, ein Beitrag zur Geistesgeschichte der nordlichen Sung," in <u>Abhandlungen für die Kunde des Morgenlandes</u>, 22 (1937): 1-85.
   A German translation of the <u>Western Inscription</u> with some of its commentaries, along with Chang's biography and a general introduction.

FUNG YU-LAN. <u>A History of Chinese Philosophy</u>. (<u>See</u> 1.2.1), Vol. 2, pp. 477-498.
   Scholarly exposition of Chang's philosophy under the headings of (a) the ether, (b) orderly sequence of things in the universe, (c) some universal phenomena, (d) celestial and terrestrial phenomena, (e) theory of the Nature, (f) unity of heaven and earth, and (g) criticism of Buddhism and Taoism.

HUANG, SIU-CHI. "The Moral Point of View of Chang Tsai," in <u>Philosophy East and West</u>, 21 (1971): 141-156.
   A very clear analysis of the moral implications of Chang's philosophy.

T'ANG CHUN-I. "Chang Tsai's Theory of Mind and Its Metaphysical Basis," in <u>Philosophy East and West</u>, 6 (1956): 113-136.
   The best essay on the metaphysics of Chang Tsai. A very scholarly attempt.

1.13.6 <u>Ch'eng Hao (1032-1085)</u>

<u>See also</u> 15.7.

CHAN, WING-TSIT. <u>A Source Book in Chinese Philosophy</u>. (<u>See</u> 1.2.1).
   Chapter 31 contains quite a long introduction to the idealistic tendency of Ch'eng Hao's "On Understanding the Nature of <u>Jen</u>" and "Reply to Master Heng-ch'ü's Letter on Calming Human Nature," as well as of selected sayings from the <u>Complete Works of the Two Ch'engs</u>.

CHANG, CARSUN. <u>The Development of Neo-Confucian Thought</u>. (<u>See</u> 1.13.1), Vol. 1.

Chapter 9 deals with the rational basis of Sung philosophy:
Ch'eng Hao, pointing out the unique philosophical contributions made by him.

CHU HSI. Reflections on Things at Hand. Tr. by Wing-tsit
Chan. Cross reference: 1.13.8.

FUNG YU-LAN. A History of Chinese Philosophy. (See 1.2.1),
Vol. 2.
The second half of chapter 12 discusses both Ch'eng Hao
and his brother Ch'eng I under the headings of (a) heavenly
principle, (b) criticism of Buddhism, (c) the physical and
the metaphysical, (d) the ether, (e) the nature, (f) fluctu-
ations of the Yin and Yang and of good and evil, (g) Ch'eng
Hao's theory of spiritual cultivation, and (h) Ch'eng I's
theory of spiritual cultivation. The similarities and differences between the two brothers are pointed out clearly to
show their respective philosophical contributions. Outstanding.

GRAHAM, A.C. Two Chinese Philosophers: Ch'eng Ming-tao and
Ch'eng Yi-ch'uan. London: Lund Humphries, 1958. 195 pp.
Probably the only available secondary source in book form
on the Ch'eng brothers. Part 1 deals with the philosophy of
Ch'eng Yi-ch'uan (Ch'eng I) in terms of li, ming (decree),
ch'i, hsing, hsin (mind), ch'eng (integrity, sincerity),
ching (composure), ke-wu (investigation of things), and criticism of Buddhism. Part 2 deals with the philosophy of
Ch'eng Ming-tao (Ch'eng Hao) in terms of jen, yi (the
changes), shen (psychic), monism and dualism, good and evil,
and Nature. Appendices include works of the Ch'eng brothers,
bibliography, etc.

1.13.7 Ch'eng I (1033-1077)

See also 15.7.

CHAN, WING-TSIT. A Source Book in Chinese Philosophy. (See
1.2.1).
Chapter 32 contains an introduction to the rationalistic
tendency in Ch'eng I, with a translation of Ch'en's "A
Treatise on What Yen Tzu (521-490 B.C.) Loved to Learn" and
"Letter in Reply to Yang Shih's (1053-1135) Letter on the
Western Inscription," as well as of his philosophical say-
ings selected from the Complete Works of the Two Ch'engs.

CHANG, CARSUN. The Development of Neo-Confucian Thought.
(See 1.13.1), Vol. 1.

Chapter 10 deals with the rational basis of Sung philosophy: Ch'eng I under the headings of (a) Ch'eng's belief in rationality, (b) his theory that human nature is reason, (c) his dual way of self-cultivation. A brief comparison of the Ch'eng brothers is also made.

CHU HSI. Reflections on Things at hand. Tr. by Wing-tsit Chan. Cross reference: 1.13.8.

FUNG YU-LAN. A History of Chinese Philosophy. (See 1.2.1). Cross reference: 1.13.6.

_____. A Short History of Chinese Philosophy. (See 1.3.1). Chapter 24 deals with Neo-Confucianism and the beginnings of the two schools, in which Fung argues that the Ch'eng brothers' divergent views of li, jen, nature, etc., led to the formation of two major Neo-Confucian schools, the idealistic wing represented by Lu Hsiang-shan and Wang Yang-ming and the rationalistic wing represented by Chu Hsi. A very interesting analysis.

GRAHAM, A.C. Two Chinese Philosophers: Ch'eng Ming-tao and Ch'eng Yi-ch'uan. Cross reference: 1.12.6.

1.13.8 Chu Hsi (1130-1200)

See also 3.4, 15.6, 15.13, 15.14.

BERNARD, HENRI. "Chi Hsi's Philosophy and Its Interpretation by Leibnitz," in T'ien Hsia Monthly, 5 (1937): 9-18.
Though not a critical study, the article tells the story of the controversy among Catholic missionaries on Chu Hsi's concept of God and Leibniz's (1646-1716) understanding of Chu Hsi's li as moral principle which is equivalent to God.

BRUCE, J. PERCY. Chu Hsi and His Masters. London: Probsthain, 1923. 336 pp.
Mainly concerned with Chu's theories of the universe, first cause, moral order, human nature, physical nature, mind, virtue, and Heaven. Objective, correct, and fairly extensive, though the author's historical and philosophical perspective is limited.

CHAN, WING-TSIT. "Chu Hsi's Appraisal of Lao Tzu," in Philosophy East and West, 25 (1975): 131-144.
Although Chu Hsi attacked Lao Tzu for the teaching of using tactics such as giving in order to get and the philosophy of non-being even more severely than his master Ch'eng I,

nevertheless he credited Lao Tzu with the concept of production and reproduction (life-giving) in the idea of the spirit
of the valley which, being empty, is therefore capable of
life-giving, thus attributing to Lao Tzu the cardinal idea
of production and reproduction in Neo-Confucianism.

_____. "Chu Hsi's Completion of Neo-Confucianism," in Sung
Studies. Ed. by F. Aubin. Ser. 2, no. 1 (1973): 59-90.
   Chu Hsi's completion of Neo-Confucian philosophy by deter-
mining its direction, by clarifying the relation between
principle and material force, by developing the concept of
the Great Ultimate, and by the culmination of the concept of
jen (humanity), his completion of the concept of the tradition of the way, or Confucian transmission, and his grouping
of the Great Learning, the Analects, the Mencius, and the
Doctrine of the Mean as the Four Books for a new basis and a
new methodology.

_____. A Source Book in Chinese Philosophy. (See 1.2.1).
   Chapter 34 contains an introductory essay describing the
great synthesis of Chu Hsi's philosophy, with a translation
of Chu's "A Treatise on Jen," "A Treatise on Ch'eng Ming-
tao's Discourse on the Nature," and "First Letter to the
Gentlemen of Hunan on Equilibrium and Harmony," as well as
selected sayings from the Chu Tzu ch'üan-shu (complete works
of Chu Hsi), rearranged under (a) moral cultivation, (b) the
relation between the nature of man and things and their destiny, (c) the nature of man and things, (d) the nature of
man and the nature of things compared, (e) physical nature,
(f) destiny, (g) the mind, (h) the mind, the nature, and the
feelings, (i) jen, (j) the great ultimate, (k) heaven and
earth, (l) spiritual beings and spiritual forces, and
(m) Buddhism.

_____. "The Study of Chu Hsi in the West," in Journal of
Asian Studies, 31 (1976): 555-577.
   The sections are on Western translations of Chu Hsi's
works, Chu Hsi's view of God, his philosophy, his debate
with Lu Hsiang-shan and Ch'en Liang, Chu Hsi and the Tradition of the Way, his criticism of Buddhism and Taoism, Chu
Hsi and Western philosophers compared, his life, his followers, and the Shushi school in Japan.

CHANG, CARSUN. The Development of Neo-Confucian Thought.
   (See 1.13.1), Vol. 1, chapter 12.
   A detailed discussion of Chu Hsi, the great synthesizer of
Sung Neo-Confucianism, under the headings of (a) Chu's boy-
hood and maturity, (b) formation of system of thought and

prolific writings, (c) administrative and political work,
(d) closing years, (e) Chu's system of philosophy, (f) the
unity of reason, (g) manifoldness of manifestations,
(h) human nature: essential and physical, (i) mind and personal cultivation, and (j) criticism of Buddhism, and work
on the Confucian classics.

CHING, JULIA. "The Confucian Way (Tao) and Tao-t'ung," in
Journal of the History of Ideas, 35 (1974): 371-388.
    How the Neo-Confucianists formulated the Confucian Way and
the tao-t'ung (Transmission of the Way) are told under the
topics of the historical pattern, the challenge of Taoism
and Buddhism, the failure of T'ang and Sung Confucianism,
the new synthesis by Chu Hsi, the new metaphysics of Chou
Tun-i, Chang Tsai, Ch'eng Hao and Ch'eng I, new method of
cultivation, the transmission determined by Chu Hsi, the
controversies between Chu and Lu Hsiang-shan, and Chu Hsi's
political philosophy.

_____. "The Goose Lake Monastery Debate," in Journal of
Chinese Philosophy, 1 (1973-1974): 161-178.
    An interesting reexamination of the famous debate between
Lu Hsiang-shan and Chu Hsi at the Goose Lake Monastery
signaling the separation of the two schools of Sung Neo-
Confucianism.

CHU HSI. Djin-sï lu. Tr. by Olaf Graf. Tokyo: Sophia University Press, 1953. 3 vols. Vol. 1, 297 pp. Vol. 2, 786 pp.
Vol. 3, 545 pp.
    (See under Chu, above). Vol. 1 is devoted to the text and
its ideas and a comparison between Neo-Confucianism and
Spinoza (1632-1677) and St. Thomas Aquinas, Vol. 2 to the
translation of the text and Yeh Ts'ai's (fl. 1248) commentary, which was very popular in Japan but not in China, and
Vol. 3 completely to notes. Analysis of the text is detailed
and sources of ideas are carefully noted.

_____. The Philosophy of Human Nature, by Chu Hsi. Tr. by
J.P. Bruce. London: Probsthain, 1922. 444 pp.
    The only translation, not without errors and with only
very few textual, linguistic, or philosophical notes, of
chapters 42-48 on principle and nature of Chu's Complete
Works. Generally reliable.

CHU HSI, in collaboration with Lü Tsu-ch'ien. Reflections on
Things at Hand: The Neo-Confucian Anthology. Tr. by Wing-
tsit Chan. New York: Columbia University Press, 1967.
441 pp.

This Neo-Confucian anthology, the Chin-ssu-lu, compiled by
Chu Hsi and his friend Lü Tsu-ch'ien,(1137-1181), has been
the most celebrated work in Neo-Confucianism, containing the
most important philosophical passages from the writings of
Chou Tun-i, Chang Tsai, and the Ch'eng brothers, arranged
under 14 categories, such as "on the substance of the Way,"
"the essentials of learning," "the investigation of things
and the investigation of principles to the utmost," etc. The
work reflects Chu's own profound knowledge and understanding
of the four Neo-Confucian philosophers in the northern Sung
Dynasty. In the translation, many comments are selected
from Chu Hsi and many Chinese, Korean, and Japanese commen-
tators on passages of the anthology.

FUNG YU-LAN. A History of Chinese Philosophy. (See 1.2.1),
Vol. 2.
    In chapter 13, Fung gives a detailed discussion of Chu's
philosophy in terms of (a) principle and the supreme ultimate, (b) the ether, (c) cosmology, (d) the nature in men
and other creatures, (e) ethics and theory of spiritual cultivation, (f) political philosophy, and (g) criticism of
Buddhism.

_____. A Short History of Chinese Philosophy. (See 1.3.1).
    Chapter 25 deals with Chu's philosophy as that of Platonic
ideas. Topics include (a) position of Chu in Chinese history,
(b) the Supreme Ultimate, (c) ch'i, or matter, (d) nature
and mind, (e) political philosophy, and (f) method of spiritual cultivation. Fung's regarding Chu's school as that of
Platonic ideas is too misleading.

GEDALECIA, DAVID. "Excursion into Substance and Function:
The Development of the t'i-yung Paradigm in Chu Hsi," in
Philosophy East and West, 24 (1974): 443-452.
    Explains how Chu Hsi developed his doctrine of t'i (sub-
stance) and yung (function) in relation to T'ai-chi (Great
Ultimate) through four stages and how he finally overcame
their dichotomy, which Wang Pi was unable to do. There is
also a brief but good discussion on Chu Hsi's theory of mind
with respect to t'i-yung and his idea of ethical conduct and
the sage.

HOCKING, W.E. "Chu Hsi's Theory of Knowledge," in Harvard
Journal of Asiatic Studies, 1 (1936): 109-127.
    The first essay on the subject in a Western language by
the first Western philosopher to write on the subject. Its
thesis is that Chu Hsi is basically an empiricist who
demanded moral action as a requirement in the investigation
of things.

NEEDHAM, JOSEPH. Science and Civilisation in China. (See
1.6.1), Vol. 2, History of Scientific Thought, pp. 455-505.
   Some of the topics treated here are: Chu Hsi and his predecessors, the study of universal pattern, involving the concepts of ch'i and li, evolutionary naturalism in a cyclical
setting, the denial of immortality and deity, Chu Hsi's philosophy of organism, and Leibnitz. Based on extensive
scholarship and critical analysis, although the materialistic
interpretation is questionable.

PANG, CHING-JEN. L'idée de Dieu chez Malebranche et l'idée de
Li chez Tchou Hi. Paris: Librairie Philosophique J. Vrin,
142. 128 pp.
   Compares the ideas of God in Malebranche and Chi Hsi and
points out their similarity. Contains a French translation
of the Chu Tzu ch'üan-shu, chapter 49 on li and ch'i, most
important subjects in Chu Hsi's philosophy not included in
J.P. Bruce's Philosophy of Human Nature by Chu Hsi.

SARGENT, GERENT E. "Les Débats Personnels de Tchou Hi en
Matière de Méthodologie," in Journal Asiatique, 243 (1955):
213-228.
   A good documentation of how Chu Hsi arrived at his method
of cultivation, that of investigation of things and the
rectification of the heart.

SCHIROKAUER, CONRAD M. "Chu Hsi as an Administrator, a Preliminary Study," in Sung Studies, ser. i, no. 3 (1976):
207-236.
   A detailed, analytical, and well-documented study of Chu
Hsi's accomplishments in the three areas of education,
political economy, and justice. Issues are carefully examined and Chu Hsi's measures and reforms are objectively
evaluated.

_____. "Chu Hsi's Political Career: A Study in Ambivalence,"
in Confucian Personalities. Ed. by Arthur F. Wright.
Stanford: Stanford University Press, 1962. Pp. 162-188.
   Shows extensive consultation and judicious use of standard Chinese source materials. The most detailed and best
account of Chu Hsi's political life and decisions in a
Western language.

TILLMAN, HOYT CLEVELAND. Values in History and Ethics in
Politics: Issues Debated between Chu Hsi and Ch'en Liang.
Harvard University Ph.D. thesis, 1976.
   Challenging Chu Hsi's synthesis of the humanistic values
of antiquity, Ch'en Liang (1143-1194) made a brilliant

ethical and metaphysical apologia for a pragmatic approach
to utility. Rejecting the diffuse intellectual climate of
the middle decades of the twelfth century, each thinker
sought to develop a more systematic and defined approach to
problems, thereby augmenting their differences towards
politics and values.

TU WEI-MING. "Reconstituting the Confucian Tradition," in
Journal of Asian Studies, 33 (1974): 441-454.
   Not only a general review of Ch'ien Mu's monumental and
epoch-making five-volume work, Chu Tzu hsin hsüeh-an (a new
scholarly record on Chu Hsi), but a study that makes clear
how Ch'ien Mu has put Chu Hsi's doctrinal development in
proper historical setting and logical perspective, covering
subjects like Chu Hsi's synthesis of Neo-Confucian philosophy, establishing the authentic line of Confucian transmission, formulating his own philosophy of mind and principle,
his debates with Lu Hsiang-shan, his scholarship, commentaries, new interpretations of classics, and other innovations.

YU, DAVID C. "Chu Hsi's Approach to Knowledge," in Chinese
Culture, 10, no. 4 (December, 1969): 1-14.
   Chu Hsi's approach is discussed under the topics of self-
cultivation, the practical and cognitive function of the
mind, the external world, ways of attaining knowledge, and
thorough-comprehension. The conclusion is drawn that in
spite of Chu Hsi's emphasis on pursuit of knowledge, the
goal of knowledge is beyond the intellectual or the moral:
it is a realization that results in freedom and spontaneity.

1.13.9 Lu Hsiang-shan (Lu Chiu-yüan) (1139-1193)

See also 15.6, 15.13.

CADY, LYMAN van LAW. The Philosophy of Lu Hsiang-shan, A Neo-
Confucian Monistic Idealist. New York: Union Theological
Seminary thesis, 1939. 451 pp.
   A selection of Lu's sayings and letters. The most exten-
sive and generally accurate translating of Lu's works so far.

CHAN, WING-TSIT. A Source Book in Chinese Philosophy. (See
1.2.1).
   Chapter 33 contains an introduction to Lu's philosophy of
the unity of mind and principle, with a translation of Lu's
selected sayings from his Complete Works.

CHANG, CARSUN. The Development of Neo-Confucian Thought.
(See 1.13.1), Vol. 1.

Chapter 13 deals with the philosophy of Lu Hsiang-shan by focusing on the philosophical debate between Lu and Chu. A very good analysis.

CHING, JULIA. "The Goose Lake Monastery Debate." Cross reference: 1.13.8.

FUNG YU-LAN. A History of Chinese Philosophy. (See 1.2.1), Vol. 2.
Chapter 14 deals with Lu, Wang Yang-ming, and Ming idealism. Fung regards Lu as the precursor of Ming idealism led by Wang Yang-ming. Yang Chien's (1140-1228) philosophy is also dealt with, and a good comparison of Lu and Chu is also made.

HUANG, SUI-CHI. Lu Hsiang-shan, A Twelfth Century Chinese Idealist Philosopher. New Haven: American Oriental Society, 1944. 116 pp.
The only monograph in a Western language on Lu. Comprehensive, systematic, clear, and objective, with extensive quotations.

1.13.10 Other Sung Thinkers

LO, WINSTON W. "Wang An-shih and the Confucian ideal of "inner sageliness'," in Philosophy East and West, 26 (1976): 41-53.
Lo addresses himself to a facet of Wang An-shih's personality, which hitherto has not been drawn into any controversy, in terms of the Confucian ideal of "inner sageliness."

1.14 YÜAN (1271-1368) PHILOSOPHY

GEDALECIA, DAVID. Wu Ch'eng: A Neo-Confucian of the Yüan. Harvard University Ph.D. thesis, 1971. 481 pp.
Wu (1249-1333) criticized textual criticism and urged moral cultivation. He synthesized Chu Hsi's approach through knowledge seeking and Lu Hsing-shan's approach through cultivation of the virtuous nature, but tipped the scale toward the side of cultivation. In emphasizing the development of the intuitively good knowledge rather than rote study, Wu influenced Wang Yang-ming's more refined version of this idea.

1.15 MING (1368-1644) PHILOSOPHY

1.15.1 Ming Philosophy in General

See also 3.2, 7.9.1, 7.9.2, 15.5, 15.13.

CHAN, WING-TSIT. "The Ch'eng-Chu School of Early Mind," in
Self and Society in Ming Thought. Ed. by Wm. Theodore
de Bary (see below), pp. 29-52.
   Deals with Ts'ao Tuan (1376-1434), Wu-Yü-pi (1391-1469),
Hsüeh Hsüan (1392-1464), and Hu Chü-jen (1434-1484), who
have generally been regarded as continuing the tradition of
Ch'eng I and Chu Hsi, and shows how they, though remaining
in the tradition, deviated from it by emphasizing more on
the mind and less on such metaphysical concepts as the Great
Ultimate and thus contributed to the growth of the School of
Mind led by Wang Yang-ming.

de BARY, WM. THEODORE. "Individualism and Humanitarianism in
Late Ming Thought," in his Self and Society in Ming Thought
(see below), pp. 145-240.
   This long treatise deals specifically with Wang Ken (1483-
1540) (the common man as sage, celebration of self, self-
mastery and self-enjoyment, the common man and the grand
unity), Ho Hsin-yin (1517-1579) (the hero and the natural
man, from desirelessness to desirefulness, the individual
and community), and Li Chih (1527-1602) (the arch-individual-
ist, innocence and intelligence, a new look at human relations, the importance of being selfish, the individual in
history, and Li as the idealist, the totalitarian, the monk
and the martyr).

de BARY, WM. THEODORE, ed.   Self and Society in Ming Thought.
New York: Columbia University Press.   550 pp.
   This is the collection of papers presented at the Conference on Ming Thought held in 1966.   The five philosophical
papers are by Chan, de Bary (see both, above), Jen (see below), T'ang (see 1.15.3), and Okada (see 1.15.4).   In his long
introductory chapter, the editor goes into the "emptiness"
or openness of Ming thought, its vitality and diversity,
the situation of the Ming intellectual, the burden of culture in the Ming, the Ming experience of the self, the
experience of oneness with all creation, quietism and activ-
ism, mind and body, and the new "liberalism" and "pragmatism"
in the late Ming.

OKADA, TAKEHIKO. "The Chu Hsi and Wang Yang-ming Schools at
the end of the Ming and Tokugawa Periods (1603-1868)," in
Philosophy East and West, 23 (1973): 139-163.
   A most substantial survey of the three different schools
among the followers of Wang Yang-ming, namely, the Existential or Realization School, the Quietist or Tranquility
School, and the Cultivation School, which emphasize, respectively, immediate intuition and vitality of the mind,

the practice of quietly gathering or collecting one's mind,
and quietly cognizing one's own heart, and mental causation
and concrete experience. A large number of Japanese followers of Chu Hsi and Wang Yang-ming are covered in the deliberation. Much of the material is new to the West.

WILHELM, HELLMUT. "On Ming Orthodoxy," in <u>Monumenta Serica</u>,
29 (1970-71): 1-25.
   Beginning with a translation of the thumb-nail sketch of
the intellectual development in Ming times from a chapter of
the history of Ming, the paper brings out the several characteristics of the Ch'eng I and Chu Hsi scholars of Ming. The
paper, however, is mainly on Wu Yü-pi. With a lengthy translation from his <u>Jih-lu</u> (daily records), Wu's emphasis on
holding on to reverence, cultivating the personality, control of the mind, etc. are clearly explained. A good
contribution to the understanding of this outstanding Neo-
Confucianist.

1.15.2 Various Ming Philosophers

BLOOM, IRENE TILENIUS. <u>Notes on Knowledge Painfully Acquired.</u>
<u>A Translation and Analysis of the K'un-chih chi by Lo</u>
<u>Ch'in-shun (1465-1547)</u>. Columbia University Ph.D. thesis,
1976. 415 pp.
   Besides the fully annotated translation of this key Ming
Neo-Confucian work, there is a 151-page study which analyzes
the intellectual debate on such basic issues as principle
and material force, the self and the world, mind and human
nature, the inner and the outer, methods of learning, intellectual and anti-intellectualism, taking into account Lo's
intellectual heritage from Sung Neo-Confucianism and his
debate with Wang Yang-ming.

CHAN, WING-TSIT. "Chan Jo-shui's Influence on Wang Yang-ming,"
in <u>Philosophy East and West</u>, 23 (1973): 9-30.
   Considers the influence of Chan on Wang under the headings
of "Taoist Practice to Nourish Life," "Sitting in Quiet
Meditation," "The Unity of Knowledge and Action," "The Extension of Innate Knowledge," and "Forming One Body with
Heaven, Earth, and All Things." The general conclusion is
that there is a definite influence though Wang himself was
silent on it and his followers all denied it.

HANDLIN, JOANNA FLUG. <u>Lü K'un (1536-1618): The Reorientation</u>
<u>of a Scholar-Official</u>. University of California, Ph.D.
thesis, 1975. 125 pp.

This study briefly outlines the biography of Lü K'un and
analyzes his writings on self-cultivation, his response to
late-Ming intellectual relativism, his attitudes towards
women, and his approach to local government. The study shows
that in response to the restless masses Lü at times wrote in
the vernacular, appealed to the emotions, stressed concrete
everyday events rather than abstract philosophical principles,
and diffused responsibilities among the common people. The
final chapter discusses Ming-Ch'ing continuity.

JEN YU-WEN. "Ch'en Hsien-chang's Philosophy of the Natural,"
in Self and Society in Ming Thought. Ed. by Wm. Theodore
de Bary. (See 1.15.1), pp. 53-92.
    The only treatise on Ch'en Hsien-chang (1428-1500) in
Western language, the essay covers the background of Ch'en's
life and thought, his biography, his philosophy of the
natural (tzu-jan), his doctrine of principle and mind, and
of emptiness and quiescence, his doctrines of quiet-sitting,
self-acquisition, and union with the universe. Necessary
reading to understand the philosophy of Chan Jo-shui and
helpful in a comparative study of Wang Yang-ming.

LI SHEN-I. "The Original Meaning and the Real Idea of 'Unifying Two into One' in the Tung-hsi chün," in Chinese Studies
in Philosophy, 6, no. 1 (1974): 61-83.
    The real meaning of Fang I-chih's (1611-1671) "unifying
two into one" is the obliteration of all contradictions in
the real world and return to the spiritual category of
"grand one," "great ultimate," or "great nothingness," essentially a theory of compromise within the tradition of idealistic metaphysics.

TAYLOR, RODNEY L. The Cultivation of Sagehood as a Religious
Goal in Neo-Confucianism: A Study of Selected Writings of
Kao P'an-lung (1562-1626). University of Montana Press
(forthcoming). 367 pp.
    Chiefly on Kao's religious practices and experience, mak-
ing use of his friendship with others and his personal
letters but based on his essays here translated. Kao's ideas
on unity, reverence, returning to quietude, transformation,
and the relation between the inner and outer are briefly
discussed, as are his sense of history and aesthetic sensitivity toward nature.

_____. "Neo-Confucianism, Sagehood and the Religious Dimen-
sion," in Journal of Chinese Philosophy, 2 (1975): 389-413.
    On Kao P'an-lung's (1562-1626) search for sagehood, which
to him is the focus and aim of learning and self-cultivation

process. This religious goal contains certain forms of the
religious dimension not readily associated with the Confucian
tradition, namely a sense of transcendence and an element of
personal faith.

1.15.3 <u>Wang Yang-ming (Wang Shou-jen) (1472-1529)</u>

<u>See also</u> 2.7, 15.13, 15.14.

CHAN, WING-TSIT. "How Buddhistic is Wang Yang-ming?" in
<u>Philosophy East and West</u>, 12 (1962): 203-216.
   An analysis of the attacks on Wang's Buddhistic tendencies,
an examination of his use of Buddhist idioms and technique
and his visits to Buddhist temples, and a discussion of his
criticism of the basic tenets of Ch'an Buddhism.

_____. <u>A Source Book in Chinese Philosophy</u>. (<u>See</u> 1.2.1).
   Chapter 35 contains an introduction to the dynamic idealism of Wang Yang-ming, with the translation of the complete
text of the <u>Ta-hsüeh wen</u> (inquiry on the <u>Great Learning</u>), as
well as of selected passages from the <u>Ch'uan-hsi lu</u> (<u>Instruc-
tions for Practical Living</u>), Wang's major work. Comments
and footnotes added.

_____. "Wang Yang-ming: A Biography," in <u>Philosophy East and
West</u>, 22 (1972): 63-74.
   Based on various sources about the life and times of Wang
Yang-ming.

_____. "Wang Yang-ming: Western Studies and an Annotated Bib-
liography," in <u>Philosophy East and West</u>, 22 (1972): 75-92.
   An annotated bibliography regarding Western studies and
publications on Wang Yang-ming.

CHANG, CARSUN. <u>The Development of Neo-Confucian Thought</u>.
(<u>See</u> 1.13.1), Vol. 2.
   A detailed and outstanding discussion of Wang's philosophy
as well as of the development and downfall of Wang's school
in the Ming Dynasty, in four full chapters (2, 3, 4 and 5).

_____. <u>Wang Yang-ming: Idealist Philosopher of Sixteenth Cen-
tury</u>. New York: St. John's University Press, 1962. 102 pp.
   A comprehensive account of Wang Yang-ming under the headings of (a) the life of Wang Yang-ming, (b) his system of
philosophy, (c) his position in Neo-Confucianism, (d) the
philosophic dialogues, and (e) a study of Chinese
institutionism.

CHENG, CHUNG-YING. "Unity and Creativity in Wang Yang-ming's
Philosophy of Mind," in Philosophy East and West, 23 (1973):
49-72.
    Wang's philosophy of mind is discussed under the following
headings: (a) Non-substantial substance (Original Reality)
of the Mind; (b) Original Reality of Mind as Manifested in
Innate Knowledge of the Good; (c) On the Will as Activation
of Mind as a Form of Creativity; (d) Unity and Creativity of
Mind in its Activation: Unity of Knowledge and Action;
(e) More Philosophical Points about the Unity of Knowledge
and Action; (f) Unity and Creativity of Mind in Consummation:
Fulfilling Innate Knowledge of the Good; and (g) Tranquility
and Harmony. Cheng holds that Wang's philosophy of mind is
best understood in his view of the unity and creativity of
an ultimate reality, leading to his notion of mind.

CHING, JULIA. "All in One--The Culmination of the Thought of
Wang Yang-ming (1472-1529)," in Oriens Extremus, 20 (1973):
137-159.
    A brief but well-rounded presentation on Wang Yang-ming's
doctrine of forming one unity with heaven, earth and all
things. The concepts of jen versus love, loving the people,
joy, the original substance of the innate knowledge of the
good, principle of life, consciousness, a self-transcending
state, and a higher reality are clarified and supported with
passages in Chinese characters and their translations.

_____. "Beyond Good and Evil, The Culmination of the Thought
of Wang Yang-ming (1472-1529)," in Numen, 22 (1973): 127-134.
    After stating the problem of evil in Wang Yang-ming, who
regarded that human nature-in-itself is beyond good and evil,
the author goes on to compare the opposing interpretations
of Wang's Four Maxims by his two pupils, Wang Chi and Ch'ien
Te-hung (1496-1574), and finally points out the similarity
of Wang's method of cultivation with those of Chuang Tzu and
Ch'an Buddhism.

_____. To Acquire Wisdom: The Way of Wang Yang-ming (1492-
1529). New York: Columbia University Press, 1977. 373 pp.
    A total view of the life and teachings of Wang. The
major chapters are devoted to the Confucian Way (Tao) and
its transmission (tao-t'ung), Wang as a man of "mad ardour"
and as a philosopher, his doctrine of the mind, his opposition to Chu Hsi's theory of investigation of things, his
doctrine of extension of the innate knowledge of the good,
the culmination of his philosophy in all-in-one and in the
doctrine of beyond good and evil.

FANG, THOMÉ. "The Essence of Wang Yang-ming's Philosophy in a Historical Perspective," in <u>Philosophy East and West</u>, 23 (1973): 73-90.

Wang's various doctrines are put against the background of the <u>Great Learning</u>, with comparison with Lu Hsiang-shan, Chu Hsi, Ch'an, Hua-yen Buddhism, and Taoism. Such key ideas of Wang's as investigation of the mind, Heavenly Principle versus human desires, the highest good, manifesting the clear character, forming one unity with all things, dissolution of all duality, unity of knowledge and action, centrality and harmony, and innate knowledge of the good are put in proper perspective. In his discussion of Wang's contribution, Fang holds that all the Neo-Confucian philosophers finally concur in the unitive system of radical Rationalism embedded in the perfect awareness of conscientious wisdom as advocated by Wang Yang-ming.

FUNG YU-LAN. <u>A History of Chinese Philosophy</u>. (<u>See</u> 1.2.1), Vol. 2.

Chapter 14 contains a good discussion of Wang Yang-ming in terms of (a) questions on the <u>Great Learning</u>, (b) unity of knowledge and conduct, (c) Chu Hsi and Wang compared, (d) criticism of Buddhism and Taoism, (e) the gradations of love, (f) origin of evil, (g) unity of activity and quiescence, (h) reactions against Wang's idealism, and (i) Wang Chi (Wang Lung-ch'i or Lung-hsi, 1498-1583) and Wang Ken, the two important disciples of Wang.

_____. <u>A Short History of Chinese Philosophy</u>. (<u>See</u> 1.3.1), chapter 26.

A much simpler account than that in the above-mentioned work, of Wang's philosophy in relation to Lu's idealism.

IKI, HIROYUKI. "Wang Yang-ming's Doctrine of Innate Knowledge of the Good," in <u>Philosophy East and West</u>, 11 (1961): 27-33.

On Wang's ideas of the relation between the nature of the innate knowledge of the good and the effort to extend it in actual practice, with special reference to Chu Hsi and Buddhism.

JUNG, HWA YOL. "Wang Yang-ming and Existential Phenomenology," in <u>International Philosophical Quarterly</u>, 5 (1965): 612-636.

Emphasizing Wang's central doctrine of philosophy, like that of phenomenology, is "an adventure of consciousness." Many phenomenological and existential elements are pointed out in Wang's philosophy, such as the rejection of the dichotomy of subject and object, mind and body, etc.

McMORRAN, IAN. "Late Ming Criticism of Wang Yang-ming: The
Case of Wang Fu-chih," in Philosophy East and West, 23 (1973):
91-102.
   The author tries to show something of the influence which
Wang Yang-ming may have exerted on Wang Fu-chih.

NIVISON, DAVID S. "Moral decision in Wang Yang-ming: The Problem of Chinese 'Existentialism'," in Philosophy East and
West, 23 (1973): 121-138.
   A very interesting comparison between Wang Yang-ming's
doctrine and existentialism, pointing out both similarities
and differences, with frequent references to Sartre, Husserl,
and Kierkegaard (especially the latter). Wang's moral decision is analyzed. All this is related to Wang's doctrines
of the innate knowledge of the good, the unity of knowledge
and action, and the famous "Four Propositions." A fresh
attempt at interpreting Wang Yang-ming as a Confucian "existentialist" in terms of moral decision.

T'ANG CHUN-I. "The Criticism of Wang Yang-ming's Teachings as
Raised by his Contemporaries," in Philosophy East and West,
23 (1973): 163-186.
   Criticism of Wang by Lu Ching-yen (Lu Nan, 1479-1542),
Huang Wan (1477-1551), and Lo Ch'in-shun. Wang's teachings
are compared with those of Chan Jo-shui. Discusses Nieh
Piao's (1487-1563) "Back to Tranquillity" and Wang Chi's two
kinds of learning as containing implicit criticisms of their
master; Wang-I-an's (Wang Tung, 1503-1581) thought about
the will as a directive principle or moral mind to supplement Wang's teachings; T'ang Shih-huai's (1522-1605) thoughts
about the pre-heaven nature and its relation to pure knowing and "constant will"; and the general trends of thought
to save the idea of will and good in Confucian schools of
the late Ming.

_____. "The Development of the Concept of Moral Mind from
Wang Yang-ming to Wang Chi," in Self and Society in Ming
Thought. Ed. by Wm. Theodore de Bary. (See 1.15.1),
pp. 92-120.
   The paper is divided into four parts on Lu Hsiang-shan's
concept of original mind as a basis for Wang Yang-ming's
"realization" of liang-chih (innate knowledge of the good),
the latter as synthesis of Chu Hsi's and Lu Hsiang-shan's
moral mind and moral cultivation, Wang's liang-chih as beyond good and evil and Wang's teaching about "learning prior
to Heaven." The conclusion is that Wang Chi, Wang Yang-
ming's pupil, developed his master's ideas to a much higher
level.

TU WEI-MING. "An Inquiry into Wang Yang-ming's Four-Sentence
Teaching," in The Eastern Buddhist, 7, no. 2 (October, 1974):
31-48.
    A penetrating analysis of Wang Chi's interpretation of
Wang Yang-ming's famous four-sentence teaching about the
mind-in-itself, the activation of intention, the faculty of
innate knowledge of the good, and the rectification of
things. Wang Lung-hsi's interpretation of them as "fourfold
nothingness," as against Ch'ien Te-hung's interpretation of
them as fourfold beingness is viewed from various angles,
such as Buddhist and Taoist influence, the nature of mind,
the innate knowledge of the good, self-cultivation, the
vital force, ways of learning, etc. The most thorough-going
treatise on the subject in a Western language.

_____. Neo-Confucian Thought in Action: Wang Yang-ming's
Youth (1472-1509). Berkeley: University of California Press,
1976. 222 pp.
    A penetrating study of the interaction between Wang's inner
identity and the development of his famous doctrine of the
unity of knowledge and action. Wang's search in his younger
years, his decision, and his enlightenment are examined in
light of this development. The meaning of this development
is viewed in its relevance to Lu Hsiang-shan, its challenge
to Chu Hsi, and the issue of the investigation of things.

_____. "Subjectivity and Ontological Reality--An Interpreta-
tion of Wang Yang-ming's Mode of Thinking," in Philosophy
East and West, 23 (1973): 187-207.
    A reconstruction of Wang's philosophy in terms of the in-
separable relation between subjectivity and ontological
reality. Primarily a study of Wang's famous doctrine of the
unity of knowing and acting, then shows its relation with
the thought of Lu Hsiang-shan, and finally discusses the
challenges of Chu Hsi and Wang's response, especially over
the issue of "investigation of things" (which for Chu Hsi
meant external investigation of principle in things, but for
Wang meant the investigation of the mind).

WANG YANG-MING. Instructions for Practical Living and Other
Neo-Confucian Writings by Wang Yang-ming. Tr. by Wing-tsit
Chan. New York: Columbia University Press, 1963. 358 pp.
    A translation of the most important and influential work
of Neo-Confucianism in China and Japan in the last 450 years.

_____. The Philosophical Letters of Wang Yang-ming. Tr. by
Julia Ching. Canberra: Australian National University Press,
1972. 142 pp.

A translation of 72 letters with slight omissions here and
there. Notes, Chinese characters, and an explanation of the
translation of certain terms are provided. Although the let-
letters are short and only slightly philosophical, they are
a good supplement to the Instructions for Practical Living
in which the most philosophical and long letters are included.

_____. The Philosophy of Wang Yang-ming. Tr. by F.G. Henke.
Chicago: Open Court, 1916. 512 pp. Reprinted in New York:
Paragon.
Well selected material but inaccurate translation.

WIENPAHL, PAUL. "Spinoza and Wang Yang-ming," in Religious
Studies, 3 (1969): 19-27.
Points out some similarities between the two: (1) Both were
pragmatists; (2) Both identified knowledge with action;
(3) Both taught extending innate knowledge. Essentially the
article is on Spinoza.

_____. "Wang Yang-ming and Meditation," in Journal of Chinese
Philosophy, 1 (1974): 199-227.
Having appraised what several writers have said about Wang
Yang-ming with reference to meditation, the author asserts
that Wang was crucially concerned with the practice of meditation in both his life and his teaching, that he became
aware of and continually took steps to correct what may be
called "mere meditation," and that his doctrines of extension
of innate knowledge of the good and "one must always be doing
something" are based on the insight that all of life is
meditation.

1.15.4 Followers of Wang Yang-ming

ARAKI, KENGO. "Confucianism and Buddhism in late Ming," in
The Unfolding of Neo-Confucianism. Ed. by Wm. Theodore
de Bary. (See 1.16.1), pp. 39-66.
The main attention is given to the two schools of mind in
the Ming: the Confucian school and that of Ch'an Buddhism.
The two polar figures in the relationship between Buddhism
and Confucianism in late Ming, namely Li Chih and Kuan Chih-
tao (1536-1608), are extensively discussed, showing the influence of Wang Chi, Wang Yang-ming's pupil, and the Ch'an
monk Ta-hui Tsung-kao (1089-1163) on Li Chih, and how Kuan
Chih-tao, advancing from the Wang Yang-ming School of Mind,
reached out to the Buddhist School of Mind.

CHANG, CHUNG-YUAN. "'The Essential Source of Identity' in
Wang Lung-ch'i's Philosophy," in Philosophy East and West,
23 (1973): 31-48.

Pointing out the Buddhist influence on Wang Chi, the author goes on to show that Wang's direct approach to liang-chih was different from that of his master Wang Yang-ming, and that his theory of the mind of the absolute present provides the first extensive treatment of this idea in Neo-Confucian philosophy. The author then goes on to discuss Heidegger in an attempt to point out similarities with Wang. Actually the paper is more on the Western thinker than on the Neo-Confucianist.

de BARY, WM. THEODORE. "Individualism and Humanitarianism in Late Ming Thought." Cross reference: 1.15.1, especially for Wang Ken, Ho Hsin-yin, and Li Chih.

_____. "Li Chih: A Chinese Individualist," in Asia, 14 (Spring, 1969): 51-68.
Li's alienation and rebellion, his concern for the average man, the individual and his fulfillment in society, his stress on spontaneity, his belief in self-expression as the basis for true morality, his rejection of traditional reform, etc.

DIMBERG, RONALD G. The Sage and Society: The Life and Society of Ho Hsin-yin. Honolulu: The University of Hawaii Press, 1974. 175 pp.
After reviewing the traditional view of the sage and society and the eventful life of Ho Hsin-yin, the author goes into a detailed discussion of Ho's ideas of human nature, human desires, the relation between physical and moral self, self-fulfillment, the emphasis on the individual in the familial relationship, the value of the relationship between teacher and student and among colleagues and associates, and the sage as a social reformer as well as a teacher. The author also defends Ho against criticisms of being Buddhist and a political adventurer.

MOU TSUNG-SAN. "The Immediate Successor of Wang Yang-ming: Wang Lung-hsi and his Theory of ssu-wu," in Philosophy East and West, 23 (1975): 103-120.
A thorough analysis, examination, and appraisal of Wang Chi's famous teaching of the four items of mind (ssu-wu-- fourfold nothingness), volition, innate knowledge of the good, and things, all of which are in the state of nothingness. This was evolved out of his unique interpretation of Wang Yang-ming's famous philosophical poem. Comparison is made with Wang Yang-ming and Buddhism. Wang Lung-hsi's ideas on investigation of things, substance and function,

mind, good and evil, the will and things, gradual awakening
and sudden awakening, and the innate knowledge of the good
are gone into.

OKADA, TAKEHIKO. "Wang Chi and the Rise of Existentialism,"
in Self and Society in Ming Thought. Ed. by Wm. Theodore
de Bary. (See 1.15.2), pp. 121-144.
 A close examination of Wang Chi's controversy with Ch'ien
Te-hung over Wang Yang-ming's doctrine of the original substance of the mind, Wang Chi's insistence of it as transcending good and evil, the latter's doctrine of direct
apprehension of the innate knowledge not through effort but
through immediate realization of non-being as the original
substance of the mind.

T'ANG CHUN-I. "The Development of the Concept of Moral Mind
from Wang Yang-ming to Wang Chi." Cross reference: 1.15.3.

1.16 CH'ING (1644-1912) PHILOSOPHY

1.16.1 Ch'ing Dynasty Neo-Confucianism

CHAN, WING-TSIT. "The Hsing-li ching-i and the Ch'eng-Chu
School of the Seventeenth Century," in The Unfolding of Neo-
Confucianism. Ed. by Wm. Theodore de Bary. (See below),
pp. 543-579.
 Treats the intellectual background, political factors, and
personalities leading to the compilation of the book (Essential Ideas of Nature and Principle). Pro-Chu Hsi thinkers
like Lu Shih-i (1611-1672), Chang Lü-hsiang (1611-1674), Lu
Lung-ch'i (1630-1693), and Li Kuang-ti (1642-1718), and
anti-Chu Hsi thinkers like Yen Yüan and Wang Fu-chih are discussed. The book is compared with other anthologies to show
its new methodology, its new philosophical orientation, and
its influence on subsequent Neo-Confucian anthologies.

CHENG, CHUNG-YING. "Reason, Substance, and Human Desires in
Seventeenth-Century Neo-Confucianism," in The Unfolding of
Neo-Confucianism. Ed. by Wm. Theodore de Bary. (See below),
pp. 469-509.
 The indeterminate substance and the "reason-substance"
relationship in Wang Fu-chih, the reason-desires relation-
ship in him, the reason-substance and reason-desire relation-
ship in Yen Yüan, Li Kung, Huang Tsung-hsi (1610-1695),
Ch'eng Ch'üeh (1604-1677), Li Erh-ch'ü (1627-1705), and Fang
I-chih are discussed.

de BARY, WM. THEODORE. "Neo-Confucian Cultivation and the
Seventeenth-Century 'Enlightenment'," in The Unfolding of
Neo-Confucianism. Ed. by Wm. Theodore de Bary. (See below),
pp. 141-216.
   A comprehensive discussion under the topics of traditional
and modern enlightenment, Japanese enlightenment, Neo-
Confucianism as a school of the mind and as a form of spiri-
tuality, the relevance of sagehood, Neo-Confucian enlightenment and "having no mind," quiet-sitting, the content and
experience of Neo-Confucian enlightenment, intellectual
"enlightenment," aesthetic enlightenment, Neo-Confucian
"emptiness," Buddhism and the new "enlightenment," the re-
assessment of Neo-Confucianism, Neo-Confucian vitalism and
reaction to Ming "Idealism," new historical awareness, and
the new naturalism.

de BARY, WM. THEODORE, ed.   The Unfolding of Neo-Confucianism.
New York: Columbia University Press, 1975.   593 pp.
   Papers presented at the 1970 conference dealing with phi-
losophy are on: Confucianism and Buddhism (K. Araki, see
1.15.4), cultivation and enlightenment (de Bary, see above),
Liu Tsung-chou's doctrine of moral mind and practice (T'ang
Chun-i, see below), Fang I-chih (Willard J. Peterson, see
below), Wang Fu-chih and the Neo-Confucian tradition (Ian
McMorran, see 1.16.2), reason, substance and human desires
(Chung-ying Cheng, see above), inner experience and lived
concreteness in Yen Yüan (Wei-ming Tu, see 1.15.3), and the
Hsing-li ching-i and the Ch'eng-Chu school (Wing-tsit Chan,
see above).

PETERSON, WILLARD J.   "Fang I-chih (1611-1671): Western Learning and the 'Investigation of Things'," in The Unfolding of
Neo-Confucianism.   Ed. by Wm. Theodore de Bary.   (See above),
pp. 369-411.
   By drawing upon Western natural philosophy and science,
Fang redirected the Confucian tendency in "investigation of
things" from the exclusive emphasis of moral purpose to the
intellectual importance of things.   Centering on investigation of physical objects, technology, and natural phenomena,
Fang showed the investigation of "things" as implicitly
worthy, and by stressing evidence and selective use of
Western learning, he turned the Confucian investigation of
things away from the Wang Yang-ming idealistic orientation.

T'ANG CHUN-I.   "Liu Tsung-chou's (1576-1645) Doctrine of
Moral Mind and Practice and His Critique of Wang Yang-ming,"
in The Unfolding of Neo-Confucianism.   Ed. by Wm. Theodore
de Bary.   (See above), pp. 305-331.

The Tung-lin school's criticism of Wang Yang-ming, Liu's opposition to Wang's "idea of beyond good and evil," Liu's critique of Wang's idea of the primacy of knowing good and evil, Liu's emphasis on the practice of self-reverence, Liu's four-sentence teaching versus Wang's four-sentence teaching, and the historical significance of Liu's criticism in contrast to that of other seventeenth-century critics are analyzed.

1.16.2 Wang Fu-chih (1619-1692)

BLACK, ALISON H. The Concept of the Mandate of Heaven in the Political Thought of Wang Fu-chih (1619-1692). University of Glascow M. Lit. thesis, 1970. 271 pp.
   A study of the political thought of Wang Fu-chih in terms of the Mandate of Heaven. Some good discussion on this fresh subject, which needs to be further explored.

CHAN, WING-TSIT. A Source Book in Chinese Philosophy. (See 1.2.1).
   Chapter 36 contains an introduction to Wang's materialism, with the translation of selected passages from the Surviving Works of Wang Fu-chih, rearranged under the philosophical headings of (a) the world of concrete things, (b) substance and function, (c) being and non-being, (d) principle and material force, (e) unceasing growth and man's nature and destiny, and (g) history and government.

CHANG, CARSUN. The Development of Neo-Confucian Thought. (See 1.13.1), Vol. 2.
   In chapter 11, Chang gives a comprehensive discussion of Wang Fu-chih as the advocate of realism and change. A good account.

HOU WAI-LU and CHANG CH'I-CHIH. "The Philosophical Thoughts of Wang Fu-chih," in Chinese Studies in History and Philosophy, 1, no. 3 (1968): 12-28.
   A Marxist interpretation of Wang's philosophy as basically materialistic, his idea that motion is absolute and based on its internal opposition, his doctrine of concrete objects, theory of human nature, etc.

McMORRAN, IAN. "Late Ming Criticism of Wang Yang-ming: The Case of Wang Fu-chih," (see 1.15.3).
   Special attention is focused on Wang Fu-chih's criticism of Wang Yang-ming's doctrine of the unity of knowledge and action, with an emphasis on Wang Fu-chih's insistence that while knowledge may precede action, action is more important.

Wang Fu-chih also criticized Wang Yang-ming's doctrine of
principle, stressing the point that everything consists of
material force.

_____. "Wang Fu-chih and the Neo-Confucian Tradition," in The
Unfolding of Neo-Confucianism. Ed. by Wm. Theodore de Bary.
(See 1.16.1), pp. 413-467.
   After a lengthy biography and a survey of his intellectual
background, the main discussion is on Wang's cosmology based
on the philosophy of ch'i and the identification of Tao with
ch'i (concrete objects), under the influence of Chang Tsai,
on whose main work Wang wrote a commentary in which he developed his own philosophy.

1.16.3 Yen Yüan (1635-1704)

See also 6.22.

BRAGG, GERALD ERNEST. The Life and Thought of Yen Hsi-chai
   (1635-1704). University of Arizona Ph.D. thesis, 1974.
   348 pp.
   Yen Yüan's life is described as a series of traumas and as
molded by local Ming Dynasty eremites who personally advocated practical learning.

CHAN, WING-TSIT. A Source Book in Chinese Philosophy. (See
   1.2.1).
   Chapter 37 introduces the practical Confucianism of Yen,
with the translation of selected passages from his writings
arranged under the philosophical headings of (a) in defense
of physical nature, (b) the identity of principle and material force, and (c) learning through experience.

CHANG, CARSUN. The Development of Neo-Confucian Thought.
   (See 1.13.1), Vol. 2, chapter 12.
   A good account of Yen Yüan the pragmatist, with generous
quotations from the philosophical writings of Yen.

FREEMAN, MANSFIELD. "Yen Hsi Chai, a Seventeenth-Century
   Philosopher," in Journal of the North China Branch of the
   Royal Asiatic Society, 59 (1935): 70-91.
   Considers Yen Yüan essentially a conservative, though he
insisted on practical results. Fails to comprehend Yen's
historical place and philosophical contribution.

TU WEI-MING. "Yen Yüan: From Inner Experience to Lived Concreteness," in The Unfolding of Neo-Confucianism. Ed. by
   Wm. Theodore de Bary. (See 1.16.1), pp. 511-541.

The increasing recognition of Yen's importance by modern
scholars, Yen's biography, Yen's attack on the rationalistic
and speculative Chu Hsi School, his emphasis on practice as
fundamental to self-cultivation as well as reform, Yen's
views on human nature, his stress on feelings as the manifes-
tation of the inherent moral propensity of man and physical
nature as the instrumentality of self-realization, and his
demand for active participation in daily affairs in place of
quiet-sitting, meditation, and book reading.

YEN YÜAN. Preservation of Learning. Tr. by Mansfield Freeman.
Los Angeles: Monumenta Serica Institute, 1972. 215 pp.
    A translation of one of the four Preservations, the most
important works of the most outstanding, independent Neo-
Confucian thinker of the seventeenth century. There is a
biography of Yen gleaned from Yen's own diaries and earlier
biographies. The introduction also includes Yen's thoughts
on education, personal cultivation, religion, human nature,
government, etc., but does not go into the intellectual currents either before or after Yen.

1.16.4 Tai Chen (1723-1777)

CHAN, WING-TSIT. A Source Book in Chinese Philosophy. (See
1.2.1).
    Chapter 38 contains an introduction to Tai's philosophy of
principle as order, with a translation of selected passages
from Tai's Commentary on the Meng Tzu tzu-i shu-cheng (meanings of terms in the Book of Mencius), under the headings of
(a) on principle, (b) on nature, (c) on capacity, (d) on
humanity, righteousness, propriety, and wisdom, and (e) on
the variety of circumstances.

CHANG, CARSUN. The Development of Neo-Confucian Thought.
(See 1.13.1), Vol. 2.
    Chapter 14 deals with the school of philological and in-
vestigatory study and Tai Chen the philologist-naturalist,
and gives a good analysis of the philosophical meanings of
Tai's Yüan-shan (inquiry into goodness) as well as of his
Meanings of Terms in the Book of Mencius.

FUNG YU-LAN. A History of Chinese Philosophy. (See 1.2.1),
Vol. 2, pp. 651-672.
    A very philosophical exposition of Tai's philosophy in
terms of (a) Tao and principle, (b) the nature and capacity,
(c) methodology for seeking principle, (d) origin of evil,
and (e) comparison of Tai Chen and Hsün Tzu.

TAI CHEN. Tai Chen's Inquiry Into Goodness. Tr. by Chung-ying
Cheng. Honolulu: East-West Center Press, 1971. 176 pp.
   A translation of Tai Chen's treatise on goodness in three
parts. Contrary to the title, the treatise deals with not
only ethics but also metaphysics, including such concepts as
creativity, what is above and what is within form, what is
natural, human nature, the mind, etc. In each case, a passage from the Classics is cited as a starting point from
which Tai argues against the Sung Neo-Confucianists. There
is a long introduction to the translation.

WU, BRUC YEN-LIN. Tai Chen: Confucian Classics and Philosophy.
Ann Arbor: University of Michigan Ph.D. thesis, 1966. 251 pp.
   Mostly a translation of an important study of Tai, includ-
ing many excerpts from his three philosophical works.

1.17   K'ANG YU-WEI and T'AN SSU-T'UNG

   1.17.1 K'ang Yu-wei (1858-1927)

   See also 10.12.1.

   CHAN, WING-TSIT. "K'ang Yu-wei and the Confucian Philosophy
   of Humanity (Jen)," in K'ang Yu-wei: A Biography and a
   Symposium. (See below), pp. 355-374. Reprinted in Chan,
   Neo-Confucianism, Etc. (See 1.13.1), pp. 247-280.
      K'ang's theory of jen as the mind that cannot bear to see
   the suffering of others, as love for one's own kind, as
   power of attraction, as ether or electricity, as forming one
   body with all, as the principle of production and reproduction, as derived from heaven, and as having gradation. Also,
   the doctrine developed by his pupil, T'an Ssu-t'ung.

   _____. A Source Book in Chinese Philosophy. (See 1.2.1).
      Chapter 39 introduces Kang's philosophy of the great
   unity, with the translation of selected passages from his
   writings under the headings of (a) the Three Ages, (b) Confucius' institutional reforms, (c) the mind that cannot
   bear to see the suffering of others, (d) the age of great
   unity, and (e) humanity.

   CHANG, CARSUN. The Development of Neo-Confucian Thought.
   (See 1.13.1), Vol. 2.
      Some good discussion of Kang's position in chapter 17, en-
   titled Chinese Thought Under the Impact of the West.

   FUNG YU-LAN. A History of Chinese Philosophy. (See 1.2.1),
   Vol. 2, pp. 673-691.

A reliable account of K'ang as the leader of the New Text school, under the headings of (a) Confucius as a religious leader and political reformer, and (b) Ta-t'ung shu (book of the great unity).

K'ANG YU-WEI. Ta T'ung shu, the One-world Philosophy of K'ang Yu-wei. Cross reference: 10.12.1.

HOWARD, RICHARD C. "K'ang Yu-wei (1885-1927): His Intellectual Background and Early Thought," in Confucian Personality. Ed. by A.F. Wright and D. Twitchett. Stanford: Stanford University Press, 1962. Pp. 294-316.
   A careful biographical study showing how K'ang was influenced by certain 19th century Confucianists and a discussion on his moral and social ideas in terms of "universal laws" before he evolved the theory of "grand unity."

LO, JUNG-PANG, ed. K'ang Yu-wei: A Biography and a Symposium. Tucson: University of Arizona Press, 1967. 541 pp.
   The important, chronological autobiography of K'ang is here published for the first time. The symposium includes articles on K'ang's Ta-t'ung shu and the Communist manifesto, his doctrine of humanity, and his excursion into science.

LO, JUNG-PANG. "K'ang Yu-wei and His Philosophy of Political Change and Historical Progress," in Symposium on Chinese Studies. Department of Chinese, University of Hong Kong, 1968. Pp. 70-81.
   K'ang's idea of historical progress through stages is carefully explained, his idea of a utopia is clearly presented, his theoretical basis and program for reform succinctly outlined, and his political ideas are compared with several Western thinkers.

1.17.2   T'an Ssu-t'ung (1865-1898)

See also 3.2.

CHAN, WING-TSIT. A Source Book in Chinese Philosophy. (See 1.2.1).
   Chapter 40 introduces the philosophy of humanity in T'an, with a translation of selected passages from T'an writings under the headings of (a) ether and humanity, (b) the principle of nature and human desires, (c) neither production nor extinction, and (d) daily renovation.

FUNG YU-LAN. A History of Chinese Philosophy. (See 1.2.1), Vol. 2, pp. 691-705.

A fairly good account of T'an's thought under the headings
of (a) love and ether, (b) being and non-being, production
and destruction, (c) government in the great unity, and
(d) regarding religious leaders.

OKA, TAKASHI. "The Philosophy of T'an Ssu-t'ung," in <u>Papers
on China</u>. Harvard University Committee on Regional Studies,
9 (1955): 1-47.
A careful investigation into the ideas expressed in T'an's
<u>Jen-hsüeh</u> (a study of benevolence), without, however, ade-
quate reference to the historical and philosophical currents
by which these ideas were molded.

1.18   CONTEMPORARY PHILOSOPHY IN CHINA

1.18.1   The Intellectual Climate

CHOW, TSE-TSUNG. "The Anti-Confucian Movement in Early Repub-
lican China," in <u>The Confucian Persuasion</u>. Ed. by A. Wright.
Stanford: Stanford University Press, 1960. Pp. 288-312.
A scholarly and objective treatment of the subject by a
noted specialist in the intellectual history of modern China,
under the headings of (a) the rise of the anti-Confucian tide,
(b) the arguments for and against a Confucian state religion,
(c) Confucianism and the democratic way of life, (d) the
attack on the old ethics, and (e) Confucian issues redefined.

_____. <u>The May Fourth Movement: Intellectual Revolution in
Modern China</u>. Stanford: Stanford University Press, 1960.
486 pp.
The best scholarly work on the subject in the English language. Topics include the initial phase of the movement,
early literary and intellectual activities, the May Fourth
incident, student demonstration and strikes, expansion of
the New Culture Movement, the ideological and political
split, 1919-1921, the literary revolution, the new thought
and re-evaluation of the tradition, the new thought and later
controversies, etc.

de BARY, WM. THEODORE, WING-TSIT CHAN, and BURTON WATSON, comps.
<u>Sources of Chinese Tradition</u>. (<u>See</u> 1.2.1).
Chapters 20-24 contain a lucid and reliable translation of
well selected writings and documents in the intellectual
history of modern China, with clear analyses. Topics include reform and reaction under the Manchus, the Nationalist
revolution, the New Culture Movement, etc. A useful source
for college students.

JEANS, ROGER BAILEY, JR. Syncretism in Defense of Confucianism:
An Intellectual and Political Biography of the Early Years of
Chang Chun-mai, 1887-1923. George Washington University Ph.D.
thesis, 1974. 598 pp.
    Describes Chang's (1887-1969) early years in three stages:
the first, the 1910s, as absorption of Western learning;
1919-1921 as defense of Confucianism; and 1922-23 as syn-
cretic, that is, combining Chinese spiritual civilization
and moral values with Western influences.

LEVENSON, JOSEPH R. Confucian China and Its Modern Fate: A
Trilogy. Berkeley: University of California Press, 1968.
579 pp.
    Originally published in three separate volumes: The Prob-
lem of Intellectual Continuity (Vol. 1, 1958), The Problem
of Monarchical Decay (Vol. 2, 1964), and The Problem of
Historical Significance (Vol. 3, 1965). An outstanding examination of the decline of the Confucian tradition under
the impact of the West as well as of the intellectual climate
in modern turbulent China.

_____. Liang Ch'i-ch'ao and the Mind of Modern China.
Berkeley: University of California Press, 1959. 256 pp.
    A very interesting study of the life and times of Liang
Ch'i-ch'ao (1873-1929), a disciple of K'ang Yu-wei, as well
as of the formation of the modern intellectual mind since
1873.

1.18.2 Hu Shih (1891-1962)

CHAN, WING-TSIT. "Hu Shih and Chinese Philosophy," in Philosophy East and West, 6 (1956): 3-12. Reprinted in Chan,
Neo-Confucianism, Etc. (See 1.13.1), pp. 281-298.
    The leading Chinese thinker's role in and contributions to
the introduction of Western philosophy, the downfall of Confucianism, and the reconstruction of Chinese traditional
philosophy. The second part is overstressed, for while Hu
joined other intellectuals in the attack on Confucianism, he
gave due credit to Confucius, as in his The Development of
the Logical Method, and Confucianism has not fallen.

FAN, KUANG-HUAN. A Study of Hu Shih's Thought. New York
University Ph.D. thesis, 1963. 312 pp.
    A good account of Hu's thoughts on religion, science,
civilization, social immortality, literature, and politics,
but virtually nothing on his studies of, contributions to,
or works on Chinese philosophy and Buddhism.

ROY, A.T. "Liang Shu-ming and Hu Shih on the Institutional
Interpretation of Confucianism," in Chung Chi Journal, 1
(1962): 139-157.
    A comprehensive review of Liang Shu-ming's thoughts and
his criticism of Hu's social and practical interpretation
of Confucian jen (humanity).

1.18.3 Chang Tung-sun (1886-1962)

CHAN, WING-TSIT. A Source Book in Chinese Philosophy. (See
1.2.1).
    Chapter 41 introduces Chang's theory of knowledge, with
the translation of selected passages from his Chih-shih yü
wen-hua (knowledge and culture).

CHANG, TUNG-SUN. "A Chinese Philosopher's Theory of Knowledge,
Etc.," in A Review of General Semantics, 9 (1952): 203-226.
Reprinted in Our Language and Our World, Selections from
Etc.: A Review of General Semantics. Ed. by S.I. Hayakawa.
New York: Harper, 1959. Pp. 299-323.
    A leading Chinese philosopher presents here his own theory
of knowledge and logic with illustrations from Chinese sentences and concepts, emphasizing that while Western logic is
fundamentally identity-logic, that of China is correlation-
logic.

1.18.4 Hsiung Shih-li (1883-1968)

CHAN, BENJAMIN CHUN-PIU. The Development of Neo-Buddhist
Thought of Modern China as Represented in the Philosophy of
Hsiung Shih-li: The Identity of Reality and Function. Temple
University Ph.D. thesis, 1968. 226 pp.
    This first systematic interpretation and assessment of
Hsiung, an Idealist Neo-Confucian philosopher, who identified reality and function, views Hsiung from two angles. As
a philosopher, Hsiung synthesizes the Absolute and the self,
the other world and this world, reality and phenomenon, and
the Buddhist School of Being and the Buddhist School of Non-
being, thereby creating a new cosmology. As a religious
person, Hsiung has deep convictions and aims at spiritual
liberation.

CHAN, WING-TSIT. A Source Book in Chinese Philosophy. (See
1.2.1).
    Chapter 43 introduces Hsiung's new idealistic Confucianism,
with a translation of selected passages from Hsiung's major
work, Hsin wei-shih lun (new doctrine of Consciousness-Only),

under the headings of (a) "closing and opening," (b) the
unity of principle and material force, (c) the mind and
humanity, (d) the unity of substance and function. Comments
and footnotes added.

LIU, SHU-HSIEN. "The Contemporary Development of Neo-Confucian
    Epistemology," in Inquiry, 14 (1971): 1940. Also in Naess,
    Arne, and Alastair Hannay, Invitation to Chinese Philosophy.
    Oslo: Universitetsfordget, 1972. Pp. 19-40.
      Extending the thesis presented in the below-mentioned
    article into a general survey of the formation of contem-
    porary Neo-Confucian theory of knowledge under the influences
    of Hsiung Shih-li's philosophy.

_____. "Hsiung Shih-li's Theory of Causation," in Philosophy
    East and West, 19 (1969): 399-407.
      A good study of Hsiung's theory of knowledge and metaphysics
    in terms of his idea of causation by way of the profound in-
    fluences of the school of Consciousness-Only in Mahāyāna
    Buddhism.

1.18.5 Fung Yu-lan (1895-   )

See also 15.12.

CHAN, WING-TSIT. A Source Book in Chinese Philosophy. (See
    1.2.1).
      Chapter 42 introduces the new rationalistic Confucianism
    of Fung, with the translation of selected passages from Fung's
    earlier work, the Hsin li-hsüeh (new rational philosophy),
    under the headings of (a) the world and principle, (b) prin-
    ciple and material force, (c) Tao, substance and function,
    and universal operation, (d) principle and the nature, and
    (e) serving Heaven and jen.

FUNG YU-LAN. "I Discovered Marxism-Leninism," in People's
    China, 1, no. 6 (1950): 10-11, 21.
      Confesses that his New Rational Philosophy is but a twi-
    light of old Chinese philosophy, which is comparable to
    medieval medicine, whereas Marxism-Leninism is comparable to
    modern medicine.

_____. "Philosophy in New China According to Fung Yu-lan," in
    Philosophy East and West (Rome) (July, 1952): 105-107.
      Maintains that there is also the dialectic in Confucianism
    and Taoism, though rudimentary, and that we should select
    the desirable and reject the undesirable from traditional
    Chinese philosophy.

FUNG YU-LAN. <u>A Short History of Chinese Philosophy</u>. (<u>See</u>
1.3.1).
   In chapter 28, entitled "Chinese Philosophy in the Modern
World," Fung presents his own philosophy in terms of the
Four Spheres of Living, methodology of metaphysics, the task
of the historian of philosophy, etc.

_____. <u>The Spirit of Chinese Philosophy</u>. (<u>See</u> 1.4.3).
   In chapter 10, on "A New System," Fung outlines his own
New Rational Philosophy as presented in the <u>Hsin-li-hsüeh</u> to
demonstrate his own creative inheritance of Ch'eng-Chu Neo-
Confucianism in a modern manner. He has totally rejected
his "new system" since 1949.

JAN YÜN-HUA. <u>Problems of Tao and Tao Te Ching</u>. Cross
reference: 7.3.

WYCOFF, W.A. <u>The New Rationalism of Fung Yu-lan</u>. Columbia
University Ph.D. thesis, 1975. 338 pp.
   Fung's New Rationalism is here presented not as an outline
or a summary of Fung's major work, the <u>Hsin-li-hsüeh</u>, but as
an analytical reconstruction of the philosophy with materials
from Fung's other philosophical works. There is also a long
account of Fung's self-criticism before 1959.

1.19 CHINESE PHILOSOPHY AND MARXISM

<u>See also</u> 10.11, 15.11.

CH'EN, JEROME, ed. <u>Mao</u>. New Jersey: Prentice-Hall, 1969.
   A good collection of Mao Tse-tung's (1893-1976) own words and
several scholars' articles evaluating Mao.

_____. <u>Mao Papers: Anthology and Bibliography</u>. London: Oxford
University Press, 1970. 221 pp.
   A good collection of Mao's writings and instructions between 1917
and 1969, with an introductory essay on Mao's literary style and an
excellent chronological bibliography of Mao's writings.

CHU PO-K'UN. "Problems of the History of Chinese Philosophy are Discussed by Peking's Philosophy Circle," in <u>Chinese Studies in History
and Philosophy</u>, 2 (1968-69): 98-104.
   Philosophers in Peking discussed the struggle in the history of
philosophy, the evaluation of idealism and materialism in philosophy,
the question of continuing the heritage of philosophy, and the
objective of the history of Chinese philosophy.

DOW, TSUNG-I. "Some Affinities Between Confucius and Marxian Philosophical Systems," in <u>Asian Profile</u>, 1 (1973): 247-259.
    An interesting discussion of the philosophical similarity between
traditional Confucianism and the dialectical system of Marxism-
Leninism, though the similarity in question is somewhat exaggerated.

Foreign Language Press, ed. <u>Selected Articles Criticizing Lin Piao
and Confucius</u>. Peking, Foreign Language Press, 1974-1975. 2 vols.
211 pp. and 229 pp.
    An official collection of anti-Confucian essays by the Maoists
and eminent scholars like Fung Yu-lan and Kao Heng. Note in particular Yang Jung-kuo's and Fung Yu-lan's essays.

FU, CHARLES WEI-HSUN. "Confucianism, Marxism-Leninism and Mao: A
Critical Study," in <u>Journal of Chinese Philosophy</u>, 1 (1974): 339-372.
    This article exposes the underlying structure of Marxism-Leninism-
Maoism as fundamentally a moralistic working ideology, and analyzes
the peculiar idealogical relation between Mao and Confucianism,
thereby shedding some light on the political-ideological implications of the present anti-Confucianism campaign in China.

_____. "Contemporary Chinese Philosophy," in <u>Handbook of Contemporary
Developments in Philosophy</u>. Ed. by John Burr, Jr. Connecticut:
Greenwood Press, 1978.
    A philosophical account of the essentials of Mao Tse-tung's
thought, his three major struggles with the revisionist line on
China's philosophical front, as well as his confrontation with
traditional Chinese philosophy.

_____. "Marxism-Leninism-Maoism As an Ethical Theory," in <u>Journal of
Chinese Philosophy</u>, 5 (1978).
    A critical exposition of Marxism-Leninism-Maoism as an ethical
theory in six sections: introduction, the highest governing principle of proletarian morality, the Maoist reorientation of proletarian morality, democratic centralism and its moral dilemma, the
Marxist-Leninist-Maoist framework of moral reasoning, and critical
postscript.

_____. "Rejoinder to Professor Howard Parsons' Critical Remarks," in
<u>Journal of Chinese Philosophy</u>, 1 (1975): 114-121.
    Counter-argues against Parsons' defense of Marxism-Leninism that
the ultimate meaning of dialectical and historical materialism consists in its functioning as a moralistic working ideology, and that
Mao's Cultural Revolution finally disclosed Mao's persistent determination to carry out the dictatorship of the proletariat in terms
of day-to-day moral transformation of man in the proletarian way.

FUNG YU-LAN. "Contemporary Chinese Philosophy: The Development of
  Marxism-Leninism in China," in Philosophy in the Mid-Century. Ed.
  by Raymond Klibansky. Firenze: La Nuova Italia Editrice, 1959.
  Vol. 4, pp. 252-262.
    Discusses Mao Tse-tung's "On Practice" in which he explains the
  origin of knowledge and the criteria of truth, and his "On Contradiction" in which he explains the two opposing metaphysical and
  materialistic-dialectic outlooks.

_____. "The Legacy of Chinese Philosophy: The Question of Continuity,"
  in Chinese Studies in History and Philosophy, 2 (1968-69): 23-34.
    Fung says we should distinguish the concrete meaning and abstract
  meaning of philosophy and continue the latter as Chinese heritage.
  For example, in the doctrine of the innate knowledge of the good,
  its concrete meaning is none other than the feudalistic morality of
  the time, but in its abstract meaning, it is the doctrine that all
  people can be sages. An earlier translation of the original Chinese
  treatise appears in the same journal, 1 (1968): 92-102, under the
  title "The Problems of Succession to the Legacy of Chinese
  Philosophy."

_____. "The Struggle between Materialism and Idealism in the History
  of Chinese Philosophy in Terms of Several Major Problems in Chinese
  Philosophy," in Chinese Studies in History and Philosophy, 2 (1969):
  3-27.
    The problems of Heaven, especially in Confucius, Mencius, Taoism,
  and Hsün Tzu, of material force in Taoism, the Book of Changes, Wang,
  Ch'ung, and Tung Chung-shu, of the mind in Buddhism and Fan Chen,
  and of li, especially in Neo-Confucianism.

_____. "Two Problems in the Study of the History of Chinese Philos-
  ophy," in Chinese Studies in History and Philosophy, 2 (1968-69):
  5-22.
    On the scope of the struggle between idealism and materialism.
  Fung thinks that the struggle has extended to all realms of thought.
  He gives many examples from the history of Chinese philosophy and
  cites many examples to show how frequent struggles between opposite
  schools or theories took place and how they proceeded.

GRIFFITH, WILLIAM E. Sino-Soviet Relations, 1964-1965. Cambridge,
  Mass.: M.I.T. Press, 1967. 504 pp.
    Continued discussion of the Sino-Soviet dispute during 1964-65.
  Should be read with its sister book, The Sino-Soviet Rift (see
  below). Well-analyzed and documented.

_____. The Sino-Soviet Rift. Cambridge, Mass.: M.I.T. Press, 1964.
  508 pp.

A detailed analysis of the Sino-Soviet idealogical dispute reaching its climax in 1963. With important documents in English translation.

Joint Publications Research Service, tr. Miscellany of Mao Tsetung Thought (1949-1968). Reproduced by National Technical Information Service, U.S. Department of Commerce, Springfield, Virginia, 1974. Parts 1 and 2.
    A substantial translation of Long Live Mao Tsetung Thought, the original text of which was unofficially circulated among the Red Guards during the Cultural Revolution. An extremely important material for a clear understanding of the development of Mao's thought since the Liberation.

KUAN FENG and LIN YÜ-SHIH. "Third Discussion of Lao Tzu," in Chinese Studies in Philosophy. Cross reference: 1.4.2.

MAO TSE-TUNG. Selected Readings from the Works of Mao Tsetung. Peking: Peking: Foreign Language Press, 1971. 504 pp.
    Most readings are selected from the below-mentioned Works. There are about ten essays after 1949 not originally included in the Selected Works, such as "On the Correct Handling of Contradictions among the People (1957)."

_____. Selected Works. Peking: Foreign Language Press, 1961. 4 vols.
    The most important primary sourcebook on Mao's thought, selected, arranged, and translated by the Foreign Language Press.

_____. Selected Works. Volume V. Peking: Foreign Language Press, 1977. 518 pp.
    The long-awaited volume posthumously edited and published shortly after the post-Mao power struggle on the highest level of the Communist Party of China. This volume includes many important speeches and writings of Mao Tse-tung between 1949 and 1957.

MUNRO, DONALD J. "Chinese Communist Treatment of the Thinkers of the Hundred Schools Period," in The China Quarterly, 24 (1965): 119-141.
    Confucius as an idealist, Mencius as subjective, Hsün Tzu as a major materialist, uncertain qualities in the Taoists and Legalists.

SCHRAM, STUART, ed. Chairman Mao Talks to the People: Talks and Letters, 1956-71. New York: Pantheon Books, 1974. 352 pp.
    A good collection and translation of Mao's sayings and writings on questions of philosophy, the Cultural Revolution, China's socialist reconstruction, etc.

SCHRAM, STUART. Mao Tse-tung. Baltimore: Penguin Books, 1967.
372 pp.
   Probably the most comprehensive and reliable biography in English,
covering the life and times of Mao until the Cultural Revolution.

_____. The Political Thought of Mao Tse-tung. Rev. ed. New York:
Praeger, 1969. 479 pp.
   In his extensively revised introduction to this enlarged collec-
tion of documents, the author re-examines the development of Mao's
thought, assesses its originality, and traces the direction of
China under Mao. Authoritative and comprehensive.

TU WEI-MING. "Confucianism: Symbol and Substance in Recent Times,"
in Asian Thought & Society, 1 (1976): 42-66.
   A fresh and serious inquiry into the symbol and substance of Confucianism in light of the Cultural Revolution and the ensuing
events, with a series of reflections on the relevance of Confucian
symbolism in identifying substantive issues in China's quest for a
new value system.

WAKEMAN, FREDERIC, JR. History and Will: Philosophical Perspectives
of Mao Tse-tung's Thought. Berkeley: University of California
Press, 1973. 392 pp.
   A scholarly attempt to reconstruct Mao's thought in relation to
Marxism and Chinese tradition.

WHITEHEAD, RAYMOND L. Love and Struggle in Mao's Thought. Maryknoll:
Orbis Books, 1977. 166 pp.
   A sympathetic emphasis on the ethical dimension of Mao's thought.
The book is divided into (1) a fighter's philosophy, (2) the struggle
ethic and social conflict, (3) the struggle ethic and personal transformation, (4) a revolution in lifestyle, (5) the struggle ethic
and liberal values, and (5) struggle and hope.

2. Human Nature

2.1 THE UNIQUENESS OF THE THEORY OF HUMAN NATURE IN CHINESE PHILOSOPHY

CHAN, WING-TSIT, tr. and comp. <u>A Source Book in Chinese Philosophy</u>.
New Jersey: Princeton University Press, 1963. 856 pp.
On human nature, <u>see</u> p. 18 (Confucius), p. 51 (Mencius), pp. 95-
98 (<u>Doctrine of the Mean</u>), pp. 128-135 (Hsün Tzu), pp. 253-254 (Han
Fei), pp. 274-278 (Tung Chung-shu), p. 289 (Yang Hsiung), p. 293
(Wang Ch'ung), pp. 456-459 (Han Yü), p. 462 (Chou Tun-i), p. 484
(Shao Yung), p. 496 (Chang Tsai), p. 522 (Ch'eng I), p. 574 (Lu
Hsiang-shan), p. 593 (Chu Hsi), and pp. 717-719 (Tai Chen).

DUBS, HOMER H. "Mencius and Sun-dz on Human Nature," in <u>Philosophy
East and West</u>, 6 (1956): 213-222.
Hsün Tzu's doctrine of human nature is understood to be intended
to support Confucius' authoritarianism. Dubs suggests that Chu Hsi
was closer to Hsün Tzu than Mencius.

GRAHAM, A.C. "The Background of the Mencian Theory of Human Nature,"
in <u>Tsing Hua Journal of Chinese Studies</u>, n.s., 6, nos. 1-2 (1967):
215-274.
A well-documented treatise arguing that before Mencius, <u>hsing</u>
(nature) was understood in the sense of life, and that discussions
centered not on whether it is good or evil but on how to nourish
and preserve life, and that even Mencius and Hsün Tzu talked about
the good and evil nature of man only in debates.

KING CHIEN-KUN. "The Confucian Concept of Human Nature," in <u>T'ien
Hsia Monthly</u>, 11 (1940): 119-127.
An interesting interpretation of Confucius' and Tzu-ssu's (492-
431 B.C.) ideas on conceiving human nature to be the universal
element of activity manifested as "the principle of life" in man
and expressed chiefly in imagination.

LAU, D.C. "Theories of Human Nature in Mencius and Shyuntzyy," in
<u>Bulletin of the School of Oriental and African Studies</u>, 15 (1953):
541-565.

The opposing theories of the two Confucian followers on human nature are carefully examined with the conclusion that they were not really as much opposed as in their theories of morality. Hsün Tzu is looked upon as inferior to Mencius in inspiring people to great deeds.

LOJUANG, STANISLAUS. "Human Nature and Human Person in Confucianism," in Chinese Culture, 2, no. 1 (1959): 4-9.
   A short but substantial account of Chinese traditional doctrines of human nature, noting a contrast between Chu Hsi on the one hand and Aristotle and St. Thomas on the other with reference to essence and concrete form.

MUNRO, DONALD J. The Concept of Man in Early China. Stanford: Stanford University Press, 1969. 256 pp.
   Ancient Chinese views on man's possibility and limitations, his relation with others and the universe, the natural equality of all men, and the Confucian and Taoist ways of cultivation to realize one's nature.

SARGENT, G.E. "Les Débats entre Meng-tseu et Siun-tseu sur la Nature Humaine," in Oriens Extremus, 3 (1956): 1-17.
   A good exposition, noting both similarities and differences, with special consideration of the meaning of the word hsing (birth, nature).

WU, JOHN. "Mencius' Philosophy of Human Nature and Natural Law," in Chinese Culture, 1, no. 1 (1957): 1-19.
   A distinguished student of law analyzes Mencius' doctrine of human nature in relation to the prescriptive and normative will of God and concludes that Mencius' philosophy of Natural Law is no different from the classical Natural Law tradition of the West.

2.2 THE RELATIONS BETWEEN THEORY OF HUMAN NATURE AND ETHICS

"The Book of Mencius," in Mencius. Tr. by D.C. Lau. Baltimore: Penguin Books, 1970. 280 pp. Also as "The Works of Mencius by James Legge," in The Chinese Classics. Oxford: Clarendon Press, 1895. 402 pp. Vol. 2.
   On nature, human, and innate virtue, see: 6A: 1-6, 2A: 6, 4B: 26. On humanity and righteousness, see: 6A: 1, 4, 8, 10, 11, 18, 19, 1A: 1, 2A: 2, 4A: 10, 20, 27.

CHAN, WING-TSIT. A Source Book in Chinese Philosophy. (See 2.1), pp. 128-135.
   See Chan's translation of Hsün Tzu's most important essay on human nature, "The Nature of Man is Evil," for his alternative way of dealing with the relation between theory of human nature and ethics.

CHENG, CHUNG-YIN. "Dialectics of Confucian Morality and Metaphysics
of Man," in Philosophy East and West, 21 (1971): 111-123.
Discusses the three stages of development of Confucian morality
looked upon as three dimensions of the Confucian moral theory. A
philosophical comparison of Confucian morality with the Kantian
morality is also given.

SCHAEFER, T.E. "Perennial Wisdom and the Sayings of Mencius," in
International Philosophical Quarterly, 3 (1963): 428-444.
An appreciative study of Mencius' ideas of the goodness of human
nature, the perfect man, and moral goodness through propriety and
charity (jen), supported by quotations.

TU WEI-MING. "The Neo-Confucian Concept of Man," in Philosophy East
and West, 21 (January, 1971): 79-87.
A short essay throwing light on the relation between human nature
and ethics from the Neo-Confucian point of view. Tu argues that
the point of departure in Confucianism is self-cultivation rather
than social responsibility, and that the perfectibility of man
through self-effort becomes a defining characteristic of Confucian
humanism and the real strength of the Neo-Confucian development of
the Confucian concept of man.

2.3 THE MANDATE OF HEAVEN (*T'IEN-MING*)

See also 3.1.1, 10.9, 14.2.2.

CHAN, WING-TSIT. A Source Book in Chinese Philosophy. (See 2.1),
chapter 1.
Note the meaning of t'ien-ming in relation to human nature in
some poems Chan translates from the Book of Poetry for a clear
understanding of how the pre-Confucian Chinese people thought about
the subject.

"The Doctrine of the Mean," in Wing-tsit Chan, A Source Book in
Chinese Philosophy. (See 2.1), p. 98. Also in James Legge, The
Chinese Classics. Oxford: Clarendon Press, 1895. Vol. 1,
pp. 382-434.
One of the most important treatises in early Confucianism on the
relation between human nature and the t'ien-ming. Note the first
sentence of the Doctrine of the Mean: "What Heaven (T'ien, Nature)
imparts to man is called human nature."

T'ANG CHUN-I. "The T'ien-ming (Heavenly Ordinance) in Pre-Ch'in
China," in Philosophy East and West, 11 (1962): 195-218 and 12
(1962): 29-49.
A penetrating investigation of the doctrine of ming in the ancient
classics and in the teachings of Confucius, Mo Tzu, Mencius, Chuang
Tzu, Lao Tzu, and Hsün Tzu.

2.4 SINCERITY (*CH'ENG*)

CHANG TSAI. "Correcting Youthful Ignorance," in Wing-tsit Chan, A
   Source Book in Chinese Philosophy. (See 2.1), pp. 507-514.
      Chapter 2, entitled "Enlightenment Resulting from Sincerity,"
   shows Chang's original interpretation of the meaning of sincerity
   in the Doctrine of the Mean as well as of his own theory of human
   nature in accordance with the idea of absolute sincerity.

CHOU TUN-I. "Penetrating the Book of Changes," in Wing-tsit Chan, A
   Source Book in Chinese Philosophy. (See 2.1), pp. 465-467.
      Chapters 1-3 show Chou's unique insights into the metaphysical
   and moral meaning of sincerity in ancient Confucian texts, especially in the Book of Changes.

The Doctrine of the Mean. (See 2.3).
      Note in particular some important sentences, such as "Sincerity
   is the Way of Heaven. To think how to be sincere is the way of
   man" (chapter 2), or "It is due to our nature that enlightenment
   results from sincerity. It is due to education that sincerity
   results from enlightenment" (chapter 21).

GRAHAM, A.C. Two Chinese Philosophers: Ch'eng Ming-tao and Ch'eng
   Yi-ch'uan. London: Lund Humphries, 1958. 195 pp.
      See in particular Graham's interpretation of Ch'eng I's understand-
   ing of ch'eng translated by Graham as "integrity" instead of
   "sincerity" (p. 67 ff.).

"The Great Learning," in Wing-tsit Chan, A Source Book in Chinese
   Philosophy. (See 2.1), chapter 4 and pp. 659-667.
      Compare the respective interpretations of the meaning of "making
   the will sincere" as the third step in the Eight Steps of the Great
   Learning given by both Chu Hsi and Wang Yang-ming.

LI AO. "The Recovery of the Nature," part 2, in Wing-tsit Chan, A
   Source Book in Chinese Philosophy. (See 2.1), pp. 456-459.
      Li's most celebrated essay dealing with the way to recover one's
   original nature. Note in particular Li's words: "...to realize that
   originally there is no thought in the mind and that it is completely
   free from tranquillity and activity--that is absolute sincerity"
   (p. 457).

2.5 THREE TYPES OF THEORY OF HUMAN NATURE (CONFUCIANISM)

2.5.1 Original Goodness

The Book of Mencius. (See 2.2).
      Note in particular Book 6, part 1, as well as 2A: 6 and
   4B: 26.

CHU HSI, in collaboration with Lü Tsu-ch'ien. <u>Reflections on</u>
<u>Things at Hand: The Neo-Confucian Anthology</u>. Tr. by Wing-
tsit Chan. New York: Columbia University Press, 1967.
441 pp.
    Chapter 1 on the substance of the Way and chapter 2 on the
essentials of learning are especially important for a good
understanding of the Neo-Confucian theory of original goodness metaphysically established by Chou Tun-i, Chang Tsai,
and the Ch'eng brothers, philosophically rearranged by Chu
Hsi.

<u>The Doctrine of the Mean</u>. Cross reference: 2.3.

KING CHIEN-KUN. "The Confucian Concept of Human Nature."
Cross reference: 2.1.

LAU, D.C. "On Mencius' Use of the Method of Analogy in Argument," in <u>Asia Minor</u>, n.s., 10 (1963): 133-194. Reprinted
in <u>Mencius</u>, Penguin Books, pp. 235-263.
    Uses the <u>Book of Mencius</u>, 4A: 17 and 6A: 1-5 to show how
Mencius skillfully used analogy to throw light on philosophical issues.

_____. "Theories of Human Nature in Mencius and Shyuntzyy."
Cross reference: 2.1.

WU, JOHN. "Mencius' Philosophy of Human Nature and Natural
Law." Cross reference: 2.1.

2.5.2 <u>Original Evil</u>

CHANG, ANDREW CHIH-YI. <u>Hsuntzu's Theory of Human Nature and</u>
<u>Its Influence on Chinese Thought</u>. Peking: privately pub-
lished, 1928. 84 pp.
    A quite reliable account of the doctrine of human nature
in Hsün Tzu in particular and in other Chinese philosophers
in general.

DUBS, HOMER H. "Mencius and Sun-dz on Human Nature." (<u>See</u>
2.1).
    Maintains that Hsün Tzu's theory was to support Confucius'
authoritarianism and radically suggests that Chu Hsi was
closer to Hsün Tzu than Mencius.

FUNG YU-LAN. <u>A History of Chinese Philosophy</u>. Tr. by Derk
Bodde. Princeton, New Jersey: Princeton University Press,
1952-53. 2 vols. Vol. 1, 455 pp. Vol. 2, 783 pp.

In volume 1, chapter 13 on Han Fei and other Legalists, Fung devotes one section to Han Fei's conception of the evilness of human nature, mostly using direct quotations from the Han Fei Tzu.

LAU, D.C. "Theories of Human Nature in Mencius and Shyuntzyy." Cross reference: 2.1.

SARGENT, G.E. "Les Débats entre Meng-tseu et Siun-tseu sur la Nature Humaine." Cross reference: 2.1.

2.5.3 Both Good and Evil ("Mixed" Theory)

CHAN, WING-TSIT. A Source Book in Chinese Philosophy. (See 2.1).
    Chapter 15 contains a translation of selected passages from Yang Hsiung's works. Yang Hsiung is one of the earliest exponents of the "mixed" theory, as is evidenced by such words as "Man's nature is a mixture of good and evil."

FUNG YU-LAN. A History of Chinese Philosophy. (See 2.5.2), Vol. 2, pp. 32-37.
    Fung gives a clear account here of Tung Chung-shu's "mixed" theory of human nature and the feelings.

HAN YÜ. "An Inquiry on Human Nature," in Wing-tsit Chan. A Source Book in Chinese Philosophy. (See 2.1), pp. 451-454.
    A very important essay expressing Han's view of the three grades of human nature: good, indifferent, and evil.

TUNG CHUNG-SHU. "Luxurian Gems of the Spring and Autumn Annals," in Wing-tsit Chan, A Source Book in Chinese Philosophy. (See 2.1), pp. 273-279.
    Chapter 35 of the Luxurian Gems, entitled "The Profound Examination of Names and Appellations," is particularly important for a good understanding of Tung's "mixed" theory of human nature.

2.6 DOCTRINE OF "FOUR BEGINNINGS"

The Book of Mencius. (See 2.2).
    Note in particular 2A: 6 and 6A: 6 for Mencius' own words on the doctrine.

CHANG, CARSUN. "Mencius' Theory of Liang-chih and the Intuitive School of Ethics in Contemporary Britain," in Tsing Hua Journal of Chinese Studies, n.s., 4, no. 2 (1964): 175-184.

A general comparison between several British philosophers, chiefly
G.E. Moore, who distinguish good and right, and Mencius, in whom
liang-chih (innate knowledge of the good) is both right and good.

_____. "The Significance of Mencius," in Philosophy East and West,
8 (1958): 37-48.
A fresh approach to Mencius, considering him to be the first in
China to have built a system based upon the doctrine of ideas,
assigned to thinking the vital role of philosophizing, used logical
ideas, and developed a theory of mind. Makes too much of Mencius'
logic, but is helpful in correcting the impression that Mencius'
intuitionism is irrational.

FUNG YU-LAN. A History of Chinese Philosophy. (See 2.5.2), Vol. 1.
In section 4 of chapter 6, a very clear analysis of the Mencian
doctrine of Four Beginnings is given in relation to the theory of
the goodness of human nature.

2.7 INNATE KNOWLEDGE OF THE GOOD AND INNATE ABILITY TO DO GOOD

The Book of Mencius. (See 2.2).
See also 2.6. Note in particular 6A: 1-6; 2A: 6; and 4B: 26.

CADY, LYMAN van LAW. Wang Yang-ming's Doctrine of "Intuitive Knowledge." Peking: privately published, 1936. 44 pp. Somewhat
enlarged as "Wang Yang-ming's 'Intuitive Knowledge,'" in The
Monist, 38 (1928): 263-291.
A comprehensive study and careful evaluation of Wang's doctrine
of innate knowledge.

CHANG, CARSUN. Wang Yang-ming: Idealist Philosopher of Sixteenth-
Century China. New York: St. John's University Press, 1962. 106 pp.
A short account of Wang's life and an outline of his basic doctrines, emphasizing the mind and the realization of the innate
knowledge of the good supported by citing passages.

CHENG, CHUNG-YING. "Conscience, Mind and Individual in Chinese
Philosophy," in Journal of Chinese Philosophy, 2 (1974): 3-40.
Deliberations include the two types of theories of mind, conscience (liang-chih, innate knowledge of the good) in relation to
principle (li) as represented by Chi Hsi and Wang Yang-ming, theory
of mind as ontological ground of theory of liang-chih and chih-
liang-chih (extension of liang-chih), understanding the individual
in the theory of mind, and sociological basis of Confucian conscience, mind, and individual.

_____. "Unity and Creativity in Wang Yang-ming's Philosophy of Mind,"
in Philosophy East and West, 23 (1973): 49-72.

Wang's philosophy of mind is discussed under the following headings: (1) Non-substantial substance (Original Reality) of the Mind;
(2) Original Reality of Mind as Manifested in Innate Knowledge of
the Good; (3) On the Will as Activation of Mind as a Form of Creativity; (4) Unity and Creativity of Mind in its Activation: Unity
of Knowledge and Action; (5) More Philosophical Points about the
Unity of Knowledge and Action; (6) Unity and Creativity of Mind in
Consummation: Fulfilling Innate Knowledge of the Good; and (7) Tranquillity and Harmony. Cheng holds that the best spirit of Wang's
philosophy of mind is found in his understanding the unity and
creativity of an ultimate reality, which contributes to his notion
of mind.

FUNG YU-LAN. "The Legacy of Chinese Philosophy: The Question of
    Continuity," in <u>Chinese Studies in History and Philosophy</u>, 2, no. 2
    (1968-69): 23-34.
    Fung says we should distinguish the concrete meaning and abstract
    meaning of philosophy and consider the latter as the continuing ele-
    ment of Chinese heritage. For example, in the doctrine of the innate
    knowledge of the good, its concrete meaning is none other than the
    feudalistic morality of the time, but in its abstract meaning it is
    the doctrine that all people can be sages. An earlier translation
    of the original Chinese treatise appears in the same journal, 1,
    no. 4 (Summer, 1968): 92-102, under the title, "The Problems of
    Succession to the Legacy of Chinese Philosophy."

IKI, HIROYUKI. "Wang Yang-ming's Doctrine of Innate Knowledge of the
    Good," in <u>Philosophy East and West</u>, 11 (1960): 27-33.
    On Wang's ideas of the relation between the nature of the innate
    knowledge of the good and the effort to extend it in actual prac-
    tice, with special reference to Chu Hsi and Buddhism.

T'ANG CHUN-I. "The Development of the Concept of Moral Mind from
    Wang Yang-ming to Wang Chi," in <u>Self and Society in Ming Thought</u>.
    Ed. by Wm. Theodore de Bary. New York: Columbia University Press.
    Pp. 92-120.
    The paper is divided into four parts on Lu Hsiang-shan's concept
    of original mind as a basis for Wang Yang-ming's realization of
    <u>liang-chih</u>, the latter as synthesis of Chu Hsi's and Lu Hsiang-shan's
    moral mind and moral cultivation, Wang's <u>liang-chih</u> as beyond good
    and evil, and Wang's teaching about "learning prior to Heaven."
    The conclusion is that Wang Chi, Wang Yang-ming's pupil, developed
    his master's ideas to a much higher level.

WANG YANG-MING. <u>Instructions for Practical Living and Other Neo-
    Confucian Writings by Wang Yang-ming</u>. Tr. by Wing-tsit Chan. New
    York: Columbia University Press, 1963. 358 pp.

An annotated translation of the most important work on the innate knowledge of the good since Mencius.

2.8 MORAL PERFECTIBILITY OF MAN (SAGEHOOD)

The Analects of Confucius. Tr. by Arthur Waley. London: Allen and Unwin, 1938. 268 pp. Also "Confucian Analects," tr. by James Legge in The Chinese Classics. Oxford: Clarendon Press, 1895. Vol. 1, pp. 137-354.
  Note in particular sections on education and learning, humanity, love and golden rule, mean and central thread, human nature, righteousness, and superior man. See the list of references on these subjects in Wing-tsit Chan, A Source Book in Chinese Philosophy. (See 2.1), p. 18.

The Book of Mencius. (See 2.2).
  Note in particular sections on equality, great man, humanity and righteousness, human nature and innate virtue, unbearing mind, undisturbed mind, and references in Wing-tsit Chan, A Source Book in Chinese Philosophy. (See 2.1), p. 51.

CHU HSI. Reflections on Things at Hand. (See 2.5.1).
  Note in particular chapters 1, 2, 3, 4, 5, 6, and 12 for a good understanding of the Neo-Confucian approach to the problem of man's moral perfection or perfectibility.

The Doctrine of the Mean. (See 2.3).
  Note the important words in the Doctrine of the Mean, chapter 1, regarding sagehood or the moral perfectibility of man, such as "What Heaven imparts to man is called human nature. To follow our nature is called the Way. Cultivating the Way is called education."

The Great Learning. (See 2.4).
  Note in particular the "three items" and "eight steps" in the text of the Great Learning.

WANG YANG-MING. Instructions for Practical Living and Other Neo-Confucian Writings. Cross reference: 2.7.

2.9 MORAL NATURE VERSUS PHYSICAL NATURE

See also 7.9.2.

CHAN, WING-TSIT. A Source Book in Chinese Philosophy. (See 2.1).
  Note in particular chapter 32 on Ch'eng I and chapter 34 on Chu Hsi for a clear understanding of how the Ch'eng-Chu rationalists approach the problem of twofold nature of man in relation to other

philosophical doctrines, such as "Principle is one but manifestations are many" or the doctrine of li-ch'i, or principle-matter
duality.

CHU HSI. Reflections on Things at Hand. (See 2.5.1). (See also 2.8).
   Note in particular chapters 1 and 2 for the Neo-Confucian approach
to the twofold nature of man.

FUNG YU-LAN. A History of Chinese Philosophy. (See 2.5.2), Vol. 2.
   Chapters 12 and 13 contain Fung's clear discussion of the theory
of twofold nature in Chang Tsai, Ch'eng I, and Chu Hsi, with many
quotations from their writings.

GRAHAM, A.C. Two Chinese Philosophers: Ch'eng Ming-tao and Ch'eng
   Yi-ch'uan. (See 2.4).
   Note in particular chapter 4 of Part 1 on Ch'eng I's (Ch'eng
Yi-ch'uan's) conception of man's twofold nature. A scholarly
analysis.

TU WEI-MING. "The Neo-Confucian Concept of Man." Cross reference:
   2.2.

2.10 THE WAY TO CULTIVATE MORAL NATURE

CHAN, WING-TSIT. A Source Book in Chinese Philosophy. (See 2.1).
   Note in particular chapters 31, 33, and 35 for a clear understanding of the idealistic approaches to the way to cultivate the moral
nature by Ch'eng Hao, Lu Hsiang-shan, and Wang Yang-ming.

The Doctrine of the Mean. (See 2.3).
   Note in particular the famous words, "the superior man honors the
moral nature and follows the paths of study and inquiry" (chapter
27), which suggests the two different approaches through "honoring
the moral nature" and "following the path of inquiry and study."
The former is emphasized by the Mind school as the way to cultivate
the moral nature.

HUANG, SIU-CHI. Lu Hsiang-shan: A Twelfth Century Chinese Idealist
   Philosopher. New Haven: American Oriental Society, 1944. 116 pp.
   Note in particular pp. 57-67. A very clear analysis of Lu's
method of the moral cultivation of the self under the three headings
of (a) self-understanding, (b) self-establishment, and (c) practical
moral conduct.

T'ANG, CHUN-I. "The Development of the Concept of Moral Mind from
   Wang Yang-ming to Wang Chi." Cross reference: 2.7.

TU WEI-MING. "The Neo-Confucian Concept of Man." Cross reference:
2.2.

2.11 TRANSFORMATION OF PHYSICAL NATURE

CHAN, WING-TSIT. A Source Book in Chinese Philosophy. (See 2.1).
    It is logical that Chang Tsai, Ch'eng I, and Chu Hsi reach the
conclusion about the transformation of the physical nature on the
basis of their theory of twofold nature.

CHU HSI. Reflections on Things at Hand. (See 2.5.1).
    See chapter 2, 80-82 for Chang Tsai's theory.

FUNG YU-LAN. A History of Chinese Philosophy. (See 2.5.2), Vol. 2.
    See pp. 477-498 for a discussion of Chang Tsai's theory.

TU WEI-MING. "The Neo-Confucian Concept of Man." Cross reference:
2.2.

2.12 PRINCIPLE OF NATURE (*T'IEN-LI*)

CHAN, WING-TSIT. A Source Book in Chinese Philosophy. (See 2.1).
    Consult chapters 30, 31, 32, 33, 34, and 35 for the Neo-Confucian
understanding of the principle of nature in two different ways, the
one identifying principle, nature, and the mind (the Mind school of
Ch'eng Hao, Lu Hsiang-shan, and Wang Yang-ming), while the other
identifies principle with nature only (the rationalist school of
Ch'eng I and Chu Hsi). Also see pp. 316, 329, 332, 334 (Neo-Taoism),
493-494 (Shao Yung), 509, 512 (Chang Tsai), 522 (Ch'eng Hao), 594,
598, 603, 605-608, 613, 618, 652 (Chu Hsi), 692, 700-701 (Wang
Fu-chih), and 712-713 (T'an Ssu-t'ung).

CHU HSI. Reflections on Things at Hand. (See 2.5.1).
    See "Principle of Nature" on p. 433 for detailed references.

FUNG YU-LAN. A History of Chinese Philosophy. (See 2.5.2), Vol. 2.
    Note in particular chapter 12 on Chang Tsai (pp. 488-496) and the
Ch'eng brothers (pp. 500-520), chapter 13 on Chu Hsi (pp. 534-542,
551-558), chapter 14 on Lu Hsiang-shan (pp. 572-579), and Wang
Yang-ming (pp. 596-610).

_____. A Short History of Chinese Philosophy. New York: Macmillan,
1948. 368 pp.
    A much simpler treatment of the subject in chapters 24-26.

HU SHIH. "The Natural Law in the Chinese Tradition," in Natural Law
Institute Proceedings. Ed. by Edward F. Barrett. Notre Dame:
University of Notre Dame Press, 1953. Vol. 5, pp. 119-153.

According to the writer, the Chinese idea of Principle of Heaven, or Natural Law, is expressed in the concept of Tao of Heaven or Nature, in the concept of the will of Heaven, in the Confucian Canon as the vehicle of universal truth, and in the Neo-Confucian concept of li (reason, law, Principle).

TU WEI-MING. "The Neo-Confucian Concept of Man." Cross reference: 2.2.

WANG YANG-MING. Instructions for Practical Living and Other Neo-Confucian Writings. (See 2.7).
    See "Principle of Nature" on p. 355 for detailed references.

2.13 EXPLANATION OF (MORAL) EVIL

The Book of Mencius. (See 2.2).
    Note in particular 6A: 2, 6, 7, 8, 10, 11, 13, 15, 17; 7A: 5 for a clear understanding of the Mencian explanation of (the origin of) evil.

CHAN, WING-TSIT. "The Neo-Confucian Solution of the Problem of Evil," in Studies Presented to Hu Shih on His Sixty-fifth Birthday. Bulletin of the Institute of History and Philology, Academia Sinica, Taipei, 1957. Pp. 773-791.
    Pre-Sung theories of evil (Mencius, Hsün Tzu, Tung Chung-shu, Wang Ch'ung, Han Yü, etc.), Chang Tsai's epoch-making doctrine of transformation of man's physical nature, and the concepts of jen and life-force (creativity or production) of Ch'eng Hao and Ch'eng I.

_____. A Source Book in Chinese Philosophy. (See 2.1).
    Note in particular chapters 3, 6, 12, 14, 15, 16, 27, 30, 32, 34, and 35 for primary sources regarding the subject dealt with by Mencius, Hsün Tzu, Han Fei, Tung Chung-shu, Yang Hsiung, Wang Ch'ung, Han Yü, Chang Tsai, Ch'eng I, Chu Hsi, and Wang Yang-ming.

CHING, JULIA. "Beyond Good and Evil, The Culmination of the Thought of Wang Yang-ming (1472-1529)," in Numen, 22 (1973): 127-134.
    After stating the problem of evil in Wang Yang-ming, who regarded human nature-in-itself as beyond good and evil, the author goes on to compare the opposing interpretations of Wang's Four Maxims by his two pupils, Wang Chi and Ch'ien Te-hung, and finally points out the similarity of Wang's method of cultivation with those of Chuang Tzu and Ch'an Buddhism.

HSU, SUNG-PENG. "Lao Tzu's Conception of Evil," in Philosophy East and West, 26 (1976): 301-316.

Hsu argues that Lao Tzu recognizes two kinds of evil: (1) the evils that directly cause human suffering in the world, and (2) the human suffering caused by the first kind.

HUANG, SIU-CHI. Lu Hsiang-shan: A Twelfth Century Chinese Idealist Philosopher. (See 2.10).
 Note in particular pp. 47-56 on Lu's doctrine of evil. Huang observes that in his doctrine of evil, Lu largely follows Mencius, though he seems to lay more emphasis on it than Mencius did, in the sense that "he goes a step beyond Mencius by postulating the necessary existence of evil, in order thereby to make the concept of goodness assume meaning" (p. 53). Huang also raises a critical point that Lu "seems to be unaware of the incompleteness of Mencius' doctrine of human nature, and thus falls into the mistake of neglecting to give an adequate explanation of desire, which he considers to be the chief cause of evil" (p. 56).

2.14 THEORY OF BUDDHA-NATURE OR TATHĀGATA-GARBHA

AŚVAGHOSHA (c. 100 A.D.). The Awakening of Faith. Tr. by Y.S. Hakeda. New York: Columbia University Press, 1967. 128 pp.
 A generally accurate translation of one of the most important works on the innate capacity to become a Buddha, or Tathāgata-garbha, much studied in China and Japan, with useful notes and bibliography.

FU, CHARLES WEI-HSUN. "Buddhist Approach to the Problem of God," in God in Contemporary Thought: A Philosophical Perspective. Ed. by Sebastian Matczak. New York: Learned Publications, 1977. Pp. 155-181.
 A philosophical clarification of the Mahāyāna conception of Buddha-nature or Tathāgata-garbha near the end of the article.

HSÜAN-TSANG. Ch'eng Wei-shih lun--Doctrine of Mere-Consciousness. Tr. by Wei Tat. Hong Kong: The Ch'eng Wei-shih lun Publication Committee, 1973. 818 pp. Cross reference: 1.11.4.

The Lankāvatāra-sūtra. Tr. by D.T. Suzuki. London: Routledge, 1932. 295 pp. Also published in New York: Humanities Press, 1966.
 A reliable translation, with scholarly introduction and notes, of one of the most influential works in the idealistic tradition of Mahāyāna Buddhism much studied by early Zen Buddhists in China.

SUZUKI, D.T. Studies in the Lankāvatāra Sūtra. London: Routledge, 1930. 464 pp.
 A technical and penetrating study. Many fundamental Mahāyāna doctrines are discussed in this scholarly work, among which is the teaching of Buddha-nature or Tathāgata-garbha.

2.15 UNITY OF NATURE (OR HEAVEN) AND MAN

CHAN, WING-TSIT. A Source Book in Chinese Philosophy. (See 2.1).
    For the doctrine of unity of Heaven and man, see the following
    pages: 40 (Confucius), 292 (Han Confucianism), 516 (Chang Tsai),
    522 (Ch'eng Hao), 574 (Lu Hsiang-shan), 595 (Chu Hsi), 659 (Wang
    Yang-ming), 752, 762 (Fung Yu-lan), and 763 (Hsiung Shih-li).

CHING, JULIA. "All in One--The Culmination of the Thought of Wang
    Yang-ming (1472-1529)," in Oriens Extremus, 20 (1973): 137-159.
    A brief but well-rounded presentation on Wang Yang-ming's doctrine
    of forming one unity with heaven, earth, and all things. The con-
    cepts of jen (humanity) versus love, loving the people, joy, the
    original substance of the innate knowledge of the good, principle
    of life, consciousness, a self-transcending state, and a higher
    reality are clarified and supported with passages in Chinese char-
    acters and their translations.

CHU HSI. Reflections on Things at Hand. (See 2.5.1).
    See pp. 19, 58, 62, 74, 76, 88, 93, 284, 287, and 303 for the
    doctrine of Heaven and man forming a unity taught by Chou Tun-i,
    Ch'eng Hao, Ch'eng I, and Chang Tsai.

FANG, THOMÉ. The Chinese View of Life: The Philosophy of Comprehen-
    sive Harmony. Hong Kong: The Union Press, 1957. 274 pp.
    A very inspiring work on the Chinese view of life in terms of the
    comprehensive harmony of man and Nature, the central theme through-
    out the book. Note chapter 3 on analysis of human nature.

_____. "A Philosophical Glimpse of Man and Nature in Chinese Culture,"
    in Journal of Chinese Philosophy, 1 (1973): 3-26.
    "The rational nature of Western man, in the self-consciousness of
    Pascal, is reduced to inherent contradiction. I think the Chinese
    philosophers can come to the rescue of this contradiction." This
    quotation sums up the thesis of the paper. Based on ancient Con-
    fucianism and Taoism, Nature is conceived of as the confluence of
    universal life, a harmonious system, a blissful place of sacrament,
    and in unity with the whole man.

MEI, Y.P. "Man and Nature in Chinese Philosophy," in Indian Univer-
    sity Conference on Oriental-Western Literary Relations. Ed. by
    Horst Frenz and G.L. Anderson, 1955. Pp. 151-160. (The University
    of North Carolina Studies in Comparative Literature, 13).
    A non-technical and appreciative account of the spirit of the
    harmony of man and Nature in Chinese thought.

NAKAMURA, HAJIME. Ways of Thinking of Eastern Peoples. Honolulu:
    East-West Center Press, 1964. 712 pp.

An interesting discussion of the subject in chapter 24, entitled "Esteem for Nature." The author especially points out that "The more important fact is that the long history of China has been comparatively peaceful because the Chinese identified nature with man" (p. 281).

WANG YANG-MING. Instructions for Practical Living and Other Neo-Confucian Writings. (See 2.7), pp. 56, 118-121, 166-167, 170, 219, 221-223, 226-227, 257-258, and 273-280.
   The Neo-Confucian perennial doctrine of forming one body with Heaven, Earth, and all things culminated in Wang Yang-ming, especially in his "Inquiry on the Great Learning," on pp. 273-280.

2.16 THE THEORY OF YIN YANG AND FIVE ELEMENTS

See also 1.6, 1.8.1, 1.8.2.

CHAN, WING-TSIT. A Source Book in Chinese Philosophy. (See 2.1).
   Note in particular chapter 13 on the philosophy of change, chapter 14 on the Yin Yang Confucianism of Tung Chung-shu, chapter 28 on the Neo-Confucian metaphysics and ethics in Chou Tun-i (especially Chou's "Explanation of the Diagram of the Great Ultimate"), chapter 29 on the numerical and objective tendencies in Shao Yung, chapter 30 on Chang Tsai's philosophy of material force, chapter 32 on the rationalistic tendency in Ch'eng I, chapter 34 on the great synthesis of Chu Hsi, and chapter 43 on the new idealistic Confucianism of Hsiung Shih-li, for the various approaches to or understandings of the ideas of Yin Yang and Five Elements.

ERKES, E. "Die Dialektik als Grundlage der chinesischen Weltanschauung," in Sinologica, 2 (1949): 31-43.
   Explains clearly how the Yin Yang doctrine forms the basis of the world-views in Tung Chung-shu, Shao Yung, Chu Hsi, and later Neo-Confucianists.

FORKE, ALFRED. The World-Conception of the Chinese. London: Probsthain, 1925. 300 pp.
   A clear statement on pp. 227-261 on the Five-Element theory, its origin, description, and relation to other social and philosophical concepts.

FUNG YU-LAN. A History of Chinese Philosophy. (See 2.5.2).
   Note in particular chapter 15, Vol. 1, on the Appendices of the Book of Changes and the cosmology of the Huai-nan Tzu, as well as chapter 2, Vol. 2 on Tung Chung-shu, chapter 3 on prognostigation texts, apocrypha, and numerology during the Han Dynasty, and chapters 11-13 on the Neo-Confucian approaches to the problem. A very useful secondary source on the subject.

IKEDA, SUETOSHI. "The Origin and Development of the <u>Wu-hsing</u> (Five
Elements) Idea: A Preliminary Essay," in <u>Philosophy East and West</u>,
16 (1966): 297-309.
A historical study emphasizing the social and religious conditions
of the fourth and third centuries B.C.

NEEDHAM, JOSEPH. <u>Science and Civilisation in China</u>. Cambridge,
England: Cambridge University Press, 1954-1962. 4 vols. Vol. 2:
<u>History of Scientific Thought</u>. 696 pp.
An excellent study of the scientific and pseudo-scientific aspects
of the theory of Yin and Yang and of Five Elements almost throughout
the work. Note in particular chapter 13, entitled "The Fundamental
Ideas of Chinese Science" for a detailed and scholarly treatment of
the subject.

3. Ethics

3.1.1 Mandate of Heaven

See also 2.3, 10.1.

CHAN, WING-TSIT, tr. and comp. A Source Book in Chinese Philosophy. New Jersey: Princeton University Press, 1963.
856 pp.
   Note in particular chapter 1 on the growth of humanism,
chapter 2 on the humanism of Confucius (see p. 18), chapter
3 on Mencius, chapter 4 on the Great Learning, chapter 5 on
the Doctrine of the Mean, chapter 13 on the Book of Changes,
chapter 14 on Tung Chung-shu, and chapter 34 on Chu Hsi for
most important primary sources on the subject. Check also
the index of the Source Book regarding the subject.

CHENG, CHUNG-YING. "Dialectics of Confucian Morality and
Metaphysics of Man," in Philosophy East and West, 21 (1971):
111-123.
   Discusses the three stages of development of Confucian
morality looked upon as three dimensions of the Confucian
moral theory. A philosophical comparison of Confucian morality with the Kantian morality is also given.

FUNG YU-LAN. A History of Chinese Philosophy. Tr. by Derk
Bodde. Princeton, New Jersey: Princeton University Press,
1952-1953. 2 vols. Vol. 1, 455 pp. Vol. 2, 783 pp.
   Note in particular Vol. 1, pp. 30-31, 129, 285, 370, 374-
375, 384-385, and Vol. 2, pp. 60, 62, 71-73, 75, 129-130,
and 193 for Fung's discussion of the various approaches to
the idea of Heavenly Mandate in the whole history of Chinese
philosophy.

_____. "The Struggle between Materialism and Idealism in the
History of Chinese Philosophy in Terms of Several Major Problems in Chinese Philosophy," in Chinese Studies in History
and Philosophy, 2, no. 4 (Summer, 1969): 3-27.

The problems of Heaven, especially in Confucius, Mencius, Taoism, and Hsün Tzu, of material force in Taoism, the Book of Changes, Wang Ch'ung, and Tung Chung-shu, of the mind in Buddhism and Fan Chen, and of li, especially in Neo-Confucianism.

HATTORI, UNOKICHI. "Confucius' Conviction of his Heavenly Mission," in Harvard Journal of Asiatic Studies, 1 (1936): 96-108.
     By an eminent Japanese scholar who has excellent historical and documentary support for his discussion of the subject.

T'ANG CHUN-I. "The T'ien-ming (Heavenly Ordinance) in Pre-Ch'in China," in Philosophy East and West, 11 (1962): 195-218 and 13 (1962): 29-49.
     A penetrating investigation on the doctrine of ming in the ancient classics and in the teachings of Confucius, Mo Tzu, Mencius, Chuang Tzu, Lao Tzu, and Hsün Tzu.

3.1.2 Human Nature

See category 2. and all the related references under 2.1, 2.2, 2.3, 2.4, 2.5.1, 2.6, 2.7, 2.9, 2.10, 2.11, 2.12, 2.15.

CHENG, CHUNG-YING. "Dialectics of Confucian Morality and Metaphysics of Man." Cross reference: 3.1.1.

3.1.3 Filial Piety and Sacrificial Rites

CHAN, WING-TSIT. A Source Book in Chinese Philosophy. (See 3.1.1).
     Note in particular chapter 2 on Confucius (1:2, 6, 11; 2:5, 7; 4: 18, 19, 20 in the Analects), chapter 3 on Mencius (3A: 4; 3B: 2, 9; 4A: 17, 18, 26; 4B: 30 in the Book of Mencius), chapter 4 on the Great Learning, and chapter 5 on the Doctrine of the Mean for early Confucian primary sources on the subject.

CHU HSI, in collaboration with Lü Tsu-ch'ien. Reflections on Things at Hand: The Neo-Confucian Anthology. Tr. by Wing-tsit Chan. New York: Columbia University Press, 1967. 441 pp.
     For the subject of filial piety, note pp. 26, 66, 77, 78n, 80-81, 174, 181, 209, 219, 236, and 300. For religious sacrifices, note 218n, 226, 229, 230, 231, and 240. This anthology reflects the general Neo-Confucian approach to the subject.

3. Ethics

The Hsiao Ching. Tr. by Sister Mary Lella Marka. New York:
St. John's University Press, 1961. 67 pp.
The translation of the Classic of Filial Piety is simple
and clear. It is not an analytical study, but there is deep
and sympathetic understanding. The Chinese text is included.

HSIEH, YU-WEI. "Filial Piety and Chinese Society," in Philosophy and Culture. Ed. by Charles Moore. Honolulu: University of Hawaii Press, 1962. Pp. 411-427. Reprinted in his
The Chinese Mind. Honolulu: East-West Center Press, 1967.
Pp. 167-187.
On the basis of ancient Confucian classics, the paper explains that filial piety is the root of benevolence which is
a primary virtue to the Chinese. The influence of the concept of filial piety on Chinese society is also discussed.

Hsün Tzu: Basic Writings. Tr. by Burton Watson. New York:
Columbia University Press. 177 pp. Also in combined edition
of Basic Writings of Mo Tzu, Hsün Tzu, and Han Fei Tzu, 1967.
The fundamental ideas of various Confucian rites are expressed here even better than in the Book of Rites (Li chi,
see below).

Li chi. "The Li Ki," in The Sacred Books of the East. Tr. by
James Legge. Oxford: Clarendon Press, 1885. Vols. 27 and
28. Vol. 27, 480 pp. Vol. 28, 491 pp. Also edited by Ch'u
Chai and Winberg Chai. New Hyde Park, New York: University
Books, 1967. Chapters 8-9, 20-22, and 30-32.
This book, the Book of Rites, contains the most important
source material on Chinese traditional ideas on sacrificial
rites. Though translated long ago, it is still reliable.
The editors have added a helpful introduction.

MAHOOD, GEORGE H. "Human Nature and the Virtue in Confucius
and Aristotle." Cross reference: 3.3.

THOMPSON, LAURENCE G. Chinese Religion: An Introduction.
Belmont: Dickenson Publishing Co., 1969. 119 pp.
Chapters 3-5 contain a good discussion of ancestor worship,
filial piety, sacrificial rites in the state and the family,
etc. in terms of the religious dimension rather than the
philosophical one.

YANG, C.K. Religion in Chinese Society: A Study of Contemporary
Social Functions of Religion and Some of Their Historical
Factors. Berkeley: University of California Press, 1961.
473 pp.

> Chapter 2, entitled "Religion in the Integration of the
> Family," contains a very interesting discussion of the sub-
> ject from the standpoint of sociology of religion under the
> headings of (a) general importance and nature of ancestor
> worship, (b) sacrificial rites, etc.

3.2 *JEN* (HUMANITY, LOVE, BENEVOLENCE)

See also 3.4.

CHAN, WING-TSIT. "Chinese and Western Interpretations of Jen
 (Humanity)," in Journal of Chinese Philosophy, 2 (1975): 107-129.
  Chinese interpretations discussed are: Confucius' jen as the
general virtue; jen as love; the identification of jen with nature
and principle and the doctrine of "Principle is one but its manifestations are many"; the man of jen regards Heaven and Earth and the
ten thousand things as one body; jen and the process of production
and reproduction; and jen as "the character of the mind and the
principle of love" in Chu Hsi. Western interpretations discussed
are: jen as general virtue; jen as the Silver Rule: jen as love with
distinctions; and jen as the principle of production and reproduction.

_____. "The Evolution of the Confucian Concept Jen," in Philosophy
 East and West, 4 (1955): 295-319.
  The article traces the thirteen stages through which the Confucian
concept of jen has evolved.

_____. "K'ang Yu-wei and the Confucian Philosophy of Humanity (Jen),"
 in K'ang Yu-wei: A Biography and a Symposium. Ed. by Jung Pang Lo.
Tuscon: The University of Arizona Press, 1967. Pp. 355-374. Reprinted in Wing-tsit Chan, Neo-Confucianism, Etc. Essays by Wing-
tsit Chan. Ed. by Charles K.H. Chen. Hanover, N.H.: Oriental
Society, 1969. 516 plus 129 pp. Pp. 247-280.
  Explains how K'ang understood jen as "the mind that cannot bear
to see the suffering of others," as "love for one's own kind," as
"power of attraction," as ether or electricity, as "forming one
body with Heaven and Earth," as having gradation, and as production
and reproduction.

_____. A Source Book in Chinese Philosophy. (See 3.1.1).
  For the concept of jen, note in particular pp. 18, 51, 84, 115,
138, 212, 285, 454, 462, 498, 522, 547, 593, 603, 659, 719, 734,
738, and 788.

CUA, ANTONIO S. "Reflections on the Structure of Confucian Ethics,"
 in Philosophy East and West, 21 (1971): 125-140.

Jen is discussed as an internal criterion of morality. It is an
inclusive virtue but a practical rather than a formal principle of
morality. Li (rites) is seen as an external criterion of morality--
neither can be without the other. The chün-tzu (perfect man) as an
ideal of a paradigmatic individual is an embodiment of jen and li.

DUBS, HOMER H. "The Development of Altruism in Confucianism," in
Radhakrishnan, Comparative Studies in Philosophy. Ed. by W.R. Inge,
et al. London: Allen and Unwin, 1951. Pp. 267-275. Reprinted in
Philosophy East and West, 1 (1951): 48-55.
  According to Dubs, although Confucius taught love for all, it was
a system of graded love opposed to the Moist doctrine of universal
love, and while some Neo-Confucianists taught universal love, and
while Chu Hsi revived the doctrine of graded love. Actually Chu Hsi
taught universal love like all Neo-Confucianists, but held its application in different relations should be different.

GRAF, OLAF. Tao und Jen, Sein und Sollen im sungchinesischen
Monismus. Wiesbaden: Otto Harrassowitz, 1970. 429 pp.
  A thorough discussion of Neo-Confucian concepts of the Great
Ultimate, principle, material force, Heaven, destiny, jen, the Four
Virtues of benevolence, righteousness, propriety, and wisdom,
equilibrium and harmony, the way of man, investigation of things,
mind and the will, the mind of Heaven and Earth, criticism of Bud-
dhism, etc., centering on Chu Hsi. Chapters are divided into
Natural Philosophy, Ethics, the Way of Man, the Confucian Classics,
and Comparison with Western Philosophy, especially Thomas Aquinas.

HANG, THADDEUS T'UI-CHIEH. "Jen Experiences and Jen Philosophy," in
Journal of the American Academy of Religion, 17 (1974): 53-65.
  Following a brief analysis of the meaning of the word jen, the
author goes on to discuss the earliest human experience and human
nature, the choice of jen and existential actualization, and finally
arrives at the cosmic and metaphysical meanings of jen which he
prefers to translate as "dianthropy" rather than the general translations of "goodness," "benevolence," "humanity," etc.

HANSEN, CHAD. "Freedom and Moral Responsibility in Confucian Ethics,"
in Philosophy East and West, 22 (1972): 169-186.
  The author argues that not only is there no philosophical debate
over the issue of freedom and moral responsibility in Confucian
thought, but there is not even a philosophical account of moral
responsibility in Confucian ethical theory.

JUNG, HWA YOL. "Jen: An Existential and Phenomenological Problem of
Intersubjectivity," in Philosophy East and West, 16 (1966): 169-188.

Comparing Chinese philosophy with existential phenomenology, the essay focuses on jen as practical activity, as sociality, and as love or feeling of commiseration which is the application of jen as intersubjectivity.

KIANG, SHAO-YUEN. "The Philosophy of Tang-Szu-Tung," in The Open Court, 36 (1922): 449-471.
    Analyzes T'an Ssu-t'ung's "Science of Love (Jen)" in nine points. Worth reading.

TAKEUCHI, TERUO. "A Study of the Meaning of Jen Advocated by Confucius," in Acta Asiatica, 9 (1966): 57-77.
    Contends that originally jen meant external beauty, but it came to mean the internalized moral character which Confucius practiced.

TALBOTT, NATHAN. "T'an Ssu-t'ung and the Ether," in Studies on Asia. Ed. by Robert K. Sakai. Lincoln: University of Nebraska Press, 1960. Pp. 20-34.
    Examines T'an's inadequate understanding of ether as a scientific concept rather than as an equivalent to the ethical concept of jen.

TONG, LIK KUEN. "Confucian Jen and Platonic Eros: A Comparative Study," in Chinese Culture, 14, no. 3 (September, 1973): 1-8.
    Both the Confucian jen and Platonic eros are understood as rational, but the accent of Confucius is on the subject, whereas the accent on Plato is on the object.

TU WEI-MING. "The Creative Tension between Jen and Li," in Philosophy East and West, 18, no. 1-2 (1968): 29-39.
    The interplay of jen and li (propriety, rites), the former being creative and providing the inner strength and substance for the latter, and the latter providing the concrete actualization of the former. Frequent comparison is made with Christian concepts.

_____. "Li as Process of Humanization." Cross reference: 3.3.

YEH, GEORGE K.C. "The Confucian Conception of Jen," in China Society Occasional Papers, n.s., 3 (1953): 5-14.
    A short and instructive lecture on Confucius', Mencius', and Chu Hsi's ideas of jen and their political implications.

3.3 *LI* (RULE OF PROPRIETY)

See also 3.11, 10.12.

CHAN, WING-TSIT. A Source Book in Chinese Philosophy. (See 3.1.1).
    For the concept of li, note in particular pp. 18 (Confucius), 99-101 and 111 (Hsün Tzu), 466, 469, and 473 (Chou Tun-i).

CUA, ANTONIO S. Reflections on the Structure of Confucian Ethics."
Cross reference: 3.2.

FUNG YU-LAN. A History of Chinese Philosophy. (See 3.1.1).
For the subject, note in particular Vol. 1, pp. 12, 36-39, 64-65,
68-74, 121, 125-127, 129, 193, 241, 282, 284, 286-288, 290, 295-
299, 301-302, 308, 313, 330, 335, 337-441 and Vol. 2, pp. 36, 40-41,
104-105, 147, 174, 211, 219, 417, 437, 521, 555, 557-559, 613, 639,
654, 661-663, 666, 680, and 714.

_____. "The Struggle between Materialism and Idealism in the History
of Chinese Philosophy in Terms of Several Major Problems in Chinese
Philosophy." Cross reference: 3.1.1.

GIMELLO, ROBERT M. "The Civil Status of Li in Classical Confucianism,"
in Philosophy East and West, 22 (1972): 203-211.
The study is made from three perspectives: li as the classical
Confucian attempt to repossess China's sacred past, as the principle
of order in society and the primary instrument of government by
exemplary virtue, and as a personal discipline in the service of
moral, intellectual and spiritual self-cultivation. Special attention is given to Hsün Tzu's doctrine of rites.

HSU, L.S. The Political Philosophy of Confucianism: An Interpretation
of the Social and Political Ideas of Confucius, His Forerunners,
and His Early Disciples. London: George Routledge, 1932. 258 pp.
Note in particular chapter 5 on the principle of li, where Hsu
makes an extensive discussion of the function of li, history and
authenticity of the Li-chi (Book of Rites), the place of li in the
development of civilization, and the practical programs of li, etc.

HSÜN TZU. Hsün Tzu. Cross reference: 3.1.3, chapter 19.

KUAN FENG and LIN YÜ SHIH. "Third Discussion on Confucius," in
Chinese Studies in Philosophy, 2 (1971): 246-263. Cross reference:
1.2.1.

Li chi. "The Li Ki," in The Sacred Books of the East. (See 3.1.3).
This is the source material for various Confucian rites or rules
of propriety on such rites as marriage, religious sacrifices, festivals, diplomatic receptions, funeral rites, capping ceremonies, etc.
The philosophical reasons for these are expressed.

MAHOOD, GEORGE H. "Human Nature and the Virtue in Confucius and
Aristotle," in Journal of Chinese Philosophy, 1 (1973-74): 295-312.

The article concentrates on a careful and analytical study of
hsiao (filial piety), hsin (truthfulness), and li. Their various
meanings, their form and content and their place in Confucian ethics
are discussed from the philosophical point of view.

TU WEI-MING. "The Creative Tension between Jen and Li." Cross
reference: 3.2.

_____. "Li as Process of Humanization," in Philosophy East and West,
22 (1972): 187-201.
    Contending that jen is not primarily a concept of human relations
but is basically linked with self-reflection and self-fulfilling,
li is an externalization of jen in a concrete social situation.
Concretely, li as a process of humanization is manifested in four
developmental stages: (a) cultivating personal life; (b) regulating
familial relations; (c) ordering the affairs of the state; and
(d) bring peace to the world. The direction of li leads to becom-
ing a sage. In the process, li is the movement of self-transformation, through which man becomes more human.

3.4 PRINCIPLE IS ONE BUT MANIFESTATIONS ARE MANY

See also 7.9.1.

CHAN, WING-TSIT. "The Evolution of the Neo-Confucian Concept Li as
    Principle," in Tsing Hua Journal of Chinese Studies, n.s., 4, no. 2
    (1964): 123-149. Reprinted in Chan, Neo-Confucianism, Etc. (See
    3.2), pp. 45-87.
    A comprehensive account and analysis of the cardinal Chinese
    philosophical concept, its development in ancient schools, its in-
    terpretation in Han times, Neo-Taoist and Buddhist contributions to
    its evolution, its Neo-Confucian elaboration, its culmination in
    Chu Hsi, and its influence in subsequent centuries. The article
    sheds some light also on the Neo-Confucian notion of "one principle
    but many manifestations."

_____. A Source Book in Chinese Philosophy. (See 3.1.1).
    For the subject, note in particular chapters 30 (Chang Tsai), 32
    (Ch'eng I), and 34 (Chu Hsi).

CHU HSI. Reflections on Things at Hand. (See 3.1.3).
    For the subject, note in particular chapters 1, 2, and 3.

GOTO, TOSHIMIDZU. "The Ontology of the 'Li' Philosophy of the Sung
    Dynasty of China," in Philosophical Studies of Japan, 2 (1960):
    119-143.

A systematic discussion of Neo-Confucian concepts like yin yang, the Great Ultimate, the Mean, life impulse, etc., but little of li (principle) itself.

HANSEN, CHAD. "Freedom and Moral Responsibility in Confucian Ethics." Cross reference: 3.2.

MIYUKI, KOKUSEN. An Analysis of Buddhist Influence on the Formation of the Sung Confucian Concept of Li-ch'i. Claremont Graduate School and University Center Ph.D. thesis, 1965. 139 pp.
    Traces the influence of the Buddhist doctrine of Buddha-nature (Tathāgata-garbha) on the Neo-Confucian theory of man's inner world of consciousness and that of Buddhist wisdom and meditation on Ch'eng I's and Chu Hsi's doctrines of investigation of things and practice of seriousness. Rejects the dualistic interpretation of Chu Hsi's ideas of li and ch'i, which are a continuum.

SUN, STANISLAUS S.J. "The Doctrine of Li in the Philosophy of Chu Hsi," in International Philosophical Quarterly, 6 (1966): 155-188.
    A convenient, comprehensive, and systematic presentation of li based on extensive survey of Western sources and quotations from original texts.

3.5 MORAL CRITICISM OF MO TZU AND YANG CHU

"The Book of Mencius," in Mencius. Tr. by D.C. Lau. Baltimore: Penguin Books, 1970. 280 pp.; or in The Chinese Classics. Tr. by James Legge. Oxford: Clarendon Press, 1895. Vol. 2, The Works of Mencius, 402 pp.
    Note in particular 3A: 5; 3B: 9; 7A: 26, 45; 7B: 26 for the primary source on the subject.

FUNG YU-LAN. A History of Chinese Philosophy. (See 3.1.1), Vol. 1.
    For the subject, note in particular pp. 119-128.

MEI, Y.P. "Yangchu and Moti: Chinese Egoist and Altruist," in The Personalist, 16 (1935): 36-44.
    A summary discussion of the respective doctrines of Yang Chu and Mo Tzu.

3.6 MORAL CRITICISM OF TAOISM AND BUDDHISM

CHAN, WING-TSIT. A Source Book in Chinese Philosophy. (See 3.1.1).
    For this subject, note in particular chapter 27 on Han Yü and Li Ao, chapter 30 on Chang Tsai (see sections 3, 4, 60, 61, 63, 64, and 67 of the Correcting Youthful Ignorance), chapter 31 on Ch'eng Hao (see sections 21, 32, 46, 76, and 77 of the Selected Sayings),

chapter 32 on Ch'eng I (see sections 23, 25, 50, and 55 of the Selected Sayings), chapter 33 on Lu Hsiang-shan (see section 4), chapter 34 on Chu Hsi (see sections 134-147), and chapter 35 on Wang Yang-ming (e.g., pp. 676-677).

CHU HSI. Reflections on Things at Hand. (See 3.1.3).
Note in particular chapter 13 on the sifting the heterodox doctrines.

FU, CHARLES WEI-HSUN. "Morality or Beyond: The Neo-Confucian Confrontation with Mahāyāna Buddhism," in Philosophy East and West, 23 (July, 1973): 375-396.
A philosophical discussion of the Neo-Confucian ethico-social criticism of Mahāyāna Buddhism in China, especially Ch'an.

FUNG YU-LAN. A History of Chinese Philosophy. (See 3.1.1), Vol. 2.
Note in particular pp. 409-413 (Han Yü), 496-498 (Chang Tsai), 508-509 (the Ch'eng brothers), 566-571 (Chu Hsi), and 610-612 (Wang Yang-ming).

_____. The Spirit of Chinese Philosophy. Tr. by E.R. Hughes. London: Kegan Paul, 1947. 224 pp. Also in Beacon paperbacks.
For the Neo-Confucian moral criticism and transcendence of Mahāyāna Buddhism, especially Ch'an, read chapter 9 on the Neo-Confucian philosophy. Fung's own evaluation involved.

GRAHAM, A.C. Two Chinese Philosophers: Ch'eng Ming-tao and Ch'eng Yi-ch'uan. London: Lund Humphries, 1958. 195 pp.
For the subject, note in particular chapter 8 on Ch'eng I's criticism of Buddhism.

3.7 METAPHYSICAL PRINCIPLES OF *JEN* (HUMANITY), *I* (RIGHTEOUSNESS), *LI* (PROPRIETY), AND *CHIH* (WISDOM) IN CHU HSI

See also 3.2.

The Book of Mencius. (See 3.5).
As regards the early Confucian establishment of these cardinal virtues (as well as faithfulness, hsin), the Book of Mencius should be read for a clear understanding. See in particular 4B: 3, 6, 13, 27, 28; 4A: 10, 20, 27; 1A: 1; 2A: 2; 5B: 4, 6, 7, 9; 6A: 1, 4, 8, 10, 11, 18, 19, 6B: 1, 14. See also all entries under 2.5.

CHAN, WING-TSIT. A Source Book in Chinese Philosophy. (See 3.1.1).
Note, for example, Chu Hsi's own words: "The moral qualities of the mind of Heaven and Earth are four: origination, flourish, advantages, and firmness...in the mind of man there are also four moral qualities--namely, jen, righteousness, propriety, and wisdom-- and jen embraces them all" (p. 594).

CHENG, CHUNG-YING. "On Yi as a Universal Principle of Specific
    Application, in Confucian Morality," in Philosophy East and West,
    22 (1972): 269-280.
      In his philosophical examination of the Confucian term yi (i) as
    ethically important as jen, Cheng suggests that yi is the funda-
    mental principle of morality that confers qualities of right and
    wrong on human actions and that produces a situation which intrin-
    sically satisfies us as moral agents.

FUNG YU-LAN. A History of Chinese Philosophy. (See 3.1.1), Vol. 2.
    Note in particular section 5 of chapter 13 on Chu Hsi.

3.8 THE IDENTITY OF (MORAL) MIND AND PRINCIPLE

See also 5.10.2, as well as all the related references under 1.11.9
and 1.11.10 on the Lu-Wang school of mind.

CHAN, WING-TSIT. A Source Book in Chinese Philosophy. (See 3.1.1).
    Note in particular chapters 31, 33, and 35.

TU WEI-MING. "Subjectivity and Ontological Reality--An Interpreta-
    tion of Wang Yang-ming's Mode of Thinking," in Philosophy East and
    West, 23 (1973): 187-205.
      A reconstruction of Wang's philosophy in terms of the inseparable
    relation between subjectivity and ontological reality.

3.9 *CHUNG* (CONSCIENTIOUSNESS) AND *SHU* (ALTRUISM)

See also category 3.2 for jen, of which chung and shu are two aspects.

The Analects of Confucius. Tr. by Arthur Waley. London: Allen and
    Unwin, 1938. 268 pp. Also in The Chinese Classics. Tr. by James
    Legge. Oxford: Clarendon Press, 1895. Vol. 1, Confucian Analects,
    pp. 137-354.
      Note in particular Tseng Tzu's words: "The Way of our Master is
    none other than conscientiousness and altruism" in 4:15.

FUNG YU-LAN. A History of Chinese Philosophy. (See 3.1.1), Vol. 1.
      Note in particular section 5 of chapter 4 on the Confucian virtues
    of uprightness, human-heartedness, conscientiousness, and altruism.

_____. A Short History of Chinese Philosophy. New York: Macmillan,
    1948. 368 pp.
      A short but clear analysis of the moral meanings of chung and shu
    on pp. 43-44.

3.10 FILIAL PIETY AND BROTHERLY RESPECT

See also all the references under 3.1.3.

The Analects of Confucius. (See 3.9).
   Note in particular 1: 2, 6, 11; 2: 5, 7; 4: 18, 19, 21. See also
   3.1.

3.11 RULES OF PROPRIETY AND MUSIC

See also 3.3.

The Analects of Confucius. (See 3.9).
   Note in particular 1: 12; 2: 5; 3: 3-4, 17, 19; 6: 25; 8: 8.

HSU, L.S. The Political Philosophy of Confucianism. (See 3.3).
   On this subject, note in particular pp. 94-96 and 99-104.

3.12 OTHER CONFUCIAN VIRTUES, E.G., COURAGE, WISDOM, ETC.

The Analects of Confucius. (See 3.9).
   Note in particular 1: 4, 6, 8; 4: 12; 7: 6; 8: 5, 7, 13; 9: 4;
   13: 18, 19; 14: 33; 15: 8, 17; 16: 4, 10; 17: 6, 8.

FUNG YU-LAN. A History of Chinese Philosophy. (See 3.1.1), Vol. 1.
   Note in particular sections 4, 5, and 6 or chapter 4.

3.13 SINCERITY

See 2.4.

3.14 DISTINCTION BETWEEN RIGHTEOUSNESS AND PROFIT

The Analects of Confucius. (See 3.9).
   Note in particular Analects 2: 24; 4: 16; 13: 3, 6; 15: 17. 4: 16
   is the most important: "The superior man understands righteousness,
   the inferior man understands profit."

The Book of Mencius. (See 3.5).
   Note in particular all the sections (6A: 1, 4, 8, 10, 11, 18, 19;
   1A: 1; 2A: 2; 4A: 10, 20, 27) on benevolent government, humanity,
   and righteousness.

CHENG, CHUNG-YING. "On Yi as a Universal Principle of Specific
   Application in Confucian Morality." Cross reference: 3.7.

FUNG YU-LAN. A History of Chinese Philosophy. (See 3.1.1), Vols. 1
   and 2.

In Vol. 1, note in particular section 6 of chapter 4 on righteousness, utilitarianism, and human nature. In Vol. 2, note especially
section 1 of chapter 14 on Lu Hsiang-shan where Fung discusses Lu's
emphatic distinction between righteousness and profit.

"The Great Learning," in A Source Book in Chinese Philosophy. Tr. by
Wing-tsit Chan. (See 3.1.1). Also in The Great Learning and The
Mean-in-Action. Tr. by E.R. Hughes. New York: Dutton, 1943.
176 pp.
   The issue is clearly stated toward the end of chapter 10.

3.15 MORAL CLASSIFICATION OF MEN: SAGEHOOD, SUPERIOR MAN, INFERIOR
      MAN

See also all references under 2.8.

The Analects of Confucius. (See 3.9).
   See especially 1: 2, 8, 14; 2: 11, 13, 14; 4: 5, 11; 6: 16; 9: 13;
   13: 3, 23, 26; 14: 24, 30; 15: 17, 20, 31; 8: 6; 12: 16; and 17: 23.

The Book of Mencius. (See 3.5).
   Note in particular 6A: 7; 3A: 1; 4B: 11, 12 for Mencius' idea of
   "great man."

CHAN, WING-TSIT. A Source Book in Chinese Philosophy. (See 3.1.1).
   Note in particular chapter 27 containing Han Yu's essay, "An
   Inquiry on Human Nature," in which Han mentions three grades of
   nature (p. 451).

CUA, ANTONIO S. "The Concept of Paradigmatic Individuals in the
   Ethics of Confucius," in Inquiry, 14 (1971): 41-55. Also in Invitation to Chinese Philosophy. Ed. by Arne Naess and Alastair Hannay.
   Oslo: Universitetsfordget, 1972. Pp. 41-55.
   The paradigmatic individual is described as a man of moral virtues
   (jen), a man of propriety and righteousness, a man of catholicity
   and neutrality, and a man of his words and deeds. Many quotations
   from the Analects are given to support this argument.

"The Doctrine of the Mean," in The Chinese Classics. Tr. by James
   Legge. Oxford: Clarendon Press, 1893. Vol. 1, pp. 382-434. Also
   in Wing-tsit Chan, A Source Book in Chinese Philosophy. (See
   3.1.1), chapter 5.
   Note in particular the three types of men mentioned in section 20.

MOORE, CHARLES A., ed. The Status of the Individual in East and West.
   Honolulu: University of Hawaii Press, 1968. 606 pp.
   Included in this anthology are "The World and the Individual" by
   Thomé H. Fang, "The Individual and the World in Chinese Methodology"

by T'ang Chun-i, "The Status of the Individual in Chinese Ethics" by Hsieh Yu-wei, and "The Status of the Individual in Chinese Social Thought and Practice" by Y.P. Mei. Nowhere else has the subject of the individual in Chinese thought been studied so thoroughly. These treatises supercede E.R. Hughes' The Individual East and West, 1937.

MORTON, W. SCOTT. The Chün Tzu, Ideal Man, in the Analects of Confucius Compared to the Greek and Christian Concepts. Edinburgh: University of Edinburgh Ph.D. thesis, 1964. 162 pp.
    A careful and appreciative study of a subject much talked about but seldom analyzed.

_____. "The Confucian Concept of Man: The Original Formulation," in Philosophy East and West, 21 (1971): 69-77.
    According to the original formulation by Confucius, who gave the term chün-tzu (gentleman) a new meaning, the gentleman is (a) imperturbable and resolute, (b) conciliatory, modest, humble, and even mild, (c) has a well-balanced character, (d) is faithful, a man in whom one can place trust, (e) is conscious of faults, and (f) has independence. In both Confucius' and Aristotle's concept of man, the mean is regarded as the criterion of virtue and the following of the middle way as one of the chief marks of the good man.

3.16 ETHICAL IDEAL: "INNER SAGEHOOD AND OUTER KINGLINESS"

See also 5.9.

CHAN, WING-TSIT. A Source Book in Chinese Philosophy. (See 3.1.1).
    See in particular pp. 208-209 and p. 333 for an understanding of the term in the Taoist sense.

FUNG YU-LAN. The Spirit of Chinese Philosophy. (See 3.6).
    For Fung's interpretation or understanding of "inner sagehood and outer kingliness" see in particular the Introduction, where Fung says, for instance, that "Therefore what philosophy discusses is what the philosophers of China describe as the Tao (Way) of 'sageness within and kingliness without'" (p. 4).

WATSON, BURTON, tr. The Complete Works of Chuang Tzu. New York: Columbia University Press, 1968. 397 pp.
    The term nei-sheng wai-wang (inner sagehood and outer kingliness) first appeared: "Therefore the Way that is sagely within and kingly without has fallen into darkness and is no longer clearly perceived..." (p. 364). The Confucianists took over this Taoist term and gave a moral (Confucian) connotation to it. The term was finally adopted by the Confucian philosophers to express their ethico-political ideal.

3.17 THREE ITEMS AND EIGHT STEPS

See also 1.2.4.

FUNG YU-LAN. A History of Chinese Philosophy. (See 3.1.1), Vol. 1.
    Note Fung's discussion of the text on pp. 361-369. Clear and
    helpful.

The Great Learning. (See 3.14).
    For the very primary source on the subject, see the text.

3.18 "HONORING THE MORAL NATURE" AND "FOLLOWING THE PATH OF INQUIRY
      AND STUDY"

See also all the references under 2.10.

CHU HSI. Reflections on Things at Hand. (See 3.1.3).
    See pp. 279-281 for the position of the early Neo-Confucianists
on the moral defects of Yang Chu and Mo Ti.

The Doctrine of the Mean. (See 3.15).
    See chapter 27 for the classical statement of the two ways of
cultivation and learning.

WANG YANG-MING. Instructions for Practical Living and Other Neo-
    Confucian Writings by Wang Yang-Ming. Tr. by Wing-tsit Chan.
    Columbia University Press, 1963. 358 pp.
    See pp. 113 and 163 for a clear statement of the issue.

3.19 METHODS OF MORAL CULTIVATION: "STRONG, MOVING POWER," EXTENSION
      OF KNOWLEDGE, EXERCISE OF SERIOUSNESS (CHING), ETC.

See also 2.10, 3.17, 3.18.

The Book of Mencius. (See 3.5).
    Note in particular 2A: 2 for the subject on Mencius' "strong,
moving power" or "undisturbed mind."

3.20 CHI ("SUBTLE, INCIPIENT, ACTIVATING FORCE") OF GOOD AND EVIL

CHANG, CARSUN. The Development of Neo-Confucian Thought. New York:
    Bookman Associates, 1962. Vol. 1, 376 pp.
    Note in particular chapter 7 on Chou Tun-i. Chi is translated by
Chang as "state of subtlety" (p. 157).

CHOU TUN-I. "Penetrating the Book of Changes," tr. by Wing-tsit Chan
    in A Source Book in Chinese Philosophy. (See 3.1.1), p. 466.

Besides an English translation of the text, see chapter 28 of the
Source Book on Chou Tun-i, as well as Chan's discussion of the term
chi on p. 784.

FUNG YU-LAN. A History of Chinese Philosophy. (See 3.1.1), Vol. 2,
pp. 435-451.
  Note in particular Fung's discussion of Chou Tun-i, the first Neo-
Confucian philosopher who paid much attention to the chi ("stirrings
of activity" in Bodde's translation) of good and evil.

GRAHAM, A.C. Two Chinese Philosophers. (See 3.6).
  Note in particular Graham's translation of chi as "inward springs
of movement" or "incipient movements not yet visible outside"
(p. 35).

3.21 RECTIFICATION OF NAMES

See also 6.8.

The Analects of Confucius. (See 3.9).
  Note in particular 12: 11, 17; 13: 3, 6.

FRANKE, O. "Über die chinesische Lehre von den Bezeichnungen," in
T'oung Pao, 7 (1906): 315-350.
  A study of the doctrine of the rectification of names in ancient
Confucianism, the Logicians, and Tung Chung-shu.

FUNG YU-LAN. A History of Chinese Philosophy. (See 3.1.1), Vol. 1,
pp. 302-311.
  Note especially Fung's discussion of Confucius' idea of the
Rectification of Names (pp. 59-62) as well as that of Hsün Tzu.

HU SHIH. The Development of the Logical Method in Ancient China.
3rd ed. Shanghai: Oriental Book Co., 1928. 187 pp. Reprinted in
New York: Paragon.
  Note in particular pp. 46-52 (Confucius) and 159-169 (Hsün Tzu).

The Works of Hsuntze. Tr. by Homer H. Dubs. London: Probsthain,
1928. 336 pp. Reprinted in Taipei: Chinese Materials and Research
Aids Service Center.
  See in particular Hsün Tzu's essay on "The Rectification of Names."

3.22 MORAL EDUCATION

See all references under 2.10, 2.11, 1.2.4, 3.17, 3.18, 3.19.

3.23 BENEVOLENT GOVERNMENT (VERSUS GOVERNMENT BY LAW OR FORCE)

See also 3.17, 10.8.

CHAN, WING-TSIT. A Source Book in Chinese Philosophy. (See 3.1.1).
   Note in particular The Analects of Confucius (2: 1, 3; 3: 19; 8:
   9, 14; 12: 7, 11, 17, 19; 13: 3, 6, 16, 29, 30; 14: 45; 15: 4;
   16: 1), the Book of Mencius (1A: 1, 5, 7; 1B: 5, 7; 2A: 5; 3A: 3;
   4A: 14; 5A: 5), the Great Learning and the Doctrine of the Mean.

CHU HSI. Reflections on Things at Hand. (See 3.1.3).
   Note in particular chapters 8 and 9.

3.24 ATTACK UPON CONVENTIONAL ETHICS (NEO-TAOISM)

See also 1.9.3, 1.9.5, 1.9.6, 1.9.8.

FUNG YU-LAN. A Short History of Chinese Philosophy. (See 3.9).
   Note particularly chapters 19 and 20 for some discussion of Neo-
   Taoist transcendence of conventional ethico-social norms.

HANSEN, CHAD. "Freedom and Moral Responsibility in Confucian Ethics,"
   in Philosophy East and West, 22 (1972): 169-186.
   The general theses are that (a) since in the Confucian theory of
   ethics, social behavior is controlled by social pressure of praise
   and blame, it has no account of moral responsibility because it does
   not need one, and (b) there is no need for an external normative
   code of behavior and therefore no need for a theory of the nature of
   excuse conditions. Li (rules of decorum) and the rectification of
   names are extensively discussed.

NIVISON, DAVID S. "Protest Against Conventions and Conventions of
   Protest," in The Confucian Persuasion. Ed. by A. Wright. Stanford:
   Stanford University Press, 1960. Pp. 177-201.
   A fine discussion of the subject, citing examples from traditional
   and modern Chinese intellectuals, such as Ou-yang Hsiu (1007-1072)
   and Ku Chieh-kang.

3.25 NATURALISTIC ETHICS (TAOISM) VERSUS HUMANISTIC ETHICS
      (CONFUCIANISM)

FU, CHARLES WEI-HSUN. "Lao Tzu's Conception of Tao," in Inquiry, 16
   (July, 1973): 367-394.
   Note in particular the sections on Tao as virtue and Tao as
   technique.

FUNG YU-LAN. A History of Chinese Philosophy. (See 3.1.1), Vol. 1.
   See especially pp. 177-191 (Lao Tzu), and pp. 223-245 (Chuang Tzu).

LAO TZU. The Way of Lao Tzu. Tr. by Wing-tsit Chan. Indianapolis:
Bobbs-Merrill, 1963. 285 pp.
    Note in particular the introductory essay on the philosophy of
Tao, in which some discussion is made of Lao Tzu's naturalistic
ethics (pp. 10-22).

3.26 DAILY RENEWAL OF MAN'S MORAL CHARACTER

See also all references in 1.2.4, 1.2.5.

The Great Learning. (See 3.14).
    Note in particular the most important sentences in the second sec-
tion of the Great Learning: "If you can renovate yourself one day,
then you can do so everyday, and keep doing so day after day" and
"Arouse people to become anew."

4. Philosophy of Religion

4.1 RELIGIOUS HUMANISM

BODDE, DERK. China's Cultural Tradition. New York: Rinehart & Co., 1957. 90 pp.
In Part B on the world of the supernatural, Bodde gives a good discussion of the Chinese attitude toward religion in general (section 1) and religions of the masses and of the intellectuals (section 3), the latter expressing more the humanistic rather than supernatural nature of Chinese thought.

CHENG, CHUNG-YING. "Reality and Understanding in the Confucian Philosophy of Religion," in International Quarterly of Philosophy, 13 (1973): 33-61.
A philosophical, overall discussion of the Confucian approach to religion, in terms of reality and understanding.

HU SHIH. "Religion and Philosophy in Chinese History," in Symposium on Chinese Culture. Ed. by Sophia H. Chen Zen. Shanghai: China Institute of Pacific Relations, 1931. Pp. 31-58.
Valuable for a total perspective of Chinese philosophy, and throws some light on the nature of religious humanism of Chinese philosophy.

LIU, SHU-HSIEN. "The Religious Import of Confucian Philosophy: Its Traditional Outlook and Contemporary Significance," in Philosophy East and West, 21 (1971): 157-175.
Liu traces the development of the Confucian religious attitude and points out its general characteristics, and discusses its contemporary significance with reference to the current development of theology and religious philosophy in the West. A general survey of the religious humanism of Confucianism and Neo-Confucianism, with some comparison made with Christian religion today.

SHIGEZAWA, TOSHIO. "Development of Rationalism in Ancient China," in Philosophical Studies of Japan, 3 (1961): 79-119.
Rational thinking in moralism and interpretations of divination, the decreasing anthropomorphic character of Heaven, the rationalism of Confucius, Mencius, the Doctrine of the Mean, the Five Agents school, etc.

Religious Humanism

SHIH, VINCENT Y.C. "A Critique of Motzu's Religious Views and Related Concepts," in Symposium on Chinese Studies Commemorating the Golden Jubilee of the University of Hong Kong, 1911-1961. Hong Kong: Department of Chinese, University of Hong Kong, 1968. Vol. 3, pp. 1-17.
　　Chiefly on Mo Tzu's doctrine of T'ien as the anthropomorphic Supreme Being, its utilitarian motivation, its reactions against Confucian teachings, its interest in the common people, and its related concepts of Yin and Yang, Tao, and antifatalism.

YANG, C.K. Religion in Chinese Society: A Study of Contemporary Social Functions of Religion and Some of Their Historical Factors. Berkeley: University of California Press, 1961. 473 pp.
　　Note in particular Yang's sociological investigation of the religious aspects of Confucianism in its doctrine and practice (chapter 10) as well as of religion and the traditional moral order (chapter 11).

4.2 HARMONIOUS UNITY OF HEAVEN AND MAN

　　Readers interested in this category are referred to 2.15 where the subject is discussed in full.

4.3 CONCEPT OF HEAVEN

　　Readers interested in this topic are referred to the following sections where the subject is discussed in full: 1.2.2, 2.15, 3.1.1, and 8.1.

4.4 *MING* (FATE, DESTINY, MANDATE OF HEAVEN)

　　Readers interested in this topic are referred to 2.3, 3.1.1, and 10.1 where the subject is discussed in full.

4.5 YIN AND YANG

　　Readers interested in this topic are referred to 1.7, 1.9.1, 1.9.2, and 2.16 where the subject is discussed in full.

4.6 PHILOSOPHICAL EXAMINATION OF THE NATURE OF SPIRITUAL BEINGS

See also all references in 4.1.

YÜ, YING-SHIH. View of Life and Death in Later Han China, A.D. 25-220. Harvard University Ph.D. thesis, 1962. 201 pp.
　　An extensively documented and excellent study of the theories of cultivation of life, destiny, death, the soul, and immortality, chiefly in Han times.

4.7 MORAL JUSTIFICATION OF RELIGIOUS (SACRIFICIAL) RITES (*LI*)

Readers interested in this topic are referred to 3.1.3, 3.3, and 3.11 where the subject is discussed in full.

4.8 NATURALISTIC APPROACH TO SUPERNATURAL PROBLEMS (TAOISM, WANG CH'UNG, AND NEO-CONFUCIANISM)

See also all references under 1.4.2, 1.4.3, 1.9.5, 4.1, 4.6.

CHAN, WING-TSIT, tr. and comp. A Source Book in Chinese Philosophy. New Jersey: Princeton University Press, 1963. 856 pp.
   Note in particular chapter 34 on Chu Hsi, in which topics such as "spiritual beings and spiritual forces" (sections 130-133) are particularly important for understanding Chu Hsi's somewhat naturalistic interpretation of the supernatural.

5. Philosophical Psychology

5.1 THEORY OF HUMAN NATURE

Readers interested in this topic are referred to category 2 where this subject is discussed in full.

5.2 THE MEAN

5.2.1 Central Harmony (Chung-ho)

CHAN, WING-TSIT, tr. and comp. A Source Book in Chinese Philosophy. New Jersey: Princeton University Press, 1963. 856 pp.
　Note in particular The Doctrine of the Mean (p. 98), and Chu Hsi's "First Letter to the Gentlemen of Human on Equilibrium and Harmony" (pp. 600-602).

CUA, ANTONIO S. "Confucian vision and experience of the world," in Philosophy East and West, 25 (1975): 319-333.
　Discusses Wang Yang-ming's thought and its significance for understanding the Confucian theme of central harmony.

5.2.2 "Watch Over Oneself When Alone"

"The Doctrine of the Mean," in The Chinese Classics. Tr. by James Legge. Oxford: Clarendon Press, 1893. Vol. 1, pp. 382-434. Also in Wing-tsit Chan, A Source Book in Chinese Philosophy. (See 5.2.1), chapter 5.
　Note in particular words such as "There is nothing more visible than what is hidden and nothing more manifest than what is subtle. Therefore the superior man is watchful over himself when he is alone" (chapter 1).

"The Great Learning," in A Source Book in Chinese Philosophy. Tr. by Wing-tsit Chan. (See 5.2.1). Also in The Great Learning and The Mean-in-Action. Tr. by E.R. Hughes. New York: Dutton, 1943. 176 pp.

Note in particular words such as "What is meant by 'making the will sincere' is allowing no self-deception...the superior man will always be watchful over himself when alone" (chapter 6).

5.2.3 Sincerity (Ch'eng)

Readers interested in this topic are referred to 2.4 where this subject is discussed in full.

5.2.4 The Principle of the Squaring Measure

The Great Learning. (See 5.2.2).
Note especially the words describing the principle of the squaring measure in section 10.

5.3 UNITY OF HEAVEN AND MAN

Readers interested in this topic are referred to 2.15 where this subject is discussed in full.

5.4 TRANQUILLITY

CHAN, WING-TSIT. A Source Book in Chinese Philosophy. (See 5.2.1).
See especially chapter 7 on Lao Tzu (chapters 16, 37, 45, 57, 61), Li Ao's "The Recovery of the Nature" (pp. 456-459), chapter 28 on Chou Tun-i (pp. 463-464 and 471-472), chapter 31 on Ch'eng Hao's "Reply to Master Heng-ch'ü's Letter on Calming Human Nature" (pp. 525-526), and chapter 34 on Chu Hsi (pp. 607-608).

FUNG YU-LAN. A History of Chinese Philosophy. Tr. by Derk Bodde.
Princeton, New Jersey: Princeton University Press, 1952-1953. 2 vols. Vol. 1, 455 pp. Vol. 2, 783 pp.
Note in particular Vol. 1, pp. 175, 181, 186, 188, 291-292, 331, and 366, and Vol. 2, pp. 395, 437, 528-529, and 585. Bodde translates the Chinese term ching as "quiescence" instead of "tranquillity."

5.5 VACUITY

See also 5.4.

CHAN, WING-TSIT. A Source Book in Chinese Philosophy. (See 5.2.1).
Note especially chapter 7 on Lao Tzu (chapter 16 in particular), chapter 8 on Chuang Tzu (especially pp. 207-208), and chapter 30 on Chang Tsai (pp. 501-504, 506, and 516).

5.6 *WU-WEI* (NONACTION)

CHAN, WING-TSIT. A Source Book in Chinese Philosophy. (See 5.2.1).

Note in particular p. 43 (Confucius), chapter 4 on Lao Tzu (especially chapters 2, 3, 10, 37, 43, 48, 57, 63, 64), pp. 254-255 (the Legalists), pp. 297-299 (Wang Ch'ung), p. 322 (Wang Pi), and section 6 of chapter 19 on Kuo Hsiang.

CREEL, HERRLEE G. "On the Origin of Wu-wei," in Symposium in Honor of Dr. Li Chi on His 70th Birthday. Taipei. Part 1 (1965): 105-137. Reprinted in Creel, What is Taoism and Other Studies in Chinese Cultural History. Chicago: University of Chicago, 1970. Pp. 48-78.
An excellent investigation of the historical origin of the notion wu-wei, consulting many primary and secondary sources. Very scholarly.

FUNG YU-LAN. A History of Chinese Philosophy. (See 5.4).
Note in particular Vol. 1, pp. 175, 180, 186, 190, 224, 285, 292, 330-335, and 375 and, Vol. 2, pp. 152-153, 215-219, 223, 242, 258, 268-269, 292, 446, 474, and 612. Wu-wei is translated by Bodde as "non-action" or "non-activity."

5.7 SPONTANEITY

CHAN, WING-TSIT. A Source Book in Chinese Philosophy. (See 5.2.1).
Note in particular chapter 4 on Lao Tzu (especially chapters 17, 19, and 64), chapter 5 on Chuang Tzu, chapter 19 on Neo-Taoism (especially section 6 on Kuo Hsiang).

FU, CHARLES WEI-HSUN. "Lao Tzu's Conception of Tao," in Inquiry, 16 (July, 1973): 367-394.
Some philosophical clarification of the notion tzu-jan (spontaneity or naturalness) is made in various places in the article.

5.8 SIMPLICITY (*P'U*)

CHAN, WING-TSIT. A Source Book in Chinese Philosophy. (See 5.2.1).
Note in particular chapter 4 on Lao Tzu (especially chapters 15, 19, 28, 37, 57, and 80), chapter 5 on Chuang Tzu, and chapter 26 on the Ch'an school (especially section C on Master I-hsüan).

CHANG, CHUNG-YUAN. Original Teachings of Ch'an Buddhism. New York: Pantheon Books, 1969. 333 pp.
In various places are found a naturalistic approach to the world and man. The Tao influence on Ch'an here in terms of simplicity or spontaneity is undeniable.

FUNG YU-LAN. A History of Chinese Philosophy. (See 5.4), Vol. 1.
Note in particular chapter 8 on Lao Tzu, especially pp. 186-191, where Fung gives a good discussion of Lao Tzu's idea of p'u ("unwrought simplicity" according to Bodde's tr.).

5.9 SAGELINESS WITHIN AND KINGLINESS WITHOUT

See also 3.16.

The Complete Works of Chuang Tzu. Tr. by Burton Watson. New York:
    Columbia University Press, 1968. 397 pp.
    Note in particular chapter 33 on "The World," in which the term
"inner sagehood and outer kingliness" appears for the first time,
and has been adopted subsequently (and interestingly) by the Confucianists and the Neo-Confucianists.

FUNG YU-LAN. A History of Chinese Philosophy. (See 5.4).
    Note in particular Vol. 1, pp. 2-3, and 120, and Vol. 2,
pp. 172-173.

_____. The Spirit of Chinese Philosophy. Tr. by E.R. Hughes. London:
    Kegan Paul, 1947. 224 pp. Also in Beacon paperbacks.
    In this work, Fung maintains that the Chinese philosophical tra-
dition always attempts at "attaining to the sublime and yet perform-
ing the common task" at the same time. And he uses this as the
basic criterion to evaluate the pro's and con's of all the major
philosophical systems of China. The idea here he adapts from the
Doctrine of the Mean (chapter 27) is basically the same as that of
"inner sagehood and outer kingliness," which Fung himself also
frequently uses in his writings.

5.10 PHILOSOPHY OF THE MIND

    5.10.1 Original Mind (Mencius, Wang Yang-ming)

    See also 1.2.2, 1.15.3.

    CHAN, WING-TSIT. A Source Book in Chinese Philosophy. (See
        5.2.1).
        Note in particular chapter 3 on Mencius and chapter 35 on
    Wang Yang-ming. In Mencius, the original mind, the mind of
    jen-i (humanity and righteousness), the child's-heart, the
    goodness of human nature, and the innate knowledge of the
    good and the innate ability to do the good are all identical
    in nature. In Wang Yang-ming, the original mind is also
    called the innate knowledge or the Principle of Heaven,
    since Principle and mind are the same in Wang's moral idealism.

    CHENG, CHUNG-YING. "Unity and Creativity in Wang Yang-ming's
        Philosophy of Mind," in Philosophy East and West, 23 (1973):
        49-72. Cross reference: 1.15.3.

T'ANG CHUN-I. "The Development of the Concept of Moral Mind
from Wang Yang-ming to Wang Chi," in Self and Society in
Ming Thought. Ed. by Wm. Theodore de Bary. New York:
Columbia University Press. 550 pp. Pp. 92-120.
   The paper is divided into four parts on Lu Hsiang-shan's
concept of original mind as a basis for Wang Yang-ming's
"realization of liang-chih (innate knowledge of the good),"
the latter as synthesis of Chu Hsi's and Lu Hsiang-shan's
moral mind and moral cultivation, Wang's liang-chih as beyond
good and evil, and Wang's teaching about "learning prior to
Heaven." The conclusion is that Wang Chi, Wang Yang-ming's
pupil, developed his master's ideas to a much higher level.

5.10.2 The Identity of the Mind and Principle
          (Lu-Wang School of the Mind)

See also 1.13.9, 1.15.3.

CHENG, CHING-YING. "Unity and Creativity in Wang Yang-ming's
Philosophy of Mind." (See 1.15.3).
   Cheng holds that the best spirit of Wang's philosophy of
mind is found in his understanding of the unity and creativity
of an ultimate reality, which understandingly ultimately
accrues to his notion of mind.

FUNG YU-LAN. A History of Chinese Philosophy. (See 5.4),
Vol. 2.
   Note in particular chapter 14 on Lu Hsiang-shan, Wang
Yang-ming, and Ming idealism.

5.10.3 The Mind Unifying Nature and Feelings (Chang Tsai,
          Chu Hsi)

CHAN, WING-TSIT. A Source Book in Chinese Philosophy. (See
5.2.1).
   Note in particular Chang Tsai's words, "The mind commands
man's nature and feelings" (p. 517) and chapter 34 on Chu
Hsi (especially sections 75-94 on the mind, nature, and
feelings).

HUANG, SIU-CHI. "The Moral Point of View of Chang Tsai," in
Philosophy East and West, 21 (1971): 141-156. Cross
reference: 1.13.5.

T'ANG CHUN-I. "Chang Tsai's Theory of Mind and Its Metaphysical
Basis," in Philosophy East and West, 6 (1956): 113-136.
Cross reference: 1.13.5.

5.10.4 No-mind or the Mind of Non-abiding

HSI-YÜN. The Zen Teaching of Huang Po on the Transmission of
Mind. Tr. by John Blofeld. London: Rider, 1958. 136 pp.
Reprinted in paperback in New York: Grove Press.
   A translation of one of the most important works on Ch'an
by Hsi-yün (d. 850), which is a short but balanced exposition
of the main tenets of the school. With a helpful introduc-
tion. On pp. 27-66 is reproduced The Huang Po Doctrine of
Universal Mind. Tr. by Chu Ch'an (Blofeld). London: The
Buddhist Society, 1947.

HUI-NENG. The Platform Scripture. Tr. by Wing-tsit Chan.
New York: St. John's University Press, 1963. 193 pp.
   Note in particular pp. 14, 18, 21, 41, 53-55, 67, and
89-93.

_____. The Platform Sūtra of the Sixth Patriarch. Tr. by
Philip B. Yampolsky. New York: Columbia University Press,
1967. 216 pp.
   Note in particular pp. 80, 82-84, 115-116, 138-140, 145-
146, 158-159, and 164-169.

5.10.5 Eight Consciousnesses (Fa-hsiang School)

   Readers interested in this topic are referred to 1.11.4
where this subject is discussed in full.

5.10.6 "Three Thousand Worlds Immanent in a Single Instant of
Thought" (T'ien-t'ai School)

   Readers interested in this topic are referred to 1.11.5
where this subject is discussed in full.

5.10.7 The Tathāgata-garbha (Hua-yen School)

   Readers interested in this topic are referred to 1.11.6
and 2.14 where this subject is discussed in full.

5.10.8 The Mind of Spiritual Tower (Chuang Tzu)

The Complete Works of Chuang Tzu. Tr. by Burton Watson. New
York: Columbia University Press, 1968. 397 pp.
   Note in particular pp. 57-58 for the subject.

5.11 CULTIVATION OF THE MIND

5.11.1 Fasting of the Mind (Chuang Tzu)

The Complete Works of Chuang Tzu. (See 5.10.8).
   Note in particular pp. 57-58 for this subject.

5.11.2 Sitting-in-Forgetfulness (Chuang Tzu)

The Complete Works of Chuang Tzu. (See 5.10.8).
   Note pp. 80, 90-91, 155, 197, 200, 205-207, 219-220, 224,
   236, 302, and especially p. 90, where Yen Hui spoke of how
   he could sit down and forget everything.

5.11.3 Self-Transformation (Chuang Tzu and Kuo Hsiang)

CHAN, WING-TSIT. A Source Book in Chinese Philosophy. (See
   5.2.1).
   Note in particular section 6 of chapter 19 on Kuo Hsiang
   (sections 2, 4, 9, 13, 15, 20, 21, 27, 28, 30, and 31).

The Complete Works of Chuang Tzu. (See 5.10.8).
   Note in particular pp. 49, and 84-85.

FUNG YU-LAN. A History of Chinese Philosophy. (See 5.4).
   Note in particular Vol. 1, chapter 10 on Chuang Tzu and
   Vol. 2, pp. 207-210 on Kuo Hsiang's idea of self-
   transformation.

5.11.4 Self-Sufficiency of All Things (Kuo Hsiang)

CHUANG TZU. A New Selected Translation with an Exposition of
   the Philosophy of Kuo Hsiang. Tr. by Fung Yu-lan. Shanghai:
   Commercial Press, 1933. 164 pp. Reprinted in New York:
   Paragon.
   Note in particular chapter 1 (Kuo Hsiang's commentary on
   Chuang Tzu's "The Happy Excursion") and the Appendix on some
   characteristics of the philosophy of Kuo Hsiang.

FUNG YU-LAN. A History of Chinese Philosophy. (See 5.4),
   Vol. 2.
   Note in particular pp. 205-236 on Kuo Hsiang.

_____. A Short History of Chinese Philosophy. New York:
   Macmillan, 1948. 368 pp.
   Note in particular pp. 220-230 on Kuo Hsiang.

5.11.5 Transformation of Physical Nature (Neo-Confucianism)

Readers interested in this topic are referred to 2.9 and
2.11 where this subject is discussed in full.

5.11.6 "Strong, Moving Power" (Mencius)

Readers interested in this topic are referred to 3.14 where
this subject is discussed in full.

5.11.7 Sitting-in-Meditation (Ch'an school)

See all references under 5.11.2, for Chuang Tzu's idea of
"sitting-in-forgetfulness" made its influence upon the Ch'an
notion of "sitting-in-meditation." See also all the related
references in 1.11.7.1 for a clear understanding of Hui-neng's
radical revision of the Indian method of meditation.

CHANG, CHUNG-YUAN. Original Teachings of Ch'an Buddhism.
   (See 5.8).
   Note in particular the discussion of "silent illumination"
   on pp. 52, 54-7, 188, and 196.

WIENPAHL, PAUL. "Wang Yang-ming and Meditation," in Journal
   of Chinese Philosophy, 1 (1974): 199-227.
   Having appraised what several writers have said about Wang
   Yang-ming with reference to meditation, the author asserts
   that Wang was crucially concerned with the practice of meditation in both his life and his teaching, that he became
   aware of and continually took steps to correct what may be
   called "mere meditation," and that his doctrines of extension
   of innate knowledge of the good and "one must always be doing
   something" are based on the insight that all of life is
   meditation.

5.11.8 Oneness of Calmness and Wisdom (Ch'an School)

See all the related references on Hui-neng in 1.11.7.1.
Also note The Platform Sūtra (5.10.4) (either Chan's tr. or
Yampolsky's tr.), in which Hui-neng's revolutionary identification of calmness (ting) and wisdom (hui) is frequently
mentioned.

5.11.9 Meditation-and-Insight

See also all the related references under 1.11.5.

AŚVAGHOSHA. The Awakening of Faith. Tr. by Y.S. Hakeda.
New York: Columbia University Press, 1967. 128 pp.
Note in particular pp. 95-120 on the subject.

CHAN, WING-TSIT. A Source Book in Chinese Philosophy. (See
5.2.1).
Note in particular pp. 404-405 on Chih-i's idea of the
function of concentration and insight.

5.11.10 Seriousness (*Ching*, Reverence) (Ch'eng I and Chu Hsi)

CHAN, WING-TSIT. A Source Book in Chinese Philosophy. (See
5.2.1).
Note in particular pp. 264-265 (Book of Changes), p. 429
(Ch'an), p. 522 ff. (Ch'eng Hao), p. 547 ff. (Ch'eng I),
and p. 593 ff. (Chu Hsi). See also Chan's discussion on
the English translation of the term ching, variously tr. as
"seriousness" (Chan), "prudence" (Chai Ch'u), "composure"
(Graham), "attentiveness" and "concentration" (Carsun Chang).

GRAHAM, A.C. Two Chinese Philosophers: Ch'eng Ming-tao and
Ch'eng Yi-ch'uan. London: Lund Humphries, 1958. 195 pp.
Note in particular Graham's discussion on Ch'eng I's idea
of ching in chapter 6 of part 1.

5.11.11 Sincerity (*Ch'eng*)

Readers interested in this topic are referred to 2.4 where
this subject is discussed in full.

5.11.12 Recovery of Original Nature (Li Ao)

See also 1.12.

CHAN, WING-TSIT. A Source Book in Chinese Philosophy. (See
5.2.1).
See part 2 for the English translation of Li Ao's "The
Recovery of Nature."

5.11.13 Transformation of Consciousness into Wisdom (Fa-
hsiang School)

See also 1.11.4.

HSÜAN-TSANG. Ch'eng Wei-shih lun--Doctrine of Mere-Consciousness. Tr. by Wei Tat. Hong Kong: The Ch'eng Wei-shih lun
Publication Committee, 1973. 818 pp. Cross Reference:
1.11.4.

5.11.14 "Viewing Things From the Viewpoint of Things" (Shao Yung)

See also all related references under 1.13.4.

CHAN, WING-TSIT. A Source Book in Chinese Philosophy. (See 5.2.1).
   Note in particular chapter 29, sections 8, 24, 28, and 29 of Shao's "Supreme Principles Governing the World."

5.11.15 Daily Renewal (The *Great Learning* and the *Doctrine of the Mean*)

Besides the following entry, readers interested in this topic are referred to 3.26 where this subject is covered in full.

GRAHAM, A.C. "Chuang-tzu's Essay on Seeing Things as Equal," in History of Religions, 9 (1969): 137-159.
   A very scholarly translation of the most philosophical chapter of the Chuang-tzu, with the translator's introductory essay.

5.11.16 Rectification of the Mind

"The Book of Mencius," in Mencius. Tr. by D.C. Lau. Baltimore: Penguin Books, 1970. 280 pp. Also in The Chinese Classics. Tr. by James Legge. Oxford: Clarendon Press, 1895. Vol. 2, The Works of Mencius, 402 pp.
   Note particularly 4A: 21.

The Great Learning. (See 5.2.2).
   Note in particular section 7 of the text, in which the way to rectify the mind is for the first time mentioned. The rectification of the mind actually constitutes the fourth step of the eight steps in the Great Learning.

SHIH, VINCENT. "The Mind and the Moral Order," in Mélanges chinoise et bouddhiques, 10 (1955): 347-364.
   Considering the Neo-Confucian theory of mind as a moral order to be one-sided and a hindrance to natural science, the author offers his own theory that mind is "experience," totally possessing both an ethical nature and a scientific spirit.

Cultivation of the Mind 5.11.16

T'ANG CHUN-I. "The Development of the Concept of Moral Mind from Wang Yang-ming to Wang Chi." Cross reference: 5.10.1.

WANG YANG-MING. <u>Instructions for Practical Living and Other Neo-Confucian Writings by Wang Yang-ming</u>. Tr. by Wing-tsit Chan. New York: Columbia University Press, 1963. 358 pp. Note in particular pp. 15, 20, 55, 160, 205, 277, and 280.

6. Epistemology

6.1 INVESTIGATION OF THINGS

CHAN, WING-TSIT, tr. and comp. A Source Book in Chinese Philosophy.
New Jersey: Princeton University Press, 1963. 856 pp.
   Note in particular chapter 32 on Ch'eng I (sections 14, 16, 17,
31, 44, 47, and 62 of the Selected Sayings), chapter 34 on Chu Hsi
(sections 25-30 of the Complete Works), and chapter 35 on Wang
Yang-ming ("Inquiry on the Great Learning" and sections 6, 7, 89,
135, 262, 315, 319, and 331 of the Instructions for Practical
Living).

CHU HSI, in collaboration with Lu Tsu-ch'ien. Reflections on Things
at Hand: The Neo-Confucian Anthology. Tr. by Wing-tsit Chan. New
York: Columbia University Press, 1967. 441 pp.
   Note in particular chapter 2 on the essentials of learning and
chapter 3 on the investigation of things and the investigation of
principles to the utmost.

HOCKING, W.E. "Chu Hsi's Theory of Knowledge," in Harvard Journal
of Asiatic Studies, 1 (1936): 109-127.
   A highly discerning discussion of Chu Hsi as an empiricist who
demanded moral perfection, insight into principles, and moral
action.

HU SHIH. "The Scientific Spirit and Method in Chinese Philosophy,"
in Philosophy and Culture--East and West. Ed. by Charles A. Moore.
Honolulu: University of Hawaii Press, 1962. Pp. 199-222. Reprinted
in Moore's The Chinese Mind. Honolulu: East-West Center Press,
1967. Pp. 104-131.
   The growth and strength of the tradition of skepticism in philosophers like Wang Ch'ung, the naturalistic view of the universe in
Wang Ch'ung, Tung Chung-shu, and others, and the scientific spirit
of doubt and investigation in Chu Hsi and other thinkers like Tai
Chen in the past eight centuries.

YU, DAVID. "Chu Hsi's approach to Knowledge," in Chinese Culture,
10, no. 4 (December, 1969): 1-14.
   A general discussion of Chu Hsi's concept of knowledge in relation
to the investigation of things and principles.

6.2 EXTENSION OF KNOWLEDGE

Readers interested in this topic are referred to 1.3.4 and 6.1 where this subject is discussed in full.

6.3 INNATE KNOWLEDGE OF THE GOOD

Readers interested in this topic are referred to 2.7 where this subject is discussed in full.

6.4 UNITY OF KNOWLEDGE AND ACTION

CHENG, CHUNG-YING. "Unity and Creativity in Wang Yang-ming's Philosophy of Mind," in Philosophy East and West, 23 (1973): 49-72. Cross reference: 1.15.3.

MAO TSE-TUNG. Selected Works. Peking: Foreign Language Press, 1961. 4 vols.
   Note in particular his essays "On Practice" (Vol. 1), "The Chinese Revolution and the Chinese Communist Party" (Vol. 2), "On New Democracy" (Vol. 2), "Serve the People" (Vol. 2), "The Foolish Old Man Who Removed the Mountain" (Vol. 2), and "Reform Our Study" (Vol. 3), etc.

NIVISON, DAVID S. "The Problem of 'Knowledge' and 'Action' in Chinese Thought Since Wang Yang-ming," in Studies in Chinese Thought. Ed. by Arthur Wright. Chicago: University of Chicago Press, 1953. Pp. 112-145.
   Reviews the doctrines of "knowledge" and "action" from Wang to Sun Yat-sen (1866-1925) and Mao Tse-tung, correctly pointing out that Chinese thinkers have always emphasized action.

WANG YANG-MING. Instructions for Practical Living and Other Neo-Confucian Writings by Yang Wang-ming. Tr. by Wing-tsit Chan. New York: Columbia University Press, 1963. 358 pp.
   Note in particular pp. 9-14, 30, 82, 92-95, 99-102, 107-113, 145-147, 201, 229-230, and 250 for the subject.

6.5 EMPHASIS ON PERSONAL REALIZATION (*T'i-jen*)

CHAN, WING-TSIT. A Source Book in Chinese Philosophy. (See 6.1).
   Note in particular the discussion of the term on p. 790, emphasizing the Neo-Confucian way of using t'i-jen as a special method of knowledge.

MOORE, CHARLES A., ed. The Chinese Mind: Essentials of Chinese Philosophy and Culture. Honolulu: East-West Center Press, 1967. 402 pp.

Contains two essays, "Chinese Theory and Practice, with Special
Reference to Humanism" and "Synthesis in Chinese Metaphysics" by
Wing-tsit Chan, in both of which Chan discusses the term t'i-jen
(p. 14 and p. 145).

6.6   EQUAL EMPHASIS ON BOTH THE INTERNAL AND THE EXTERNAL (CH'ENG I)

CHAN, WING-TSIT. A Source Book in Chinese Philosophy. (See 6.1).
   Note in particular Ch'eng I's unique interpretation of "serious
in order to straighten the internal life and righteous in order to
square the external life" ("Great Appendices" of the Book of Changes)
on (e.g.) p. 560.

FUNG YU-LAN. A History of Chinese Philosophy. Tr. by Derk Bodde.
   Princeton, New Jersey: Princeton University Press, 1952-1953. 2
   vols. Vol. 1, 455 pp. Vol. 2, 783 pp. Pp. 527-532.
   Ch'eng I's theory of spiritual cultivation.

6.7   "FIVE STEPS" (THE *DOCTRINE OF THE MEAN*)

"The Doctrine of the Mean," in The Chinese Classics. Tr. by James
   Legge. Oxford: Clarendon Press, 1893. Vol. 1, pp. 382-434. Also
   in Wing-tsit Chan, A Source Book in Chinese Philosophy. (See 6.1),
   chapter 5.
   Note the "five steps" given in section 20 of the text: "Study it
(the way to be sincere) extensively, inquire into it accurately,
think over it carefully, sift it clearly, and practice it earnestly."
(See also 2.3).

FUNG YU-LAN. A History of Chinese Philosophy. (See 6.6), Vol. 1.
   Note in particular p. 373 on the subject.

6.8   RECTIFICATION OF NAMES

See also 3.21.

CHENG, CHUNG-YING. "Rectifying Names (cheng-ming) in Classical Confucianism," in Essays in Asian Studies. Ed. by Harry Lambly.
   University of Hawaii Asian Studies Publication, 1969, pp. 82-96.
   A philosophical analysis of the Confucian notion of the rectification of names.

CUA, ANTONIO S. "The Logic of Confucian Dialogues," in Studies in
   Philosophy and the History of Philosophy, 4 (1969): 18-33.
   Various characteristics of the Confucian dialogues are described
to show that the basic Confucian methodology has as its essential
conceptual element the actual priority of existence over essence.

The philosophical use of reason in Confucianism is reasonableness rather than abstract rationality. Concepts and general principles are explained by way of examples and rules. The rectification of names means that ethical concepts are governed by moral rules.

MEI, Y.P. "Some Observations on the Problem of Knowledge among the Ancient Chinese Logicians," in Tsing Hua Journal of Chinese Studies, n.s., 1, no. 1 (1956): 114-121.
    A cursory view of ancient Chinese philosophers' understanding of the nature and constitutions of the knowing experience and the social function of names.

6.9 NAME AND ACTUALITY (THE LOGICIANS)

    Readers interested in this topic are referred to 1.5.2 and 1.6 where this subject is discussed in full.

6.10 DISTINCTION BETWEEN THE FUNDAMENTAL AND THE SECONDARY (THE *Great Learning*)

FUNG YU-LAN. A History of Chinese Philosophy. (See 6.6), Vol. 1.
    Note Fung's discussion of the text on pp. 361-369.

"The Great Learning," in A Source Book in Chinese Philosophy. Tr. by Wing-tsit Chan. (See 6.1). Also in The Great Learning and The Mean in Action. Tr. by E.R. Hughes. New York: Dutton, 1943. 176 pp.
    Note in particular Chapter 1 of the text and the first four chapters of commentary rearranged by Chu Hsi.

WANG YANG-MING. Instructions for Practical Living and Other Neo-Confucian Writings by Wang Yang-ming. (See 6.4).
    Note in particular "The Inquiry on the Great Learning" (pp. 271-280), where Wang gives his own idealistic interpretation of the root (fundamental) and the branches (secondary): "The main thing is that root and branches should not be distinguished as two different things....If it is realized that manifesting the clear character is to love the people and loving people is to manifest the clear character, how can they be split in two?" (p. 276).

6.11 *MING* (INSIGHT OR ENLIGHTENMENT--LAO TZU)

FU, CHARLES WEI-HSUN. "Lao Tzu's Conception of Tao," in Inquiry, 16 (July, 1973): 367-394.
    Gives a philosophical explication of Lao Tzu's ming as basically an ontological insight, not merely a kind of enlightenment in the practical sense (see section 1).

The Way of Lao Tzu. Tr. by Wing-tsit Chan. Indianapolis: Bobbs-
    Merrill, 1963. 285 pp. Also tr. as The Way and Its Power by
    Arthur Waley. London: Allen and Unwin, 1935. 262 pp. (Also in
    Evergreen paperbacks, New York: Grove Press.) Also tr. as Tao Te
    Ching by Gia-fu Feng and Jane English. New York: Alfred A. Knopf,
    1972. 170 pp. Also tr. as The Wisdom of Laotse by Lin Yu-tang.
    New York: The Modern Library, 1948. 326 pp. Also tr. as Lao Tzu
    by John C.H. Wu. New York: St. John's University Press, 1961.
    115 pp.
    Note in particular chapters 16, 22, 24, 33, 52, and 55 of the
    text for Lao Tzu's own words on ming.

6.12 NON-KNOWLEDGE (LAO TZU, CHUANG TZU)

See also 1.4.2, 1.4.3.

The Complete Works of Chuang Tzu. Tr. by Burton Watson. New York:
    Columbia University Press, 1968. 397 pp.
    Note in particular chapters 2, 3, 16, 17, 22, and 25 of the text.
    To Chuang Tzu, non-knowledge is actually perfect knowledge about
    the nameless Tao, as in the case of Lao Tzu.

The Lao Tzu. (See 6.11).
    Note in particular chapters 3, 10, 19, 20, 48, 65, and 81 of
    the text for Lao Tzu's own words on wu-chih (non-knowledge). Note
    also another related idea, wu-yen (non-word), expressed in chapters
    2, 5, 43, 56, 73, and 81 of the same text.

6.13 EQUALIZATION OF ALL THINGS AND OPINIONS (CHUANG TZU)

CHAN, WING-TSIT. A Source Book in Chinese Philosophy. (See 6.1),
    pp. 179-191.
    Translation of the subject chapter with his own comments and
    footnotes.

CHUANG TZU. A New Selected Translation with an Exposition of the
    Philosophy of Kuo Hsiang. Tr. by Fung Yu-lan. Shanghai: Commercial
    Press, 1933. 164 pp. Reprinted in New York: Paragon.
    See especially pp. 43-64 for Fung's translation of "The Equality
    of Things and Opinions," with the additional translation of Kuo
    Hsiang's Commentary on the Chuang-Tzu. Philosophically very clear.

GRAHAM, A.C. "Chuang Tzu's Essay on Seeing Things as Equal," in
    History of Religions, 9 (1969/70): 137-159.
    A fresh and scholarly attempt at reconstruction and reinterpreta-
    tion of chapter 2, the most important chapter, of the Chuang Tzu, in
    which Chuang Tzu sets out his philosophy of seeing all things (and

opinions) as equal from the point of view of Tao. With Graham's
new translation of the chapter, rearranged in 20 sections.

6.14 "THREE STANDARDS" (MO TZU AND THE MOISTS)

HU SHIH. The Development of the Logical Method in Ancient China.
3rd ed. Shanghai: Oriental Book Co., 1928. 187 pp. Reprinted in
New York: Paragon.
   Note in particular pp. 72-82 on Mo Ti's three laws of reasoning
(three standards). Hu's analysis is very clear and scholarly, and
is probably the best on the subject.

MEI, Y.P. Motse, The Neglected Rival of Confucius. London:
Probsthain, 1934. 222 pp.
   A good discussion of Mo Tuz's methodology, and in particular, his
doctrine of the three standards appears on pp. 61-84.

Mo Tzu: Basic Writings. Tr. by Burton Watson. New York: Columbia
University Press, 1963. 140 pp. Also The Ethical and Political
Works of Motse. Tr. by Y.P. Mei. London: Probsthain, 1929.
275 pp.
   Note in particular Mo Tzu's "Attack on Fatalism" in three parts
for his doctrine of three standards. Mo Tzu says: "...for any doctrine there must be the three standards....(1) There must be a basis
or foundation. (2) There must be an examination. (3) And there
must be practical application."

6.15 "SEVEN METHODS OF ARGUMENT" (MOISM)

FUNG YU-LAN. A History of Chinese Philosophy. (See 6.6), Vol. 1.
   Note in particular pp. 257-262 on the Neo-Moist discussion on
dialectic, where Fung gives a clear account of each of the seven
methods of argument.

GRAHAM, A.C. "The Logic of the Mohist Hsiao-ch'ü," in T'oung Pao, 51
(1964): 1-54.
   Translation and discussion of chapter 45 of the Mo Tzu in terms
of Moist logic and the Chinese language, interpreting the phrase in
the chapter, "to kill a robber is not to kill a jen," to mean "not
to kill the robber as a person."

HU SHIH. The Development of the Logical Method in Ancient China.
(See 6.14).
   Book 3 of Part 3 deals with the logic of Neo-Moism, in which Hu
gives a very analytic discussion of the subject. On pp. 95-108 Hu
focuses on five methods of reasoning, i.e., hsiao (deduction), pi
(comparison), mou (parallel), yüan (analogy), and t'ui (induction).

The two other methods are <u>huo</u> (probability) and <u>chia</u> (hypothesis).
Hu's treatment of the subject is still the best and unsurpassed.

LAU, D.C. "Some Logical Problems in Ancient China," in <u>Proceedings
of the Aristotelian Society</u>, n.s., 53 (1953): 189-204.
   Examines the methods of analogy, parallel, precedent, and extension in chapter 45 (<u>Hsiao-ch'ü</u>) of the <u>Mo Tzu</u> for the practical
purpose of overcoming the opponent. Also speculates on how the
Chinese language hindered ancient logicians.

NEEDHAM, JOSEPH. <u>Science and Civilisation in China</u>. Cambridge,
   England: Cambridge University Press, 1954-1962. 4 vols. Vol. 2
<u>History of Scientific Thought (1956)</u>: 696 pp. Pp. 171-184.
   Discusses the scientific thought in the "Moist Canon" in terms of
speech, attributes, sensations, the models and methods of Nature,
classification, loose appellations, universal and particular, des-
ignation, comparison between classes, causation, part and whole,
agreement, difference, inference, contradictions, etc., and sheds
some fresh light on the Neo-Moist methods of argument.

6.16 SCEPTICISM AND NATURALISM (WANG CH'UNG)

   Readers interested in this topic are referred to 1.9.5 where this
subject is discussed in full.

6.17 TWO LEVELS OF TRUTH (CHI-TSANG)

CHANG, GARMA C.C. <u>The Buddhist Teaching of Totality: The Philosophy
of Hwa Yen Buddhism</u>. University Park: Pennsylvania State University
Press, 1971. 270 pp.
   Note pp. 103-114 on "<u>śūnyatā</u> (emptiness) and logic," where Chang
focuses on Chi-tsang's "two truths on three levels" as a philosophical elaboration on Nāgārjuna's system of the two truths, and uses
some notations of symbolic logic to show a simplification of Chi-
tsang's subject doctrine. An excellent analysis.

de BARY, WM. THEODORE, et al., eds. <u>The Buddhist Tradition in India,
China, and Japan</u>. New York: The Modern Library, 1969. 417 pp.
Pp. 144-150.
   The English translation of selected passages from Chi-tsang's
writings concerning his theory of the twofold truth.

FUNG YU-LAN. <u>A Short History of Chinese Philosophy</u>. (<u>See</u> 6.6), Vol.
   2, pp. 245-246.
   A discussion on Chi-tsang's theory of double truth. Short but
clear enough.

6.18 HARMONY OF HIGHER TRUTH, LOWER TRUTH, AND THE MEAN (T'IEN-T'AI)

Readers interested in this topic are referred to 1.11.5 where this subject is discussed in full.

6.19 HARMONY OF FACTS AND PRINCIPLES (HUA-YEN SCHOOL)

See also 1.11.6.

CHANG, CHUNG-YUAN. Original Teachings of Ch'an Buddhism. New York: Pantheon Books, 1969. 333 pp. Pp. 41-51.
    Characterization of the Ts'ao-tung school in terms of the inter-fusion of universality (principle) and particularity (facts), by way of showing the philosophical influence of the Hua-yen doctrine of unimpeded perfect mutual solution, and on the Ts'ao-tung teaching of the five relations between particularity and universality. A good treatment of the subject in its historical perspective.

SUZUKI, DAISETZ TEITARO. Essays in Zen Buddhism. London: Luzac, 1934. 392 pp. (Third Series). Reprinted in paperback in London: Rider & Co., 1970. 396 pp.
    A unique insight into the meaning of Zen in relation to the phi-losophy and religion of the prajñāpāramitā (perfection of wisdom) and to the Gandavyūha, the fundamental scripture of the Hua-yen school. Note in particular Suzuki's profound treatment of the four-fold Dharmadhātu (Realm of Dharma) on pp. 147-156 in relation to the subject.

6.20 "VIEWING THINGS FROM THE VIEWPOINT OF THINGS THEMSELVES" (SHAO YUNG)

Readers interested in this topic are referred to 1.13.4 where this subject is discussed in full.

6.21 EMPHASIS ON EMPIRICAL KNOWLEDGE (CHU HSI, TAI CHEN)

See also 1.13.8, 1.16.4, 6.1.

HU SHIH. "The Scientific Spirit and Method in Chinese Philosophy." Cross reference: 6.1.

LEVENSON, JOSEPH R. "The Abortiveness of Empiricism in Early Ch'ing Thought," in Far Eastern Quarterly, 13 (1954): 155-165. Revised in his Confucian China and Its Modern Fate, pp. 3-14.
    Maintains that while Ch'ing 17th- and 18th-century empiricists were not conducive to the birth of science, it was because their questioning began with a certain traditional, Confucian certainty. Not all the secondary sources used are first-rate.

6.22 EMPHASIS ON PRACTICE (YEN YÜAN)

See also 1.13.1.

CHENG, CHUNG-YING. "Theory and Practice in Confucianism," in Journal
of Chinese Philosophy, 1 (1974): 179-198.
   The views of Confucius, Mencius, the Great Learning, the Doctrine
of the Mean, and Wang Yang-ming are analyzed and discussed, showing
their contributions to the understanding of the relation between
theory and practice, or knowledge and action.

NIVISON, DAVID S. "The Problem of 'Knowledge' and 'Action' in
Chinese Thought Since Wang Yang-ming." (See 6.4).
   Note in particular pp. 124-126 where Nivison discusses Yen's view
of education as basically a practical matter, though Yen's thought
is still much concerned with moral self-cultivation. For him, the
purpose of investigating things is "a transcendent enlightening
experience" (p. 125).

6.23 "REFUTATION OF FALSE VIEWS IS ITSELF REVELATION OF THE CORRECT VIEW" (CHI-TSANG)

See also 1.11.3, 6.17.

TAKAKUSU, J. The Essentials of Buddhist Philosophy. 3rd ed.
Honolulu: Office Appliance Co., 1956. 221 pp.
   Note in particular pp. 100-107.

7. Metaphysics and Ontology

7.1 CONCEPT OF HEAVEN

See also 1.2.2, 2.3, 2.15, 3.1.1.

The Analects of Confucius. Tr. by Arthur Waley. London: Allen and
Unwin, 1938. 268 pp. Also published in The Chinese Classics. Tr.
by James Legge. Oxford: Clarendon Press, 1893. Vol. 1, Confucian
Analects, pp. 137-354.
For Confucius on Heaven, see 2: 4; 3: 13; 5: 12; 6: 26; 7: 22;
9: 5, 6; 11: 8; 12: 5; 14: 37; 16: 8, and 17: 19.

FUNG YU-LAN. A History of Chinese Philosophy. Tr. by Derk Bodde.
Princeton, New Jersey: Princeton University Press, 1952-1953. 2
vols. Vol. 1, 455 pp. Vol. 2, 783 pp.
Note in particular Fung's formulation in Vol. 1 of the five senses
of Heaven (t'ien) in Chinese philosophical and religious writings:
(a) a material or physical t'ien or sky, (b) a ruling or presiding
t'ien, (c) a fatalistic t'ien, equivalent to the concept of ming
(fate), (d) a naturalistic t'ien, equivalent to Nature, and (e) an
ethical t'ien, that is, one having a moral principle and which is
the highest primordial principle of the universe (p. 31). Fung's
clarification of the various meanings of Heaven in Chinese thought
is extremely important and helpful for a basic understanding of
the term.

_____. "The Struggle between Materialism and Idealism in the History
of Chinese Philosophy in Terms of Several Major Problems in
Chinese Philosophy," in Chinese Studies in History and Philosophy,
2, no. 4 (Summer, 1969): 3-27.
The problem of Heaven, especially in Confucius, Mencius, Taoism,
and Hsün Tzu, of material force in Taoism, the Book of Changes,
Wang Ch'ung, and Tung Chung-shu, of the mind in Buddhism and Fan
Chen, and of li (principle), especially in Neo-Confucianism.

Hsün Tzu: Basic Writings. Tr. by Burton Watson. New York: Columbia
University Press. 177 pp. Also published in combined edition of
Basic Writings of Mo Tzu, Hsün Tzu, and Han Fei Tzu. 1967.
See chapter 17 for Hsün Tzu's concept of Heaven.

Mo Tzu: Basic Writings. Tr. by Burton Watson. New York: Columbia
University Press, 1963. 140 pp.
   For Mo Tzu's concept of Heaven, see pp. 75-93 for the translation
of chapters 26 and 27.

SHIH, VINCENT Y.C. "A Critique of Motzu's Religious Views and Related
Concepts," in Symposium on Chinese Studies Commemorating the Golden
Jubilee of the University of Hong Kong, 1911-1961. Hong Kong:
Department of Chinese, University of Hong Kong, 1968. Vol. 3,
pp. 1-17.
   A general examination of Mo Tzu's basic doctrines, such as the
anthropomorphic Heaven, universal love, benefit for the people,
criticism of Confucianists, attack on belief in fate, wasteful festivals, warfare, etc.

7.2 THE GREAT ULTIMATE AND THE ULTIMATE OF NON-BEING

   7.2.1 The Ultimate of Non-Being or the Ultimateless (*Wu-chi*)

   CHAN, WING-TSIT, tr. and comp. A Source Book in Chinese Philosophy. New Jersey: Princeton University Press, 1963.
   856 pp.
      Note p. 460 and pp. 463-465 (Chou Tun-i's T'ai-chi-t'u
   shuo or Explanation of the Diagram of the Great Ultimate),
   p. 556 and pp. 577-578 (Chu Hsi), p. 752 and pp. 758-759
   (Fung Yu-lan's Hsin li-hsüeh or The New Rational Philosophy)
   for an understanding of the Neo-Confucian development of
   the metaphysical doctrine of wu-chi, in its relation to
   t'ai-chi (supreme ultimate), from Chou-Tun-i to Fung Yu-lan.

   CHANG, CARSUN. The Development of Neo-Confucian Thought.
   New York: Bookman Associates, Inc., 1962. Vol. 1, 376 pp.
      In chapter 7 the author gives a detailed analysis of Chou
   Tun-i's cosmological speculations in terms of wu-chi and
   t'ai-chi, and in chapter 13 he discusses in detail the
   debate between Chu Hsi and Lu Hsiang-shan, mainly with
   respect to the meaning of the first sentence in Chou Tun-i's
   T'ai-chi-t'u shuo, i.e., "The Ultimate of Non-being and also
   the Great Ultimate!" An extremely important debate regarding the ontological relation between wu-chi and t'ai-chi in
   the history of Neo-Confucian metaphysics.

   CHU HSI, in collaboration with Lü Tsu-ch'ien. Reflections on
   Things at Hand: The Neo-Confucian Anthology. Tr. by Wing-
   tsit Chan. New York: Columbia University Press, 1967.
   441 pp.
      Note in particular chapter 1 on the substance of the Way,
   where the Sung Neo-Confucian metaphysics of wu-chi and
   t'ai-chi is systematically presented by Chu Hsi.

FUNG YU-LAN. A History of Chinese Philosophy. Tr. by Derk
  Bodde. Princeton, New Jersey: Princeton University Press,
  1952-1953. 2 vols. Vol. 1, 455 pp. Vol. 2, 783 pp.
    Note in particular pp. 435-437, 441, and 444 for Fung's
  discussion of Chou Tun-i's metaphysical system in terms of
  wu-chi and t'ai-chi.

The Way of Lao Tzu. Tr. by Wing-tsit Chan. Indianapolis:
  Bobbs-Merrill, 1963. Also tr. as The Way and Its Power by
  Arthur Waley. London: Allen and Unwin, 1935. 262 pp.
  (Also in Evergreen paperbacks, New York: Grove Press).
  Also tr. as Tao Te Ching by Gia-fu Feng and Jane English.
  New York: Alfred A. Knopf, 1972. 170 pp. Also tr. as
  The Wisdom of Laotse by Lin Yu-tang. New York: The Modern
  Library, 1948. 362 pp. Also tr. as Lao Tzu by John
  C.H. Wu. New York: St. John's University Press, 1961.
  115 pp.
    The word wu-chi appeared first in chapter 28 of the Lao
  Tzu, though it was not a metaphysical notion in the strict
  sense, as in the case of Neo-Confucian philosophy.

7.2.2 The Supreme Ultimate (*T'ai-chi*)

CHAN, WING-TSIT. A Source Book in Chinese Philosophy. (See
  7.2.1).
    Note p. 263 and p. 271 (Book of Changes), pp. 463-465 and
  p. 472 (Chou Tun-i), p. 484 (Shao Yung), p. 535 (Ch'eng Hao),
  p. 585 (Lu Hsiang-shan), p. 593 (Chu Hsi), and p. 752 and
  p. 758 (Fung Yu-lan) for the subject. See also 7.2.1.

CHANG, CARSUN. The Development of Neo-Confucian Thought,
  Vol. 1. Cross reference: 7.2.1.

CHU HSI. Reflections on Things at Hand. Cross reference:
  7.2.1.

FUNG YU-LAN. A History of Chinese Philosophy. (See 7.2.1),
  Vol. 2.
    Note in particular pp. 101-102, p. 118, pp. 182-183,
  pp. 435-442, pp. 452-453, pp. 457-459, pp. 478-479,
  pp. 534-535, pp. 545-546, pp. 549-552, p. 559, pp. 589-590,
  p. 607 and p. 640 for the various approaches to the notion
  of t'ai-chi in the Book of Changes and in Neo-Confucianiam.
  See also 7.2.1.

HUANG, SIU-CHI. "The Concept of T'ai-Chi (Supreme Ultimate)
  in Sun Neo-Confucian Philosophy," in Journal of Chinese
  Philosophy, 1 (1974): 275-294.

In this philosophical clarification of the term, Huang
maintains that all the Sung thinkers are in accord (despite
the disagreement over the term wu-chi in relation to t'ai-
chi), that cosmos, in which all things come into being and
pass away, is ontologically real. Also points out the
ethical implication of the term.

7.3 TAO

CHAN, WING-TSIT. A Source Book in Chinese Philosophy. (See 7.2.1).
   Note in particular the Analects of Confucius (4: 5, 8; 7: 6; 15:
   28, 31; 17: 4), the Doctrine of the Mean (pp. 95-96, p. 98,
   p. 100), the Lao Tzu (chapters 1, 4, 8, 14, 16, 21, 23, 25, 32, 34,
   35, 37, 40-42, 51), the Chuang Tzu (pp. 202-205), the Han-fei Tzu
   (pp. 305-306), Wang Pi (pp. 321-324), Ho Yen (pp. 324-325), Kuo
   Hsiang (p. 317), Han Yü (pp. 454-455), Ch'eng Hao (sections 1, 5,
   19, 32, 41, 42, 44, and 50), Ch'eng I (sections 10, 13, 22, 26, 30,
   33, 36, 57, 69, 73, and 78), Lu Hsiang-shan (sections 1-3, 8-9, 11-
   13, 15, 17-19, 30, 33, 36, and 42), and Fung Yu-lan (p. 751,
   pp. 758-759 and p. 762). The references here in the Source Book
   are not exhaustive, since almost all Chinese philosophers, especially Confucianists and Taoists and even Buddhists, use the term
   Tao in various senses in their writings. Further, the complexity
   of the meanings of Tao always arises because of the identification
   of Tao with many other important metaphysical notions such as non-
   being, jen, li (principle), wu-chi, t'ai-chi, Nature (t'ien), the
   mind (of Tao), or pen-t'i (substance or reality), depending on how
   each Chinese philosopher approaches the problem of metaphysical
   reality in terms of Tao. It is suggested here, therefore, that
   other related topics under 7 (Metaphysics and Ontology) be checked
   as well for more references.

CHANG, CHUNG-YUAN. "The Concept of Tao in Chinese Culture," in
   Review of Religion, 17 (1953): 115-132.
   A neat description of the concept of Tao in Confucius, Lao Tzu,
   and religious Taoism and Buddhism.

_____. "Some Basic Philosophical Concepts of Confucianism and
   Taoism," in Missionary Research Library Occasional Bulletin, 6,
   no. 1 (1955): 1-13.
   On the non-differentiation of Tao and jen (equated with "psychic
   integration") and the psychic transformation of the self.

_____. "Tao: A New Way of Thinking," in Journal of Chinese Philos-
   ophy, 1 (1973-1974): 137-152.
   A comparison of Taoist thinking with the thinking of Plato, the
   Buddhists, Hegel, and Heidegger, particularly the latter. References are made to European thinkers' reactions to the Tao-te ching.

_____. "Tao and the Sympathy of All Things," in <u>Eranos-Jahrbuch</u>, 24 (1955): 407-432.
   Interprets "sympathy" as Taoist synthesis of opposites and unity in multiplicity. This state of non-being is to be known through intuition and quietude.

FU, CHARLES WEI-HSUN. "Lao Tzu's Conception of Tao," in <u>Inquiry</u>, 16 (July, 1973): 367-394. Cross reference: 1.4.2.

FUNG YU-LAN. <u>A History of Chinese Philosophy</u>. (<u>See</u> 7.2.1).
   For the notion of Tao in various senses or approaches, note in particular Vol. 1, pp. 16, 56, 59, 73, 82, 95, 103, 131, 133, 148, 153-156, 158, 170-171, 173, 175, 177-179, 180-181, 183-185, 187, 190, 193, 202-203, 223-227, 232, 236, 240-242, 245, 279, 284, 290-293, 308, 310-311, 315, 331-334, 361-362, 366, 370, 372-374, 377-378, 383-384, 391, and Vol. 2, pp. 44, 99-100, 147, 183, 207-209, 397, 399, 402-403, 406, 409-412, 501, 510-511, 538, 542, 562-563, 590-591, 633, 636-639, 642-644, 652-657.

GRAF, OLAF. <u>Tao und Jen, Sein und Sollen im sungchinesischen Monismus</u>. Wiesbaden: Otto Harrassowitz, 1970. 429 pp. Cross reference: 1.3.2.

GRAVA, ARNOLD. "Tao: An Age-Old Concept in Its Modern Perspective," in <u>Philosophy East and West</u>, 13 (1963): 235-250.
   Discusses Siegbert Hummel's interpretation of Tao as absence of conceptual perception. Attempts to interpret Tao in terms of its creative potentiality and its relational character versus later interpretations of it by some Neo-Taoists in terms of being and non-being. Only Western sources are used.

IZUTSU, TOSHIHIKO. "The Absolute and the Perfect Man in Taoism," in <u>Erans-Jahrbuch</u>, 36 (1967): 379-440.
   Exclusively dealing with Lao Tzu and Chuang Tzu, the author compares their theories of meaning to that of the Confucianists. The major topics of deliberation are ontological chaos of Taoism, Taoist metaphysics, and Taoist concepts of ecstasy and the perfect man.

JAN YÜN-HUA. "Problems of Tao and <u>Tao Te Ching</u>," in <u>Numen</u>, 22 (1975): 208-234.
   Fung Yu-lan's various descriptions of Tao are critically examined, as are interpretations of Tao by Fung's critics. The question whether ancient Taoist philosophers were influenced by Yogic techniques is also discussed, with special reference to Bagchi, Needham, Liebenthal, Eliade, etc.

7.4 UNITY OF HEAVEN AND MAN

Readers interested in this topic are referred to 2.15 where this subject is discussed in full.

7.5 THE UNIVERSAL MIND (T'IEN-T'AI AND CH'AN SCHOOLS)

FUNG YU-LAN. A History of Chinese Philosophy. (See 7.2.1), Vol. 2, pp. 360-384.
    A very philosophical account of the T'ien-t'ai school's conception of reality in terms of the mind (one mind, universal mind), the Tathāgata-garbha, the Bhūtatathatā, etc.

HUI-HAI. The Zen Teaching of Hui Hai. Tr. by John Blofeld. New York: Samuel Weiser, 1972. 160 pp.
    A revised and refined translation of Hui-hai's (750-832) text by a British Buddhist monk quite familiar with Chinese Mahāyāna Buddhism and the Book of Changes. Along with the above work, this Ch'an text is very important for a clear understanding of the Ch'an approach to the problem of (the universal) mind in relation to emptiness, Nirvāna, prajñā (wisdom), etc.

HURVITZ, LEON. Chih-i (538-595): An Introduction to the Life and Ideas of a Chinese Buddhist Monk. Bruges: Imprimerie Sainte-Catherine, 1963. 372 pp. Cross reference: 1.11.5.

HSI-YÜN. The Zen Teaching of Huang Po on the Transmission of Mind. Tr. by John Blofeld. London: Rider, 1958. 136 pp. Reprinted in paperback in New York: Grove Press.
    One of the most important Ch'an texts on the universal mind, which is no-mind or the mind of non-abiding.

TAKAKUSU, J. The Essentials of Buddhist Philosophy. 3rd ed., Honolulu: Office Appliance Co., 1956. 221 pp.
    Chapter 11 deals with the T'ien-t'ai school of Chih-i, outlining the historical background as well as analyzing the major ideas of the most important philosopher of this school.

7.6 THUSNESS (T'IEN-T'AI AND HUA-YEN SCHOOLS)

CHANG, GARMA C.C. The Buddhist Teaching of Totality: The Philosophy of Hwa Yen Buddhism. University Park: Pennsylvania State University Press, 1971. 270 pp. Cross reference: 1.11.6.

FUNG YU-LAN. A History of Chinese Philosophy. (See 7.2.1), Vol. 2.
    Note in particular pp. 361-366, 369-370, 377, and 385-386 for the T'ien-t'ai school's conception of Thusness (Bhūtatathatā). See also 1.11.5 and 7.5.

TAKAKUSU, J. The Essentials of Buddhist Philosophy. (See 7.5).
   Note in particular pp. 38-40, 45-47, 52-53, 83-86, 91, 94, 98,
   110-118, 134-137, 156, 172, and 193.

7.7 HUA-YEN SCHOOL

   7.7.1 Four Realms of Dharmas

      Readers interested in this topic are referred to 1.11.6
   and 6.19 where this subject is discussed in full.

   7.7.2 Ten Metaphysical Propositions

   See also 1.11.6.

      CHAN, WING-TSIT. A Source Book in Chinese Philosophy. (See
      7.2.1), pp. 411-424.
         A translation of "mastering the ten mysteries" and the
      Hua-yen i-hai pai-men (hundred gates to the sea of ideas of
      the Flowery Splendor Scripture) with respect to the notion
      of the ten metaphysical propositions.

      CHANG, GARMA, C.C. The Buddhist Teaching of Totality: The
      Philosophy of Hwa Yen Buddhism. (See 7.6).
         Note in particular pp. 155-167 for "an elaboration of the
      ten mysteries." An excellent account.

      FUNG YU-LAN. A History of Chinese Philosophy. (See 7.2.1),
      Vol. 2, pp. 349-355.
         Discussion of "mastering the ten mysteries" in Fa-tsang's
      "Essay on the Golden Lion."

   7.7.3 Harmony of Facts and Principles

      Readers interested in this topic are referred to 6.19
   where this subject is discussed in full.

   7.7.4 Six Characteristics

   See also 1.11.6.

      CHANG, GARMA, C.C. The Buddhist Teaching of Totality: The
      Philosophy of Hwa Yen Buddhism. (See 7.6).
         Note in particular pp. 168-170 for a very good discussion
      on "the harmonious mergence of the Six Forms."

      FUNG YU-LAN. A History of Chinese Philosophy. (See 7.2.1),
      Vol. 2.

Note in particular p. 355 for a very short discussion of
"embracing the Six Qualities" in Fa-tsang's "Essay on the
Golden Lion."

7.8 CH'I (VITAL FORCE, MATERIAL FORCE) (CHANG TSAI)

See also 7.9.2.

FUNG YU-LAN. A History of Chinese Philosophy. (See 7.2.1), Vol. 2.
   Note in particular pp. 478-482 on Fung's discussion of Chang Tsai's
   concept of Ether (ch'i) in relation to "Great Void" (t'ai-hsü),
   "transforming force" (hua), "Great Harmony" (t'ai-ho), etc. See
   also 1.11.5.

T'ANG CHUN-I. "Chang Tsai's Theory of Mind and Its Metaphysical
   Basis," in Philosophy East and West, 6 (1956): 113-136. Cross
   reference: 1.13.5.

7.9 PRINCIPLE (LI)

7.9.1 Principle in General

See also 3.4, 3.9.2, as well as the related topics 2.12 and
6.9.2. Note the complexity of the meanings of Principle, as
in the cases of Tao and Heaven or Nature.

BERNARD, HENRI. "Chu Hsi's Philosophy and Its Interpretation
   by Leibnitz," in T'ien Hsia Monthly, 5 (1937): 9-18.
      In understanding Leibnitz's interpretation of Chu Hsi's li
   and equivalent to an anthropomorphic God, Bernard does not
   quite present Leibnitz's position correctly. What Leibnitz
   meant was that although Chu Hsi's li is abstract and not
   anthropomorphic, it can also be thought of as God as Matteo
   Ricci believed.

BRUCE, J. PERCY. "The Theistic Import of the Sung Philosophy,"
   in Journal of the North China Branch of the Royal Asiatic
   Society, 49 (1948): 111-127.
      Contends that Chu Hsi's basic doctrines of li and the
   Great Ultimate are essentially moral and not materialistic,
   that li as the source of all things is religious, and that
   it is moral because it embraces humanity and righteousness.
   T'ien is the Lord, to whom man must be responsible for his
   actions.

CHAN, WING-TSIT. "The Evolution of the Neo-Confucian Concept
   Li as Principle," in Tsing Hua Journal of Chinese Studies,

n.s., 4, no. 2 (1964): 123-129. Reprinted in Chan's Neo-
Confucianism, Etc. Essays by Wing-tsit Chan. Ed. by
Charles K.H. Chen. Hanover, N.H.: Oriental Society, 1969.
516 and 129 pp. Pp. 45-87.
   A comprehensive account and analysis of the cardinal
Chinese philosophical concept, its development in ancient
schools, its interpretation in Han times, Neo-Taoist and
Buddhist contributions to its evolution, its Neo-Confucian
elaboration, its culmination in Chu Hsi, and its influence
in subsequent centuries.

_____. A Source Book in Chinese Philosophy. (See 7.2.1).
   Note in particular pp. 5-6 (The Book of Odes), p. 9
(Doctrine of the Mean), p. 269 (Book of Changes), pp. 260-
261 (Han Fei Tzu), pp. 315-316, 318, 320-324 (Wang Ch'ung),
p. 326 (Kuo Hsiang), p. 351 (Seng-chao), p. 489 (Shao Yung),
p. 504, 508-514, 517 (Chang Tsai), sections 3, 8, 15, 16,
18, 20-24, 26, 33, 34, 37, 53, 60, 62, 64, 65, 67, 69, 70-
72, 75 (Ch'eng Hao), sections 2, 17, 18, 24, 31, 34, 47, 48,
58, 62, 66, 75-77 (Ch'eng I), sections 1-3, 8-9, 11-13, 15,
17-19, 21, 30, 33, 36, 40-42 (Lu Hsiang-shan), sections 100-
113 (Chu Hsi), sections 3, 6, 7, 32-34, 53, 94, 101, 133,
135, 228 (Wang Yang-ming), pp. 692-695, 697-701 (Wang Fu-
chih), p. 703, 707 (Yen Yüan), pp. 709-710 (Tai Chen),
p. 751, 754-759 (Fung Yu-lan), and p. 767 (Hsiung Shih-li).

CHU HSI. The Philosophy of Human Nature. Tr. by J.P. Bruce.
London: Probsthain, 1922. 444 pp.
   See pp. 24-37, 47-55, 79-94, 157-160, 194-211, and 229-
241 for material on li.

GOTO, TOSHIMIDZU. "The Ontology of the 'Li' Philosophy of the
Sung Dynasty of China," in Philosophical Studies of Japan,
2 (1960): 119-143.
   A systematic discussion of Neo-Confucian concepts like yin
yang, the Great Ultimate, the Mean, life impulse, etc., but
little of li itself.

GRAHAM, A.C. "The Place of Reason in the Chinese Philosophical
Tradition," in The Legacy of China. Ed. by Raymond Dawson.
Oxford: The Clarendon Press, 1964. Pp. 28-56.
   Largely a survey of ancient Chinese philosophy, the essay
also gives a three-page summary of Neo-Confucian ideas on
li. Not specifically concerned with rational principles or
the use of reason.

_____. Two Chinese Philosophers: Ch'eng Ming-tao and Ch'eng
Yi-ch'uan. London: Lund Humphries, 1958. 195 pp.

Note in particular pp. 8-21 for the author's extensive
analysis of Ch'eng I's conception of principle. The author
says, "The great innovation of the Ch'eng brothers is to
claim that 'the innumerable principles amount to one principle,' for which 'heaven,' the 'decree,' and the 'Way' are
merely different names, thus transforming a natural order
conceived after the analogy of human society into a rational
order" (p. 11).

NEEDHAM, JOSEPH. Science and Civilisation in China. Cambridge,
England: Cambridge University Press, 1954-1962. 4 vols.
Vol. 2, History of Scientific Thought (1956): 696 pp.
Pp. 472-485 and 557-570.
Needham's opinions on the concept of li and scientific
thought.

SUN, STANISLAUS, S.J. "The Doctrine of Li in the Philosophy
of Chu Hsi," in International Philosophical Quarterly, 6
(1966): 155-188.
A comprehensive and systematic presentation of li based on
a survey of Western sources and quotations from original
texts.

7.9.2   The Relations Between *Li* (Principle) and *Ch'i* (Material
Force)

See also 2.9, 7.8, 7.9.1.

CHAI, CH'U. "Neo-Confucianism of the Sung-Ming Periods," in
Social Research, 18 (1951): 370-392.
On the Neo-Confucian concepts of li, ch'i, mind, human
nature, etc. The presentation is simple but instructive.

CHAN, WING-TSIT. A Source Book in Chinese Philosophy. (See
7.2.1), chapter 42.
Note in particular Chan's introduction to and selected
translation of Fung Yu-lan's Hsin li-hsüeh (new rational
philosophy), in which Fung re-formulates the "dualistic"
metaphysics of li and ch'i in a new light.

FUNG YU-LAN. A History of Chinese Philosophy. (See 7.2.1),
Vol. 2, pp. 534-558.
Note in particular Fung's discussion of both li (or the
T'ai-chi) and ch'i in relation to cosmology as well as to
the nature in men and other creatures. Substantiated by
abundant quotations from the original texts in Chu Hsi.

GRAHAM, A.C. Two Chinese Philosophers: Ch'eng Ming-tao and
Ch'eng Yi-ch'uan. (See 7.9.1).
    Chapters 1 and 3 of Part 1 deal with Ch'eng I's notions of
li and ch'i respectively, but the ontological relation between them is clearly pointed out in their relation to change
and transformation, material things, and human nature.

MIYUKI, KOKUSAN. An Analysis of Buddhist Influences on the
Formation of the Sung Confucian Concept of Li-ch'i.
Claremont Graduate School and University Center thesis,
1963. 139 pp.
    Traces the influence of the Buddhist doctrine of Buddha-
nature on the Neo-Confucian theory of man's inner world of
consciousness and that of Buddhist wisdom and meditation on
Ch'eng I's and Chu Hsi's doctrines of investigation of
things and practice of seriousness (ch'eng). Rejects the
dualistic interpretation of Chu Hsi's ideas of li and ch'i,
since they are a continuum.

7.9.3 "Principle is One, but Manifestations are Many"

    Readers interested in this topic are referred to 3.4
where this subject is discussed in full.

7.9.4 The Identity of Nature and Principle

    Readers interested in this topic are referred to 7.9.1
where this subject is discussed in full.

7.9.5 The Identity of (Moral) Mind and Principle

    Readers interested in this topic are referred to 3.8 where
this subject is discussed in full.

7.10 SUBSTANCE AND FUNCTION

CHAN, WING-TSIT. A Source Book in Chinese Philosophy. (See 7.2.1).
    Note in particular pp. 141 and 159 (Lao Tzu), 267 (Book of
Changes), 323 (Neo-Taoism), 344, 358, 368-369, 401, 403-404, 414-
415, 433, 435 (Buddhism), 485-489, 502, 517, 535, 541, 570, 596-
597, and 696-697 (Neo-Confucianism), and 758, 765, 767-769, and
771 (contemporary philosophy). Substance and function are two
abstract terms employed to show the inseparable metaphysical relations between non-being and being, the nameless and the named,
wu-wei (non-action) and yu-wei (having action), li and ch'i,
reality and manifestations, One and Many, or between Tao (on the
one hand) and yin yang, Five Agents, and things (on the other).

See also the related references on such topics as "Principle is one but manifestations are many" (3.4) or "The relations between li and ch'i" (7.9.2).

GEDALECIA, DAVID. "Excursion Into Substance and Function: The Development of the T'i-yung Paradigm in Chu Hsi," in Philosophy East and West, 24 (1974): 443-452.
    Explains how Chu Hsi developed his doctrine of t'i (substance) and yung (function) in relation to T'ai-chi through four stages and how he finally overcame their dichotomy (which Wang Pi was unable to do). There is also a good brief discussion on Chu Hsi's theory of mind with respect to t'i-yung and his idea of ethical conduct and the sage.

7.11 ORIGINAL NOTHINGNESS (WANG PI)

Readers interested in this topic are referred to 1.10.7 where this subject is discussed in full. For further information, see also 1.4.2.

7.12 SINCERITY (*CH'ENG*) (THE *DOCTRINE OF THE MEAN*, NEO-CONFUCIAN METAPHYSICS)

Readers interested in this topic are referred to 2.4 where this subject is discussed in full.

7.13 DUALITY OF HUMAN NATURE (CH'ENG I AND CHU HSI)

Readers interested in this topic are referred to 2.9 where this subject is discussed in full. For further information, see also the related topics 2.10, 3.4, and 7.9.2.

7.14 *MING* (FATE, DESTINY, MANDATE OF HEAVEN)

Readers interested in this topic are referred to 2.3, 3.1.1, and 10.9 where this subject is discussed in full.

7.15 ONTOLOGIZATION OF *JEN* (HUMANITY)

Readers interested in this topic are referred to 3.7 where the ontologization of jen is finally completed in Chu Hsi's li-ch'i metaphysical system. For further information, see also 3.2 and 3.4.

7.16 REVERSION AND CAUSATION

7.16.1 Principle of Reversion (Lao Tzu)

FU, CHARLES WEI-HSUN. "Lao Tzu's Conception of Tao." (See 7.3).

Note in particular the author's philosophical analysis of
"Tao as Principle (of reversion)" in section 4, where he
argues that Tao as principle is the key dimension of Tao in
the Lao Tzu.

The Lao Tzu. (See 7.2.1).
   Note in particular chapters 2 ("Being and non-being produce
each other"), 23 and 25 ("To be far-reaching is to be returning"), 40 ("All things carry the yin and embrace the
yang"), 42 ("Reversing is the movement of Tao"), and 58 and
77 of the text of the Lao Tzu.

NEEDHAM, JOSEPH. Science and Civilisation in China. (See
   7.9.1), Vol. 2, History of Scientific Thought.
   Note in particular Needham's analysis of the principle of
reversion in "change, transformation and relativity"
(pp. 74-83) of chapter 10 on Taoism. He observes that "The
Tao Te Ching describes the cyclical changes in no uncertain
terms" (p. 75), although "On the whole the Taoists avoided
the elaboration of a cosmogony, wisely considering that the
original creative operation of the Tao must remain for ever
unknowable" (pp. 77-78). Needham's rediscovery of the scientific aspect of the principle of reversion is very insightful.

7.16.2 Causation

See also 7.18.1.

CUA, A.S. "Practical Causation and Confucian Ethics," in
   Philosophy East and West, 25 (1975): 1-10.
   Discussions center around the notions of influence and
response which form the background conceptions for the Confucian vision of central harmony. The moral requirements
are expressed in terms of ritual propriety and human-
heartedness.

FU, CHARLES WEI-HSUN. "Lao Tzu's Conception of Tao." (See
   7.3).
   Fu contends in the article that there are mainly two possible hermeneutic versions of Lao Tzu's cosmological thinking, and that, philosophically speaking, the ontological
interpretation is more acceptable than the cosmological
interpretation. See also the preceding topic, 7.16.1.

The Way of Lao Tzu. Tr. by Wing-tsit Chan. Indianapolis:
   Bobbs-Merrill, 1963.
   The most important chapters on Lao Tzu's cosmology in
terms of natural causation are 1, 4, 40, 42, and 52. In his

comment on the passage "Tao produced the One..." (chapter 42), Chan says that "the evolution here (as in the Book of Changes), is natural. Production (sheng) is not personal creation or purposeful origination, but natural causation" (p. 176).

WU, JOSEPH S. "Causality: Confucianism and Pragmatism," in Philosophy East and West, 25 (1975): 13–22.
    The main theme of this article is to compare the concepts of causality in the philosophy of John Dewey (1859–1952) with the concept of causality as presupposed in the Book of Changes. While the dominant factor in Western philosophy is the instinctive belief in necessity, that of the Book of Changes is the conviction of order. However, both conceive of causality as organic, situational, contextual, instrumental, and operational.

7.17 THEORY OF CYCLES AND TIME

See also 1.7, 11.3, 11.7.5.

CAIRNS, GRACE E. Philosophies of History: Meeting of East and West in Cycles-Pattern Theories of History. New York: Philosophical Library, 1962. 496 pp.
    Chapter 8, "Organismic Cyclical Patterns of History in Chinese Thought," pp. 159–195, conveniently summarizes the Yin Yang succession theory, Tung Chung-shu's theory of Three Stages of Progress, and Shao Yung's theory of Cycles of Worlds.

CHAN, WING-TSIT. A Source Book in Chinese Philosophy. (See 7.2.1).
    On the subject, note in particular pp. 245–247 (Yin Yang school), 263 and 265 (Book of Changes), 279–284 (Tung Chung-shu), sections 1, 10–13, 21, and 23 (Shao Yung's cosmology), and 641–642 (Chu Hsi).

NEEDHAM, JOSEPH. Science and Civilisation in China. (See 7.9.1), Vol. 2, History of Scientific Thought.
    Probably the most comprehensive and scholarly treatment of the subject, clarifying the scientific and pseudo-scientific aspects of the theory of cycles in Chinese thought. Note in particular pp. 75, 78, 239, 245, 253ff, 257, 265, 404, 420, 453, 456, 485–487, and 506 on the various approaches to the subject of the Taoists, Tsou Yen, Tung Chung-shu, Shao Yung, Chu Hsi, and others.

_____. Time and Eastern Man: The Henry Myers Lecture, 1964. London: Royal Anthropological Institute of Great Britain and Ireland, 1965. 52 pp.
    Maintains that to the Chinese, time is a continuum and not atomistic; that the Chinese have treated history as a continuity; that

their cyclical concept is minor and largely Taoistic; that they
have held a single track theory of dynastic legitimacy; that they
have regarded time as going upward; but that there has been the
element of compartmentalized time which has worked against the
development of natural science.

SIVIN, NATHAN. "Chinese Conceptions of Time," in The Earlham Journal,
1 (1966): 82-91.
A reassertion of common beliefs that time is always cyclical to
the Chinese and that they look to the past. No mention of well-
known Chinese theories of history, but at least helpful for some
understanding of the background regarding the present topic. Cf.
Needham's work on time, described above.

TONG, LIK KUEN. "The Concept of Time in Whitehead and the I Ching,"
in Journal of Chinese Philosophy, 1 (1974): 373-393.
Gives an interpretation of the Book of Changes solely in terms of
its dynamic meaning, which, Tong says, is only necessary because of
the nature of Whitehead's philosophy of Creativity. Note in particular the table showing the main points of affinity between the
Whiteheadean and the I Ching metaphysical systems.

7.18 YIN YANG AND FIVE AGENTS

    7.18.1 Idea of Origination (Tsou Yen)

        Readers interested in this topic are referred to 1.7.2
    where this subject is discussed in full. For further infor-
    mation, see also the preceding topic, 7.17, for related
    references.

    7.18.2 Yin and Yang

        Readers interested in this topic are referred to 2.16
    where this subject is discussed in full.

    7.18.3 Five Agents

See also 2.16.

IKEDA, SUETOSHI. "The Origin and Development of the Wu-hsing
(Five Elements) Idea: A Preliminary Essay," in Philosophy
East and West, 16 (1966): 297-309.
A historical study emphasizing the social and religious
conditions of the fourth and third centuries B.C.

7.19   THE BOOK OF CHANGES

7.19.1   *The Book of Changes* in General

The Book of Changes.   Tr. by John Blofeld.   New York: Dutton,
   1966.   228 pp.
   Translation, generally accurate, of the texts and explanations of the hexagrams (but not the general commentaries),
with an extensive introductory discussion on the use of the
book for divination.

FU, CHARLES WEI-HSUN.   "Lao Tzu's Conception of Tao."   (See
   7.3).
   One interesting point in the article is that the author
uses the three meanings of Change to illustrate the philosophical significance of Tao as principle (of reversion) in
the Lao Tzu.   See section 4 on the subject.

The I Ching or Book of Changes.   Tr. by Cary F. Baynes from
   the German version of Richard Wilhelm.   New York: Pantheon
   Books, 1950.   2 vols.   Vol. 1, 395 pp.   Vol. 2, 376 pp.
   Also available in one complete volume in New Jersey: Princeton University Press, 1967.   740 pp.
   A generally reliable and very readable translation with
extensive comments.   On the three meanings of Change, see
pp. 280-281.

RUMP, ARIANE.   Die Verwundung des Hellen als Aspekt des Bösen
   im I ching.   Dut-Druck AG, Cham, Switzerland, 1967.   141 pp.
   An analysis and study of each of the six lines of the
thirty-sixth hexagram of the Book of Changes, the ming-i or
the Darkening of the Light as an aspect of evil, with sup-
porting materials from the Chou-i che-chung (reconciliation
of interpretations of the Book of Changes) and other Chinese
commentaries.

The Text of Yi King.   Tr. by Z.D. Sung.   Shanghai: The China
   Modern Education Co., 1935.   369 pp.
   Actually an adaptation of Legge's translation (see below),
with the Chinese text.

TONG, PAUL K.K.   "A Cross-cultural Study of I-ching," in
   Journal of Chinese Philosophy, 3 (1975): 73-84.
   Polarism versus continuumism, I ching's conception of
motion and the cosmic continuum, the continuum of good and
evil, the continuum of a psychological event and its cosmic

horizon, the continuum of cosmic and moral forces, and continuum of the conscious and the subconscious, all with comparisons with Western ideas.

WILHELM, HELLMUT. The Book of Changes in the Western Tradition: A Selective Bibliography. Seattle, 1975. 29 pp.
(Parerga, 2.).
The bibliography lists translations and other Western
scholarly contributions to our understanding of the Book of
Changes and also some titles documenting the impact of the
book, during various periods, on the Western intellectual
climate.

_____. Change: Eight Lectures on the I Ching. Tr. from the
German by Cary F. Baynes. New York: Pantheon Books, 1960.
111 pp. Also in paperback, Harper. 111 pp.
The best study of the Classic, with clear elucidation of
the concept of change, its basic principles, and its meaning for Chinese history and society. Note in particular
chapter 2 on the concept of change, in which the three senses
of change, i.e., chien-i (the easy), pien-i (the changing),
and pu-i (the constant) are fully clarified.

_____. Heaven, Earth, and Man in the Book of Changes.
Seattle: University of Washington Press, 1977. 230 pp.
Seven lectures on the concept of time, the creative prin-
ciple, human events, the interplay of image and concept, etc.

The Yi King. Tr. by James Legge in The Sacred Books of the
East. Oxford: Clarendon Press, 1882. Vol. 16, 488 pp.
Also in paperback in New York: Dover.
This needs to be revised through consultation with many
commentaries, old and new.

7.19.2 Four Forms, Trigrams, Hexagrams, and Other Metaphysical
Symbols (*The Book of Changes*)

CHAN, WING-TSIT. A Source Book in Chinese Philosophy. (See
7.2.1).
Chapter 13 contains Chan's introductory essay on the philosophy of Change, with the selected translations of Hexagram No. 1 (Ch'ien, Heaven), Hexagram No. 2 (K'un, Earth),
the "Appended Remarks," and "Remarks on Certain Trigrams."
Note in particular the footnote (p. 262) on the various
metaphysical symbols of the I ching.

FUNG YU-LAN. <u>A History of Chinese Philosophy</u>. (<u>See</u> 7.2.1),
Vol. 1.
   Chapter 15 contains Fung's extensive and clear discussion
on the "Appendices of the <u>Book of Changes</u>" under the headings of (a) origin of the <u>Book of Changes</u> and of its "Appendices," (b) the eight trigrams and the Yin and Yang,
(c) development and change of phenomenal things, (d) the
endless cycle of phenomenal change, and (e) the hexagrams
and human affairs. With many quotations from the text
itself.

NEEDHAM, JOSEPH. <u>Science and Civilisation in China</u>. (<u>See</u>
7.9.1), Vol. 2, <u>History of Scientific Thought</u>.
   An excellent analysis of the system of the <u>Book of Changes</u>
under the headings of (a) from omen proverbs to abstract
concepts, (b) a universal concept-repository, (c) significance of the trigram and hexagram symbols in later Chinese
scientific thought, (d) the <u>Book of Changes</u> as the "administrative approach" to natural phenomena, its relation to
organized bureaucratic society and to the philosophy of
organism, and (e) Addendum on the <u>Book of Changes</u> and the
binary arithmetic of Leibnitz. Needham tried hard to point
out the scientific, the pseudo-scientific, as well as the
philosophical implications of the <u>Book of Changes</u>, which is
the most difficult of all the Chinese classics.

T'ANG YUNG-T'UNG. "Wang Pi's New Interpretation of the <u>I Ching</u>
and <u>Lun-yü</u>," tr. by Walter Liebenthal in <u>Harvard Journal of
Asiatic Studies</u>, 10 (1947): 124-161.
   Sheds new light on Wang Pi as a Neo-Taoistic interpretation of Confucian classics and thus a unique philosopher in
the history of Chinese philosophy.

WILHELM, HELLMUT. <u>Change: Eight Lectures on the I Ching</u>.
(<u>See</u> 7.19.1).
   An extensive elucidation of the basic metaphysical symbols,
such as hexagrams, trigrams, and the Four Forms is made
throughout the work by a German sinologist very well versed
in ancient Chinese classics, especially the <u>Book of Changes</u>.

_____. <u>Heaven, Earth, and Man in the Book of Changes</u>. (<u>See</u>
7.19.1), pp. 3-28.
   Maintains, with cogent arguments and solid support, that
time is here conceived as a unifying and cohesive factory
as well as change. With discussion on Leibnitz, Shao Yung,
etc.

7.20 UNIVERSAL CAUSATION BY THUSNESS (HUA-YEN SCHOOL)

See also 1.11.6.

TAKAKUSU, J. The Essentials of Buddhist Philosophy. (See 7.5),
    pp. 38-41 and 113-114.
        A very good, though short, analysis of the notion.

7.21 "THREE THOUSAND WORLDS IMMANENT IN A SINGLE INSTANT OF THOUGHT"
      (T'IEN-T'AI SCHOOL)

    Readers interested in this topic are referred to 1.10.5 where
this subject is discussed in full.

8. Philosophy of Language

GRAHAM, A.C. "'Being' in Western philosophy compared with shih/fei and yu-wu in Chinese philosophy," in Asia Major, n.s., 7, parts 1/2 (1959): 79-112.
   On the functions of "to be" in Chuang Tzu, the "Moist Canon," Wang Pi, Kuo Hsiang, Chang Tsai, etc., compared with its use in English.

HANSEN, CHAD D. "Ancient Chinese Theories of Language," in Journal of Chinese Philosophy, 2, no. 3 (1975): 245-283.
   Argues that there are four major presuppositions identified as part of the Chinese general theory of language, namely (a) emotivism, (b) distinction-making, (c) conventionalism, and (d) nominalism, and tries to show how these assumptions are related to each other and to the philosophic perspectives of the pre-Han masters.

8.1 RECTIFICATION OF NAMES

See also 3.21, 6.8.

LIU, SHU-HSIEN. "The Use of Analogy and Symbolism in Traditional Chinese Philosophy," in Journal of Chinese Philosophy, 1 (1974): 313-338.
   Liu contends that as a general trend the Chinese are moving away from an analogical way of thinking toward a symbolic way of thinking through metaphorical expressions.

8.2 THE RELATIONS BETWEEN NAME (LOGICAL CONCEPT) AND REALITY (REFERENCE)

See also 1.4.2, 1.5.

CHENG, CHUNG-YING. "A Generative Unity: Chinese Language and Chinese Philosophy," in The Tsing-hua Journal of Chinese Studies, n.s., 10, no. 1 (June, 1973): 90-105.
   According to Cheng, the formation of the Chinese language and construction of the Chinese characters and grammar indicate a genuine unity between the Chinese language and Chinese thought.

CHENG, CHUNG-YING. "Logic and Language in Chinese Thought," in
  Contemporary Philosophy: A Survey. Ed. by Raymond Klibansky. Paris:
  Institut International de Philosophie.
    Chiefly on the explicit formulation of Chinese logic in the Moist
  Canon and the Kung-sun Lung Tzu in which the laws of identity, non-
  contradiction, and excluded middle are recognized. Also discussions
  on recent interpretations of basic terms in these works. Only indirectly concerned with the present subject.

LIU, SHU-HSIEN. "The Use of Analogy and Symbolism in Traditional
  Chinese Philosophy." Cross reference: 8.1.

SENG-CHAO. "Nirvāna is Nameless," tr. by Chung-yuan Chang in Journal
  of Chinese Philosophy, 1 (1973-1974): 247-274.
    A translation of one of the four important essays of Buddhist
  philosophy which comprises Chao-lun (treatise of Seng-chao) with
  the translator's introduction.

UNO, SEIICHI. "Some Observations on Ancient Chinese Logic," in Philosophical Studies of Japan, 6 (1965): 31-42.
    General summary of logical doctrines in the School of Names, the
  Legalist, Taoist, and Confucian Schools, pointing out the weakness
  in logic because of chief interest in politics. Only indirectly
  concerned with the present subject.

8.3 LOGICAL PARADOX (THE LOGICIANS)

See also 1.5.2, 1.6, 8.2.

CHENG, CHUNG-YING. "On Zen (Ch'an) Language and Zen Paradox," in
  Journal of Chinese Philosophy, 1 (1973-1974): 77-102.
    A rigorous philosophical reconstruction of Ch'an paradox and lan-
  guage by using an analytic model.

_____. "Ontological Commitment and Ch'an Paradoxes," in Journal of
  Chinese Philosophy, 1 (1973): 1-27.
    A philosophical analysis of Ch'an language in relation to paradox
  and ontological commitment. A fresh attempt.

CHMIELEWSKI, JANUSZ. "Linguistic Structure and Two-Valued Logic:
  The Case of Chinese," in To Honor Roman Jakobson: Essays on the
  Occasion of His Seventieth Birthday. The Hague and Paris: Mouton,
  1967. Pp. 475-482.
    It is concluded from an examination of the use of double negation
  in archaic Chinese that the Chinese, at an early date, had arrived
  at a fairly sophisticated formulation of the principle of non-
  contradiction. See also 1.5.1.

HU SHIH. The Development of the Logical Method in Ancient China.
3rd ed. Shanghai: Oriental Book Co., 1928. 187 pp. Reprinted in
New York: Paragon.
Note in particular chapter 4 on the inductive logic of the Moist
School and chapter 5 on Hui Shih and Kung-sun Lung, both of which
are included in Book 3. Hu sheds some fresh light on the problem
of logical paradox tackled by the Moists, Kung-sun Lung, and especially Hui Shih.

LIU, SHU-HSIEN. "The Use of Analogy and Symbolism in Traditional
Chinese Philosophy." Cross reference: 8.1.

8.4 NON-ATTACHMENT TO LANGUAGE AND THOUGHT (TAOISM, BUDDHISM)

The Complete Works of Chuang Tzu. Tr. by Burton Watson. New York:
Columbia University Press, 1968. 397 pp.
Note in particular chapter 27 on "Imputed Words" and Chuang Tzu's
autobiographic note (p. 373) in chapter 33, in both of which is
presented Chuang Tzu's philosophy of language. Non-word in Chuang
Tzu, as well as in Lao Tzu, is paradoxically the best language on
the basis of the nameless Tao. As Chuang Tzu says, "...we must
have no-words! With words that use no-words, you may speak all
your life long and you will never have said anything. Or you may
go through your whole life without speaking them, in which case you
will never have stopped speaking" (p. 304). See also 6.13.

FUNG YU-LAN. A Short History of Chinese Philosophy. New York:
Macmillan, 1948. 368 pp.
It is extremely interesting and meaningful that chapter 22 on
Ch'an Buddhism has the sub-title "the philosophy of silence,"
which shows Fung's insight into the language of Ch'an in terms of
non-word.

HU SHIH. "Ch'an (Zen) Buddhism in China: Its History and Method,"
in Philosophy East and West, 3 (1953): 3-24.
Convincingly traces the development of Ch'an as an integral part
of the general history of Chinese thought that cannot be understood
through illogical or irrational thinking. Excellent on the Seven
Schools of Ch'an and on the development of the Ch'an method regarded
as a rational method of education. In particular, the author
points out the importance of pu-shuo-p'o, "never tell too plainly,"
in Ch'an training, for, as he explains, "it is the duty of the
teacher never to make things too easy for the novice; he must not
explain things in too plain language." Pu-shuo-p'o can actually
be regarded as part of Ch'anist philosophy of silence.

The Lao Tzu, tr. as The Way of Lao Tzu by Wing-tsit Chan.
Indianapolis: Bobbs-Merrill, 1963. Also tr. as The Way and Its
Power by Arthur Waley. London: Allen and Unwin, 1935. 262 pp.

(Also in Evergreen paperbacks, New York: Grove Press). Also tr.
as Tao Te Ching by Gia-fu Feng and Jane English. New York:
Alfred A. Knopf, 1972. 170 pp. Also tr. as The Wisdom of Laotse
by Lin Yu-tang. New York: The Modern Library, 1948. 326 pp.
Also tr. as Lao Tzu by John C.H. Wu. New York: St. John's University Press, 1961. 115 pp.
   Note in particular chapters 2, 5, 43, 56, 73, and 81 of the text.
Lao Tzu is undoubtedly the first Chinese philosopher to stress the
significance and importance of "practicing the teaching of non-
word." See also 6.12.

SUZUKI, DAISETZ TEITARO. Essays in Zen Buddhism. London: Luzac,
   1927. 423 pp. (First Series). Reprinted in New York: Grove Press,
   1961. 389 pp.
   See in particular Essay 4 on the history of Zen Buddhism from
Bodhidharma (fl. 460-534) to Hui-neng. Suzuki rightly observes
that these four lines describe how the principles of Zen distinguish
themselves from other schools of Buddhism: "A special transmission
outside the scriptures; no dependence upon words and letters; direct
pointing at the soul of man; seeing into one's nature and the
attainment of Buddhahood" (p. 176).

8.5 NON-WORD

See also 8.4.

TONG, LIK KUEN. "The Meaning of Philosophical Silence: Some Reflections on the Use of Language in Chinese Thought," in Journal of
   Chinese Philosophy, 3 (1976): 169-183.
   Concentrates on the linguistic dimension of the problem of the
intentional meaning of philosophical silence in Chinese thought,
in relation to the nature and function of language.

8.6 FORGETFULNESS OF WORDS (CHUANG TZU)

The Complete Works of Chuang Tzu. Tr. by Burton Watson. (See 8.4).
   Note in particular Chuang Tzu's characterization of the true man
of old in terms of the forgetfulness of words: "...bemused, he
forgot what he was going to say" (p. 79). Chuang Tzu's "forgetfulness of words" can be regarded as part of his philosophy of forgetfulness (of language, of things, of self, of heaven and man, etc.).
For his unique idea of forgetfulness in general, see in particular
pp. 79-80, 90-91, 155, 197, 200, 205-207, 219, 220, 224, 234, 236,
and 302. See also 8.4.

8.7 IMPORTANCE OF FIGURATIVE EXPRESSIONS IN THE METAPHYSICS OF TAO,
     SUCH AS PARADOX, PARABLES, METAPHORS, REPEATED OR WEIGHTY WORDS,
     ETC.

See also 8.4, 8.6.

The Complete Works of Chuang Tzu. Tr. by Burton Watson. (See 8.4).
   Note in particular chapter 27 on "Imputed Words" and chapter 2 on
"Equality of All Things and Opinions" for the most important source
on the subject.

LIU, SHU-HSIEN. "The Use of Analogy and Symbolism in Traditional
   Chinese Philosophy." Cross reference: 8.1.

SUZUKI, DAISETZ TEITARO. Essays in Zen Buddhism. (See 8.4).
   Note in particular Essay 6 on "Practical Methods of Zen Instruction," where Suzuki stresses paradox, denial of opposites, contradiction, affirmation, repetition, and exclamation as the verbal
methods used by Zen masters to train the minds of their disciples
(pp. 268-298).

8.8 PHILOSOPHICAL SIGNIFICANCE OF *KUNG-AN* (*KŌAN*, ENIGMATIC STATE-
     MENTS OR QUESTIONS)

See also 8.4, 8.7.

CHANG, CHUNG-YUAN. Original Teachings of Ch'an Buddhism. New York:
   Pantheon Books, 1969. 333 pp.
   Another collection of the primary sources of kōan selected and
translated from the Records of the Transmission of the Lamp.
Chang's own notes are too brief and unclear, not comparable to
those in Luk, Ch'an and Zen Teaching (see below).

CHENG, CHUNG-YING. "On Zen (Ch'an) Language and Zen Paradox." Cross
   reference: 8.3.

HU SHIH. "Ch'an (Zen) Buddhism in China: Its History and Method."
   (See 8.4).
   Contains a very good account of Zen methods in terms of travel-
ing, kōan, etc.

LUK, CHARLES. Ch'an and Zen Teaching. London: Rider & Co., 1960.
   254 pp. (Second series). Reprinted in paperback in Berkeley:
Shambala Publications, 1971.
   A very good collection of many important kōans in the five Ch'an
sects after Hui-neng, the real founder of the School of Sudden
Awakening. Detailed and extremely helpful notes by the translator.

MIURA, ISSHU, and RUTH FULLER SASAKI. The Zen Kōan: Its History and Use in Rinzai Zen. New York: Harcourt, Brace & World, 1965. 156 pp.

Another important work on kōan Zen by the two famous teachers of Lin-chi (Rinzai School) Zen. Part 1 deals with the history of the kōan in Lin-chi Zen, and part 2 makes an extensive and concrete study of kōan in Lin-chi Zen under the headings of (a) the four vows, (b) seeing into one's own nature, (c) the Hosshin (Dharmakāya, Law Body) and (interlocking of differentiation) kōans, (d) the gon-sen (investigation of words) kōans, (e) the nanto (difficult to pass through) kōans, (f) the goi (five ranks) kōans, and (g) the commandments.

ROSEMONT, HENRY. "The Meaning is the Use: Kōan and Mondō as Linguistic Tools of the Zen Masters," in Philosophy East and West, 20, no. 2 (April, 1970): 110–119.

An interesting philosophical analysis of the meaning of kōan and mondō (questions and answers) in terms of the use, by relating Zen language to the ordinary language analysis of Wittgenstein and Austin.

SUZUKI, DAISETZ TEITARO. Essays in Zen Buddhism. (See 8.4).

Note in particular Essay 1 on the kōan exercise in two parts, under the various headings of (e.g.) an experience beyond knowledge, psychological antecedents of satori (awakening) prior to the kōan system, technique of Zen discipline in its early history, the growth of kōan system and its signification, practical instructions regarding the kōan exercise, the kōan exercise and the and the nembutsu (recitation of the Buddha's name), etc. The pioneer work on kōan in the English language.

_____. "Zen: A Reply to Hu Shih," in Philosophy East and West, 3 (1953): 25–46. Reprinted in Studies in Zen. New York: Dell. Pp. 129–164.

Note in particular Suzuki's unique discussion of kōan, shock therapy, etc., from the Lin-chi (Rinzai) school point of view.

8.9   THE MORAL FUNCTIONING OF LANGUAGE IN CONFUCIAN PHILOSOPHY AND LITERATURE

The Analects of Confucius. Tr. by Arthur Waley. London: Allen and Unwin, 1938. 268 pp. Also tr. by James Legge in The Chinese Classics. Oxford: Clarendon Press, 1893. Vol. 1, Confucian Analects, pp. 137–354.

Note in particular Confucius' own words on ceremonies and music, education and learning, knowledge and wisdom, literature and art, rectification of names, as well as on words and acts (see the classification and location of these subjects in Chan, Wing-tsit,

tr. and comp., A Source Book in Chinese Philosophy. New Jersey:
Princeton University Press, 1963. 856 pp. P. 18). It can be truly
said that Confucius was the first Chinese thinker to emphasize the
moral functioning of language in both philosophy and literature.

CUA, A.S. "Use of Dialogues and Moral Understanding," in Journal of
Chinese Philosophy, 2 (1975): 131-147.
  A general characterization of Confucian, Socratic, and Ch'an
dialogues and their philosophical and practical significance. The
Confucian dialogue surrounds the concepts of jen, filial piety,
ritual propriety, and the superior man and focuses on particular
situations whereas the Socratic dialogue is on the universal character of moral notions and Ch'an aims at transcending any recog-
nizable sort of knowledge. The Ch'an dialogue is paradoxical rather
than persuasive or discursive. The three different dialogues imply
three different dimensions of moral life.

de BARY, WM. THEODORE, WING-TSIT CHAN and BURTON WATSON. comps.
Sources of Chinese Tradition. New York: Columbia University Press,
1960. 976 pp.
  Note in particular pp. 371-382 on Han Yü in chapter 15, with the
translation of some important essays showing Han's "ancient-prose"
style as opposed to the elaborate parallel-prose of his day.

9. Logic

CHANG, TUNG-SUN. "A Chinese Philosopher's Theory of Knowledge," in
Etc.: A Review of General Semantics, 9 (1952): 203-226. Reprinted
in Our Language and Our World, Selections from Etc.: A Review of
General Semantics. Ed. by S.I. Hayakawa. New York: Harper, 1959.
Pp. 299-323.
   Illustrating with Chinese sentences and concepts, a leading
Chinese epistemologist and logician shows that his own theory of
knowledge brings out the difference between Western logic (which is
basically identity-logic) and Chinese logic (which is essentially
correlation-logic).

CHENG, CHUNG-YING. "Classical Chinese Logic: A Preliminary Description," in Philosophy East and West, 15, nos. 3-4 (1965): 195-216.
   A preliminary attempt at philosophical reconstruction and characterization of classical Chinese logic.

_____. "On Implications (tse) and Inference (ku) in Chinese Grammar
and Chinese Logic," in Journal of Chinese Philosophy, 2 (1975):
225-243.
   Tse and ku as homophonic types of heterogeneous tokens, logical
and grammatical functions of tse and ku, logical-grammatical distinction between tse and ku, logical relation between tse and ku,
and interpretation of Neo-Mohist logic: shuo (explanation or argument) and hsiao (following or imitation).

CHMIELEWSKI, JANUSZ. "Linguistic Structure and Two-Valued Logic:
The Case of Chinese," in To Honor Roman Jakobson: Essays on the
Occasion of His Seventieth Birthday. The Hague: Mouton, 1967.
Pp. 474-482.
   Having observed that the linguistic structure of Chinese has a
strong tendency toward two-valued logic, the author maintains that
at an early date the Chinese arrived at a fairly sophisticated
formulation of the principle of non-contradiction and that the
dialectical procedure of the Moists was based on the laws of non-
contradiction and of the excluded middle.

CHMIELEWSKI, JANUSZ. "Notes on Early Chinese Logic," in <u>Recznik</u>
  <u>Orientaistyozny</u>, 26, no. 1 (1962): 7-21, no. 2 (1963): 91-105, 27,
  no. 1 (1963): 103-121, no. 2 (1965): 87-111, 29, no. 2 (1965): 117-
  138, 30, no. 1 (1966): 31-52, 31, no. 1 (1968): 117-136, and 32,
  no. 2 (1969): 83-103.
      The purpose of the series is to single out typical forms of reason-
  ing in early Chinese philosophy, to define them in terms of elementary symbolic logic, and to find out general logical laws and notions
  underlying them. Using the <u>Kung-sun Lung Tzu</u> and the <u>Mo Tzu</u> as the
  basis, problems of the horse and whiteness, <u>hsiao</u>, and <u>chih</u> are
  discussed for the investigation of the principles of double negation,
  law of contradiction, problems of "similarity and difference," etc.

LAU, D.C. "Some Logical Problems in Ancient China," in <u>Proceedings</u>
  <u>of the Aristotelian Society</u>, n.s., 53 (1953): 189-204.
      A study of the methods of analogy, parallel, precedent, and ex-
  tension used in chapter 45 ("<u>Hsiao-ch'ü</u>") of the <u>Mo Tzu</u>, and the
  limitation the Chinese language puts on the use of those methods.

LIU, SHU-HSIEN. "The Use of Analogy and Syllogism in Traditional
  Chinese Philosophy," in <u>Journal of Chinese Philosophy</u>, 1 (1973-
  1974): 313-338.
      By investigating the logic of Hsün Tzu, the Neo-Moists, the <u>Book</u>
  <u>of Changes</u>, and Chuang Tzu, the author draws the general conclusion
  that the progress of Chinese thought seems to have moved from an
  analogical way of thinking towards a symbolic way of thinking and
  that analogies are employed as a means to learn or as expressions
  to facilitate the understanding of the Way and not to be regarded
  as a form of inference. Some comparison with Western Logical
  Positivism and Aquinas is made.

SCHWARTZ, BENJAMIN I. "On the Absence of Reductionism in Chinese
  Thought," in <u>Journal of Chinese Philosophy</u>, 1 (1973): 27-44.
      The argument here is that there has been very little reductionism,
  that is, reducing the cosmic manifold to the minimal. The ancient
  Hundred Schools offer little or no evidence of any reductionist
  impulse. Han Dynasty thought accepts a world of variety and plen-
  titude. The concepts of Tao, <u>T'ien</u> and <u>ch'i</u> can almost never be
  interpreted in a reductionist sense.

9.1 RECTIFICATION OF NAMES

Readers interested in this topic are referred to 3.21 and 6.8
where this subject is discussed in full.

9.2 THE RELATIONS BETWEEN NAME (LOGICAL CONCEPT) AND REALITY

See also 8.2.

SENG-CHAO. "Nirvana is Nameless," tr. by Chung-yuan Chang in Journal
    of Chinese Philosophy, 1 (1973-1974): 247-274.
    A fresh translation of one of the four important essays of
    Buddhist philosophy which comprises Chao-lun, with the translator's
    introduction.

9.3 LOGICAL PARADOX (HUI SHIH AND OTHER DEBATERS)

See also 8.3.

CHENG, CHUNG-YING. "On Zen (Ch'an) Language and Zen Paradox," in
    Journal of Chinese Philosophy, 1 (1973-1974): 77-102. Cross
    reference: 8.3.

9.4 DISCUSSIONS ON SOLIDITY, WHITENESS, ETC. (KUNG-SUN LUNG)

See also 1.6.2, 8.2.

CHAN, WING-TSIT, tr. and comp. A Source Book in Chinese Philosophy.
    New Jersey: Princeton University Press, 1963. 856 pp.
    See pp. 235-243 for translations of "On the White Horse," "On
    Marks (chih) and Things," "On the Explanation of Change," "On
    Hardness and Whiteness," and "On Names and Actuality" of the Kung-
    sun Lung Tzu.

HU SHIH. The Development of the Logical Method in Ancient China.
    3rd ed. Shanghai: Oriental Book Co., 1928. 187 pp. Reprinted in
    New York: Paragon.
    On the subject, note in particular pp. 118-130, where Hu Shih
    deals with the paradox of Kung-sun Lung and others.

9.5 THE "THREE STANDARDS" OF BASIS, EXAMINATION, AND APPLICATION
     (MOISM)

    Readers interested in this topic are referred to 6.14 where this
subject is discussed in full.

9.6 "SEVEN METHODS OF ARGUMENTATION" (MOISM)

    Readers interested in this topic are referred to 6.15 where this
subject is discussed in full.

9.7 TWO LEVELS OF TRUTH (CHI-TSANG)

Readers interested in this topic are referred to 6.17 where this subject is discussed in full.

9.8 "REFUTATION OF FALSE VIEWS IS ITSELF REVELATION OF CORRECT VIEW" (CHI-TSANG)

Readers interested in this topic are referred to 6.23 where this subject is discussed in full.

10. Social and Political Philosophy

10.1 <u>HUMAN RELATIONS AND UTOPIA</u>

CHING, JULIA. "Neo-Confucian Utopian Theories and Political Ethics,"
in <u>Monumenta Serica</u>, 30 (1972-1973): 1-56.
   A comprehensive survey of the Neo-Confucian political theories
in the Sung and Ming periods against the background of utopian
theories in ancient Taoism and Han Dynasty thought. The first part
deals with the political thought of Wang An-shih, Chang Tsai, Ch'eng
Hao, Ch'eng I, Li Kou (1009-1050), Hu Hung (1100-1155), Shao Yung,
Chu Hsi, Lu Hsiang-shan, and in particular, Wang Yang-ming. The
second part is on Neo-Confucian ideas on political ethics, particularly on the concepts of <u>jen</u> and loyalty.

HSU DAU-LIN. "The Myth of the 'Five Human Relations' of Confucius,"
in <u>Monumenta Serica</u>, 29 (1970-1971): 27-37.
   With extensive textual support and historical evidence, it is
convincingly shown that Confucius never taught the Five Human Relations. Neither the Five Relations nor the Three Bonds of the Han
period had currency during the four centuries following the Han.
It was during the Sung that the concept of the Five Relations came
vigorously into being through the efforts of Neo-Confucian
philosophers.

ROSEMONT, HENRY. "State and Society in the <u>Hsün Tzu</u>: A Philosophical
Commentary," in <u>Monumenta Serica</u>, 29 (1970-1971): 38-78. Cross
reference: 1.3.3.

10.2 <u>RECTIFICATION OF NAMES</u>

   Readers interested in this topic are referred to 3.21 and 6.8
where this subject is discussed in full.

10.3 <u>ETHICO-SOCIAL NORMS (<u>LI</u> [CEREMONIES] IN HSÜN TZU)</u>

<u>See also</u> 3.3, 1.3.3.

DUBS, HOMER H. <u>Hsüntze, The Moulder of Ancient Confucianism</u>.   London:
Probsthain, 1927.   308 pp.   Reprinted in New York: Paragon.

On the present subject note in particular the author's detailed analysis of the basis of ethics (chapter 7) as well as of li and jen, or the rules of proper conduct and benevolence (chapter 8).

Hsün Tzu: Basic Writings. Tr. by Burton Watson. New York: Columbia University Press. 177 pp. Also in combined edition of Basic Writings of Mo Tzu, Hsün Tzu, and Han Fei Tzu, 1967.
   For this subject, note especially chapter 6 ("A Discussion of Rites"), chapter 7 ("A Discussion of Music"), and chapter 9 ("Rectifying Names").

The Works of Hsüntze. Tr. by Homer H. Dubs. London: Probsthain, 1928. 336 pp. Reprinted in Taipei: Chinese Materials and Research Aids Service Center.
   On the present subject, note in particular Book 19, "On the Rules of Proper Conduct."

10.4 MODELING AFTER THE LATTER-DAY KINGS

FUNG YU-LAN. A History of Chinese Philosophy. Tr. by Derk Bodde. Princeton, New Jersey: Princeton University Press, 1952-1953. 2 vols. Vol. 1, 455 pp. Vol. 2, 783 pp.
   Note in particular for this subject Vol. 1, chapter 12, section 3 (pp. 282-284) for Hsün Tzu's attitude toward the Chou institutions. Short but clear.

Hsün Tzu: Basic Writings. Tr. by Burton Watson. (See 10.3).
   Note in particular chapter 3 ("The Regulations of a King").

The Works of Hsüntze. Tr. by Homer H. Dubs. (See 10.3).
   On the present subject, note in particular Book 5 ("Against Physiognomy") and Book 9 ("Kingly Government").

10.5 "RENOVATING THE PEOPLE" AND "ABIDING IN THE SUPREME GOOD"
       (*THE GREAT LEARNING*)

See also 1.3.4, 3.17.

CHAN, WING-TSIT, tr. and comp. A Source Book in Chinese Philosophy. New Jersey: Princeton University Press, 1963. 856 pp. Pp. 659-667.
   These pages deal with Wang Yang-ming's "Inquiry on the Great Learning" (translated here by Chan) and Wang Yang-ming's differences with Chu Hsi's interpretation.

"The Great Learning," in A Source Book in Chinese Philosophy. Tr. by Wing-tsit Chan. (See above). Also in The Great Learning and The Mean in Action. Tr. by E.R. Hughes. New York: Dutton, 1943. 176 pp.

"Renovating the People" and "Abiding in the Supreme Good" con-
stitute the second and the third items of the Three Items in the
text of the Great Learning.

10.6 "GOVERNING THE STATE" AND "ATTAINING THE WORLD PEACE" (*THE GREAT LEARNING*)

See also all related references under 1.3.4, 3.17.

CHAN, WING-TSIT. A Source Book in Chinese Philosophy. (See 10.5).
   Note Wang's thesis concerning the nature of the Eight Steps that
"while the order of the tasks involves a sequence of first and last,
in substance they are one and cannot be so separated. At the same
time, while the order and the tasks cannot be separated into first
and last, their function must be so refined as not to be wanting in
the slightest degree" (p. 666). See also 10.5 in particular, and
see 6.10 for a clear understanding of the issue involved between
Wang Yang-ming and Chu Hsi.

The Great Learning. (See 10.5).
   "Governing the state" and "attaining the world peace" are the
last two items of the Eight Items mentioned in the text of the
Great Learning.

10.7 THE RELATIONS BETWEEN ETHICS AND POLITICO-SOCIAL PHILOSOPHY

See also 3.16, 3.17, 3.23.

CHANG, Y.C. "Wang Shou-jen as a Statesman," in Chinese Social and
   Political Science Review, 23 (1939-1940): 30-99, 155-252, 319-375,
   and 473-517.
   A long biography, detailed and objective discussions on Wang
Yang-ming's politics in thought and action, and accurate translations of several political documents. The political career and
deeds of Wang Yang-ming exemplify the Confucian ethico-social
practice in terms of the natural extension and application of Confucian ethical teachings to politico-social philosophy.

de BARY, WM. THEODORE. "Chinese Despotism and the Confucian Ideal:
   A Seventeenth-Century View," in Chinese Thought and Institutions.
   Ed. by John K. Fairbank. Chicago: University of Chicago Press,
   1957. Pp. 163-203.
   A careful examination of Huang Tsung-hsi's political ideas involving the Confucian ideal of the non-separation of ethics and
political philosophy.

de BARY, WM. THEODORE. "Individualism and Humanitarianism in Late
Ming Thought," in Self and Society in Ming Thought. Ed. by de Bary.
New York: Columbia University Press, 1969. 775 pp.
  Focusing on the self and the individual, the essay critically
examines the rise of individualism and humanitarianism, centering
on the concepts of sagehood and active involvement in life. Emphasis is laid on Wang Ken and his doctrines of self-fulfillment, self-
expression, and direct response to life, on Li Chih's radical
individualism, and on their social and historical significance.

FANG, THOMÉ. The Chinese View of Life: The Philosophy of Comprehensive Harmony. Hong Kong: The Union Press, 1957. 274 pp.
  On the present subject, note in particular Fang's description of
Chinese moral ideas (chapter 5) as well as of Chinese political
thought (chapter 7), under the various headings of (a) ideal
politics versus "reale Politik," (b) politics and morality fused
into one spirit in the system of Confucius, (c) government by virtue
and government by cultural refinement, (d) the gap between actuality
and ideality is bridged over by political life, etc.

HSU, L.S. The Political Philosophy of Confucianism: An Interpretation of the Social and Political Ideas of Confucius, His Forerunners, and His Early Disciples. London: George Routledge & Sons,
1932. 258 pp.
  A comprehensive and readable account of the political thought of
Confucianism as a natural extension of Confucian ethics. Note in
particular chapter 6 in which the author discusses the principle of
benevolent government under the headings of (a) the five principles
of benevolent government, (b) the four evils of bad government,
(c) the rule of virtue, (d) the rule of love, (e) utilitarianism,
nationalism and imperialism, and (f) rules of public administration.

MA, HERBERT. "Law and Morality: Some Reflections on the Chinese
Experience Past and Present," in Philosophy East and West, 21,
(1971): 443-460.
  Ma's article attempts to show (a) how law became dominated by
Confucian ethics in traditional China, (b) what influence this
relationship exerted on Chinese law during and after its Western-
ization, and (c) what legal philosophy can do in reconciling traditional Chinese morals and the modern Westernized Chinese law and
legal system.

WU, JOHN C. "Chinese Legal and Political Philosophy," in Philosophy
and Culture--East and West. Ed. by Charles A. Moore. Honolulu:
University of Hawaii Press, 1962. Pp. 611-630. Reprinted in The
Chinese Mind. Ed. by Moore. Honolulu: East-West Center Press,
1967. Pp. 213-237.

On the foundation of political authority according to Lao Tzu
and Confucius, the Chinese legal system as a system of duties rather
than rights, based on morals and aiming at social harmony.

10.8 BENEVOLENT GOVERNMENT VERSUS GOVERNMENT BY LAW OR FORCE

See also 3.23 and all related references under 3.16, 3.17, 10.4, 10.5,
10.6.

CHEN, EN-CHENG. "Han Fei's Principle of Government by Law," in
  Chinese Culture, 1, no. 4 (1958): 91-103.
    A quite clear and general discussion of the subject.

10.9 THE IDENTITY OF THE MANDATE OF HEAVEN AND THE PEOPLE'S WILL
         (MENCIUS)

See also 1.3.2, 3.1.1.

CHAN, WING-TSIT. A Source Book in Chinese Philosophy. (See 10.5).
    See 1B: 7, 8; 4A: 9; 4B: 3; 5A: 5; and 7B: 14 of the Book of
  Mencius in chapter 3. Note in particular Mencius' words, such as
  "It was Heaven that gave the empire to him (Shun, the legendary
  ancient emperor-sage). It was the people that gave the empire to
  him" (5A: 5) or "(In the state) the people are the most important...
  the ruler is of slight importance" (7B: 14).

CREEL, HERRLEE G. "The Mandate of Heaven," in his The Origin of
  Statecraft in China. Chicago: The University of Chicago Press,
  1970. Vol. 1, The Western Chou Empire, pp. 81-100.
    How the doctrine developed as a result of historical conditions,
  how it is set forth in ancient documents, and how it was concerned
  with the two extremes of the king and the common people. A historical discussion rather than a philosophical one.

FUNG YU-LAN. A History of Chinese Philosophy. (See 10.4), Vol. 1.
    Note in particular pp. 111-117 where Fung discusses Mencius'
  political ideal and moral justification of revolution in terms of
  the identification of the Mandate of Heaven and the people's will.

WU, JOSEPH. "Philosophy and Revolution: Confucianism and Pragmatism,"
  in Philosophy East and West, 23 (1973): 323-332.
    An interesting comparison of the hexagram ke in the Book of
  Changes and John Dewey's pragmatism.

10.10 THE CONCEPT OF REVOLUTION

See also 10.8.

de BARY, WM. THEODORE. "Chinese Despotism and the Confucian Ideal: A
Seventeenth-Century View." (See 10.7).
   A careful examination of Huang Tsung-hsi's political ideas includ-
ing his idea of political revolution.

FAN, KUANG-HUAN, ed. Mao Tse-tung and Lin Piao: Post-Revolutionary
Writings. New York: Doubleday & Co., 1972. 536 pp.
   A good collection of the major writings of Mao and Lin Piao
(1908-1971) on revolution, with special emphasis on the Great
Proletarian Cultural Revolution.

MAO TSE-TUNG. Selected Works. Peking: Foreign Language Press, 1961.
4 vols. (The Fifth Volume was published posthumously in 1977).
   Maoist theory of revolution is probably the most important in the
history of political philosophy in China since Mencius. Note in
particular his writings such as "Problems of Strategy in China's
Revolutionary War," "On Practice," "The Chinese Revolution and the
Chinese Communist Party," and "On People's Democratic Dictatorship."

REJAI, MOSTAFA, ed. Mao Tse-tung on Revolution and War. New York:
Doubleday & Co., 1969. 452 pp.
   Readings from Mao Tse-tung's works on revolution and war, well
selected and rearranged under the headings of (a) imperialism,
revolution, and war, (b) stages of revolutionary development,
(c) dynamics of revolution: united front, (d) dynamics of revolution: the army, (e) dynamics of revolution: the Communist Party,
and (f) the global strategy. With good introductory notes in each
chapter.

10.11   JUSTIFICATION OF SPECIFIC GOVERNMENTAL MEASURES, SUCH AS THE
"WELL-FIELD SYSTEM," CONFUCIAN EDUCATIONAL SYSTEM, ETC.

CHAN, WING-TSIT. A Source Book of Chinese Philosophy. (See 10.5).
   Note in particular the Great Learning in chapter 4 and 1A: 7;
2A: 5; 3A: 3; and 3A: 4 of the Book of Mencius in chapter 3 with
respect to the early Confucian governmental measures and their
justification.

CHU HSI, in collaboration with Lü Tsu-ch'ien. Reflections on Things
at Hand: The Neo-Confucian Anthology. Tr. by Wing-tsit Chan. New
York: Columbia University Press, 1967. 441 pp.
   The most important and comprehensive primary source on Neo-
Confucian thought. Note in particular chapter 8 on the principles
of governing the state and bringing peace to the world, chapter 9
on systems and institutions, and chapter 10 on methods of handling
affairs. In these three chapters are found Sung Neo-Confucian
ideas of governmental measures and their justification.

FUNG YU-LAN. A History of Chinese Philosophy. (See 10.4), Vol. 1.
    Note in particular section 3 of chapter 6 on Mencius' ideal
political and economic measures, and section 7 of chapter 14 on the
Great Learning.

LEVENSON, JOSEPH R. "Ill Wind in the Well-Field: The Erosion of the
    Confucian Ground of Controversy," in The Confucian Persuasion. Ed.
    by A. Wright. Stanford: Stanford University Press, 1960.
    Pp. 268-287.
    An interesting discussion of the "ill wind in the well-field" in
modern China, under the headings of (a) ching-t'ien (well-field)
and Confucian reformism, (b) the socialism-ching-t'ien cliche,
(c) paradise lost and regained, (d) sentimental radicalism, (e) the
contemporaneity of Hu Shih, Hu Han-min (1879-1936), and Liao
Chung-k'ai (1876-1925), (f) the changing style of conservatism, and
(g) Confucian sound in a Marxist sense.

WANG YANG-MING. Instructions for Practical Living and Other Neo-
    Confucian Writings by Wang Yang-ming. Tr. by Wing-tsit Chan. New
    York: Columbia University Press, 1963. 358 pp.
    Note in particular Wang's writings on social and political mea-
sures on pp. 283-309.

10.12   THE WORLD OF GREAT HARMONY (*THE BOOK OF RITES*)

CHAI, CH'U and WINBERG CHAI, eds. The Humanist Way in Ancient China:
    Essential Works of Confucianism. New York: Bantam Books, 1965.
    373 pp.
    The Analects, the Book of Mencius, the Great Learning, and the
Doctrine of the Mean rearranged topically and completely translated,
plus selections from the Hsün Tzu, the Book of Rites and Tung
Chung-shu. Also the Classic of Filial Piety in its entirety. Helpful introductions but no notes. For the idea of the world of great
harmony in the Book of Rites, see pp. 338-339.

FUNG YU-LAN. A History of Chinese Philosophy. (See 10.4), Vol. 1.
    Note in particular section 9 of chapter 14 on "The Evolution of
Li" (Li-yün) in the Book of Rites. In this essay, Li-yün, the
Confucian political goal in terms of the "Period of Great Unity"
and the "Period of Small Tranquility," is mentioned for the first
time.

Li chi. "The Li Ki," in The Sacred Books of the East. Tr. by James
    Legge. Oxford: The Clarendon Press, 1885. Vol. 27, 480 pp.
    Vol. 28, 491 pp. Also edited by Ch'u Chai and Winberg Chai. New
    Hyde Park, New York: University Books, 1967. Chapters 8-9, 20-22,
    and 30-32.
    For the idea of the world of great harmony, see this source, the
Book of Rites, Vol. 27, p. 364.

10.12.1 Philosophy of Great Harmony (K'ang Yu-wei)

See also 1.17.1.

CHAN, WING-TSIT. A Source Book in Chinese Philosophy. (See
    10.5).
    Note in particular pp. 730-734 for a clear understanding
    of K'ang's discussion on the "Age of Great Unity."

CHANG, CARSUN. The Development of Neo-Confucian Thought.
    New York: Bookman Associates, Inc., 1962. Vol. 2, 521 pp.
    Note in particular Chang's detailed analysis of K'ang's
    philosophy of great harmony on pp. 412-422 as a result of
    the new impact of the West on modern China. See also 1.13.1.

FUNG YU-LAN. A History of Chinese Philosophy. (See 10.4),
    Vol. 2, pp. 684-691.
    A detailed and good account of K'ang's idea of great har-
    mony in the Ta-t'ung shu (book of the great unity).

K'ANG YU-WEI. Ta T'ung Shu, The One-World Philosophy of K'ang
    Yu-wei. Tr. by Laurence G. Thompson. London: Allen &
    Unwin, 1958. 300 pp.
    An elaborate and most radical document, with a specific
    program, on an ideal society in which all distinctions of
    race, sex, etc. will be eliminated. The translation is
    abridged to some extent and contains too many brackets to
    facilitate reading. The most important primary source on
    K'ang's political philosophy of great harmony.

LO, JUNG-PANG. "K'ang Yu-wei and His Philosophy of Political
    Change and Historical Progress," in Symposium on Chinese
    Studies. Department of Chinese, University of Hong Kong,
    1968. Pp. 70-81.
    K'ang's idea of historical progress through stages is
    carefully explained, his idea of a utopia is clearly pre-
    sented, his theoretical basis and program for reform suc-
    cinctly outlined, and his political ideas are compared with
    several Western thinkers.

10.13 INNER SAGEHOOD AND OUTER KINGLINESS

    Readers interested in this topic are referred to 3.16 and 5.1
where this subject is discussed in full.

10.14 GOVERNMENT OF *WU-WEI* (NONACTION)

See also 5.6.

CHAN, WING-TSIT. A Source Book in Chinese Philosophy. (See 10.5).
   For the various approaches to the concept of wu-wei see in particular p. 43 (Confucius), chapters 2, 3, 10, 37, 43, 48, 57, 63,
and 64 of the Lao Tzu translated in chapter 7, pp. 245-255 (the
Legalists), pp. 297-299 (Wang Ch'ung), p. 322 (Wang Pi), and p. 327
and p. 332 (Kuo Hsiang). It is interesting to note that even Confucius sometimes spoke of wu-wei as the ideal political practice,
as is evidenced by the words, "To have taken no (unnatural) action
and yet have the empire well governed, Shun was the man!" (p. 43).

CREEL, HERRLEE G. "On the Origin of Wu-wei," in his What Is Taoism?
and Other Studies in Chinese Cultural History. Chicago: University
of Chicago Press, 1970. 192 pp.
   The article focuses on the concept of wu-wei and throws some
light also on the origin of the Taoist school.

FUNG YU-LAN. A Short History of Chinese Philosophy. New York:
Macmillan, 1948. 368 pp.
   Note in particular chapters 9 (Lao Tzu), 10 (Chuang Tzu) and 19
(Neo-Taoism: The Rationalists) for a clear discussion of the Taoist
and Neo-Taoist conception of wu-wei as a political practice. Fung's
discussion of Kuo Hsiang's elaboration on the distinction between
wu-wei and yu-wei (having action) is very interesting. See
pp. 224-225.

10.15   THE GOAL OF "PROMOTING BENEFITS AND REMOVING EVIL" (MO TZU)

See also 1.5.1.

CHAN, WING-TSIT. A Source Book in Chinese Philosophy. (See 10.5).
   Note in particular Mo Tzu's "Universal Love" (pp. 213-217), "The
Will of Heaven" (pp. 217-221), as well as selected passages from
chapter 20 of the Mo Tzu (pp. 226-227) rearranged under the heading
"utilitarianism."

FUNG YU-LAN. A History of Chinese Philosophy. (See 10.4), Vol. 1.
   Note in particular section 4 (Mo Tzu's utilitarianism), section
5 (what is the great profit for the people) and section 6 (universal
love) of chapter 5 on Mo Tzu. In these sections Fung discusses
quite well Mo's idea of "promoting benefits and removing evil" as a
Moist utilitarian alternative to the Confucian theory of benevolent
government.

MEI, Y.P. Motse, The Neglected Rival of Confucius. London:
Probsthain, 1934. 222 pp.
   For the present subject, see in particular chapters 5 and 7.

10.16 ATTACKS ON WAR AND WASTEFUL FUNERALS AND MUSICAL FESTIVALS (MO TZU)

See also 1.5.1.

CHAN, WING-TSIT. A Source Book in Chinese Philosophy. (See 10.5).
Note in particular Chan's additional selections from the Mo Tzu
under the headings of "condemnation of wasteful musical activities"
(pp. 227-228) and "condemnation of elaborate funerals" (pp. 228-229).

FUNG YU-LAN. A History of Chinese Philosophy. (See 10.4), Vol. 1.
For the present topic, note in particular section 5 of chapter 5
on "what is the great profit for the people," where Fung gives a
clear account of Mo's exaltation of frugality and opposition to all
forms of extravagance from the Moist utilitarian point of view.

MEI, Y.P. Motse, The Neglected Rival of Confucius. (See 10.15).
On this topic, note in particular chapters 6 and 7.

10.17 "ELEVATING THE VIRTUOUS" AND "AGREEMENT WITH THE SUPERIOR" (MO TZU)

See also 1.5.1.

CHAN, WING-TSIT. A Source Book in Chinese Philosophy. (See 10.5),
pp. 229-231.
For the present topic, note in particular Chan's additional
selections from the Mo Tzu under the headings of "elevating the
worthy to government positions" (pp. 229-230) and "agreement with
the superior" (pp. 230-231), with Chan's comments and footnotes.

FUNG YU-LAN. A History of Chinese Philosophy. (See 10.4), Vol. 1.
Note in particular Fung's discussion of Mo's idea of "agreement
with the superior" in section 8 of chapter 5 on political sanctions.
However, Fung does not discuss Mo's idea of "elevating the virtuous"
here.

MEI, Y.P. Motse, The Neglected Rival of Confucius. (See 10.15).
For the present topic, note in particular chapter 6.

10.18 PHILOSOPHY OF POWER (THE LEGALISTS)

See also 1.8.

CHEN, EN-CHENG. "Han Fei's Principle of Government by Law."
(See 10.8).
A clear and general account of Han Fei's idea of philosophy of
power in terms of the principle of government by law.

HSIAO, KUNG-CH'UAN. "Legalism and Autocracy in Traditional China,"
in Tsing Hua Journal of Chinese Studies, n.s., 4, no. 2 (1964):
108-121.
    Maintains that in Chinese history the Confucian state utilized
Confucianism largely to support autocratic practices that were in
reality inspired by the Legalists.

10.19   CONCEPT OF LAW AND ITS ENFORCEMENT (THE LEGALISTS)

See also 1.8, 10.18.

HUGHES, E.R. "Political Idealists and Realists of China of the Fourth
and Third Centuries B.C.," in Journal of the North China Branch of
the Royal Asiatic Society, 63 (1932): 46-64.
    Rather brief but accurate accounts of Mo Tzu, Hsün Tzu, and the
Legalists. Some good discussion of the Legalist concept of law
and its enforcement.

10.20   MAOIST IDEOLOGY

    Readers interested in this topic are referred to 1.18 where this
subject is discussed in full.

11. Philosophy of History and Philosophy of Science

11.1 THE MORAL INTERPRETATION OF THE *SPRING AND AUTUMN ANNALS*

CHAN, WING-TSIT, tr. and comp. A Source Book in Chinese Philosophy.
New Jersey: Princeton University Press, 1963. 856 pp.
    In chapter 1 on the growth of humanism, Chan introduces some
important notions found in ancient China, such as T'ien (Heaven) or
the Mandate of Heaven, with a good translation of selected passages
from the Book of History, the Book of Odes, and the Tso-chuan (Tso's
commentary on the Spring and Autumn Annals), and the Kuo-yü (conversations of the states). The discussion and selected translations
provide background concerning the Confucian moral interpretation of
the Spring and Autumn Annals.

FUNG YU-LAN. A History of Chinese Philosophy. Tr. by Derk Bodde.
Princeton, New Jersey: Princeton University Press, 1952-1953. 2
vols. Vol. 1, 455 pp. Vol. 2, 783 pp.
    In Vol. 1, note in particular chapter 3 on philosophical and
religious thought prior to Confucius, where Fung throws some light
on the development of the moral and humanistic interpretation of
history, natural events, etc., as exemplified in the Tso-chuan.

PULLEYBLANK, E.G. "The Historirgraphical Tradition," in The Legacy of
China. Ed. by Raymond Dawson. London: Oxford University Press,
1964. 392 pp.
    A good discussion of the historirgraphical tradition in China,
stressing the importance of the Tso-chuan, which represents the
moral interpretation of the Spring and Autumn Annals accepted by
the orthodox Confucianists.

TAIN, TZEY-YUEH. Tung Chung-shu's System of Thought: Its Sources and
Its Influence on Han Scholars. University of California Los
Angeles Ph.D. thesis, 1974. 301 pp. Cross reference 1.9.2.

WIDGERY, ALBAN G. Interpretations of History--From Confucius to
Toynbee. London: Allen and Unwin, 1961. 260 pp.
    The chapter on "Quietist and Social Attitudes to History in
China" (pp. 15-42) deals with the Taoist concept of the impermanence

of historical events and the Confucian conviction that history pro-
ceeds on a principle of justice which has meaning only here and now.
Although the book is not directly related to the present topic, it
at least provides some background regarding the Confucian moral interpretation of history beginning with the Spring and Autumn Annals.

11.2 RECTIFICATION OF NAMES AS THE BASIC CRITERION FOR ETHICO-
HISTORICAL JUDGMENT

CHAN, WING-TSIT. A Source Book in Chinese Philosophy. (See 11.1).
    Note 12: 11, 12: 17, 13: 3, and 13: 6 of the Analects in chapter
2 for a clear understanding of the earliest presentation of the
doctrine of the rectification of names as the basic criterion for
the Confucian ethico-historical judgment.

FUNG YU-LAN. A History of Chinese Philosophy. (See 11.1), Vol. 1.
    Section 3 of chapter 4 on Confucius' rectification of names deals
with the present topic very clearly. It is a valuable secondary
source on the topic.

LANCASHIRE, D. "A Confucian Interpretation of History," in Journal
of the Oriental Society of Australia, 3 (1965): 76-87.
    An excellent discussion stressing that modern Confucianists have
always regarded historical developments as an expression of a moral
principle moving towards its goal in human history with an inner
spirit transcending dynastic successions. Although the article is
not directly concerned with the present topic, its emphasis on the
Confucial moral interpretation of history may help us understand
how and why the doctrine of the rectification of names does con-
stitute the basic criterion for the Confucian ethico-historical
judgment.

WIDGERY, ALBAN G. Interpretations of History--From Confucius to
Toynbee. Cross reference: 11.1.

11.3 THEORY OF CYCLES (TUNG CHUNG-SHU)

See also 1.7, 1.9.2, 7.17.

CAIRNS, GRACE E. Philosophies of History: Meeting of East and West
in Cycles-Pattern Theories of History. New York: Philosophical
Library, 1962. 496 pp.
    Chapter 8, "Organistic Cyclical Patterns of History in Chinese
Thought" (pp. 159-195), conveniently summarizes the Yin Yang succession theory, Tung Chung-shu's theory of Three Stages of Progress,
and Shao Yung's theory of Cycles of Worlds.

CHAN, WING-TSIT. A Source Book in Chinese Philosophy. (See 11.1).
   Note in particular pp. 287-288 on Tung's theory of historical
   cycles.

FUNG YU-LAN. A History of Chinese Philosophy. (See 11.1), Vol. 2.
   Section 11 and section 12 of chapter 2 give a detailed and scholarly discussion of Tung's philosopny of history and his unique interpretation of the meaning of the Spring and Autumn Annals in terms
   of the Three Ages. With abundant citations from Tung's writings on
   historical cycles, Fung makes Tung's philosophy of history very
   intelligible.

NEEDHAM, JOSEPH. Time and Eastern Man: The Henry Myers Lecture,
   1964. London: Royal Anthropological Institute of Great Britain and
   Ireland, 1965. 52 pp. Cross reference: 7.17.

POKORA, TIMOTEUS. "Notes on New Studies on Tung Chung-shu," in
   Archiv Orientalni, 33 (1965): 256-271. Cross reference: 1.9.2.

11.4 HISTORY AS THREE AGES OF CHAOS, SMALL PEACE, AND GREAT UNITY
      (K'ANG YU-WEI)

See also 1.17, 10.12, 11.3.

LANCASHIRE, D. "A Confucian Interpretation of History." Cross
   reference: 11.2.

11.5 THE CONCEPT OF THE TRANSMISSION OF (CONFUCIAN) TAO

CHAN, WING-TSIT. "Chu Hsi's completion of Neo-Confucianism," in
   Sung Studies. Ed. by F. Aubin. Ser. 2, no. 1 (1973): 59-90.
   Chu Hsi's determination of the tradition of the orthodox trans-
   mission of Confucian doctrines.

_____. A Source Book in Chinese Philosophy. (See 11.1).
   For the primary sources on the present topic (though not exhaustive) note in particular p. 83 (Mencius), pp. 454-456 (Han Yü),
   pp. 547-550 (Ch'eng I), and pp. 646-653 (Chu Hsi).

CHANG, CARSUN. The Development of Neo-Confucian Thought. New York:
   Bookman Associates, Inc., 1962. Vol. 1, 376 pp.
   Note in particular Chang's treatment of Han Yü, Li Ao, and Chu
   Hsi in chapters 4, 5, and 12, where some light is thrown on the
   transmission of the Confucian Way by these three important Neo-
   Confucianists in the T'ang and Sung Dynasties.

CHING, JULIA. "The Confucian Way (Tao) and Tao-T'ung," in Journal
   of the History of Ideas, 35 (1974): 371-388. Cross reference:
   1.13.8.

CHU HSI, in collaboration with Lü Tsu-ch'ien. Reflections on Things
   at Hand: The Neo-Confucian Anthology. Tr. by Wing-tsit Chan. New
   York: Columbia University Press, 1967. 441 pp.
     For the present topic, note in particular chapters 2 ("The Essen-
   tials of Learning"), 11 ("The Way to Teach"), 13 ("Sifting the
   Heterodoxical Doctrines"), and 14 ("On the Dispositions of Sages
   and Worthies"). This Neo-Confucian anthology should supplement the
   primary sources on the topic in Chan, A Source Book in Chinese Philosophy, listed above.

FU, CHARLES WEI-HSUN. "Morality or Beyond: The Neo-Confucian Confrontation with Mahāyāna Buddhism," in Philosophy East and West,
   23, no. 3 (July, 1973): 375-396.
     Note in particular sections 1 and 2, where Fu discusses the Neo-
   Confucianists' vindication and transmission of the Confucian orthodoxy as against Mahāyāna Buddhist challenge.

11.6 MAOIST EXPLANATION OF HISTORY

See also 1.19.

FEUERWERKER, ALBERT, ed. History in Communist China. Cambridge,
   Mass.: M.I.T. Press, 1968. 382 pp.
     Probably the best anthology on the subject, including very inter-
   esting and scholarly articles, such as "China's History in Marxian
   Dress" (A. Feuerwerker), "The Place of Confucius in Communist
   China" (J.R. Levenson), "Chinese Communist Treatment of the Origins
   and the Foundation of the Chinese Empire" (A.F.P. Hullsewe),
   "Chinese Communist Interpretations of the Chinese Peasant Wars"
   (J.P. Harrison), "Mao Tse-tung as Historian" (H.L. Boorman), and
   "Some Questions of Historical Science in the Chinese People's
   Republic" (Vyatkin and Tikhvinsky).

11.7 PHILOSOPHY OF SCIENCE

11.7.1 The Nature of Principles (*Li*)

See also 2.11, 3.4, 6.1, 6.19, 7.9.1, 7.9.2.

NEEDHAM, JOSEPH. Science and Civilisation in China. Cambridge,
   England: Cambridge University Press, 1954-1962. 4 vols.
   Vol. 2, History of Scientific Thought (1956): 696 pp.
     The most important work on the subject. Check the entry
   li on p. 676 for the various meanings of li functioning as
   principle or organization, pattern, etc. Needham explores
   very extensively and thoroughly the various approaches to
   (the nature of) principle taken by Taoists, Neo-Confucianists,
   Mahāyāna Buddhists such as the Hua-yen philosophers, etc.

11.7.2 "Three Standards" of Basis, Examination, and Applica-
        tion (Moism)

   Readers interested in this topic are referred to 6.14 where
this subject is discussed in full.

11.7.3 Emphasis on Empirical Evidences and Verification

   Readers interested in this topic are referred to 1.9.5
and 6.21 where this subject is discussed in full.

11.7.4 Principle of Reversion (Taoism)

   Readers interested in this topic are referred to 7.16.1
where this subject is discussed in full.

11.7.5 Yin and Yang

See also 2.16, 7.2.2.

CHENG, CHUNG-YING. "Greek and Chinese Views on Time and the
   Timeless," in Philosophy East and West, 24 (1974): 155-160.
     Critical remarks on David A. Kolb's "Time and the Timeless
   in Greek Thought" and Shu-hsien Liu's "Time and Temporality:
   The Chinese Perspective," both papers published in the same
   issue as Cheng's own.

LIU, SHU-HSIEN. "Time and Temporality: The Chinese Perspective," in Philosophy East and West, 24 (1974): 145-150.
     Liu presents in brief the Chinese views of time and makes
   some generalized statements about the special characteristics
   of these views from a comparative point of view.

TONG, LIK KUEN. "The Concept of Time in Whitehead and the
   I Ching," in Journal of Chinese Philosophy, 1 (1973-1974):
   373-394.
     A careful, philosophical comparison of Whitehead's con-
   cept of time and that of the Book of Changes. A table
   showing the main points of affinity between the Whiteheadean
   and the I Ching metaphysical systems is added.

11.7.6 Theory of Cycles

See also 1.9.2, 7.17, 11.3.

CHENG, CHUNG-YING. "Greek and Chinese Views on Time and the
   Timeless." Cross reference: 11.7.5.

LIU, SHU-HSIEN. "Time and Temporality: The Chinese Perspective." Cross reference: 11.7.5.

TONG, LIK KUEN. "The Concept of Time in Whitehead and the
I Ching." Cross reference: 11.7.5.

11.7.7 <u>Laws of Nature: The Constancy and Regularity of Nature</u>

<u>See also</u> 2.16, 7.3, 7.9.1, 7.16.1, 7.16.2, 7.17, 9.26.

CHENG, CHUNG-YING. "Greek and Chinese Views on Time and the
Timeless." Cross reference: 11.7.5.

_____. "Model of Causality in Chinese Philosophy: A Compara-
tive Study," in <u>Philosophy East and West</u>, 25 (1976): 3-20.
   Cheng attempts to deal with causality from the point of
view of Chinese philosophy, most especially classical
Chinese thought.

LIU, SHU-HSIEN. "Time and Temporality: The Chinese Perspective." Cross reference: 11.7.5.

NEEDHAM, JOSEPH. <u>Science and Civilisation in China</u>. (<u>See</u>
11.7.1), Vol. 2, <u>History of Scientific Thought</u>.
   The most important source on the subject, especially the
second volume.

TONG, LIK KUEN. "The Concept of Time in Whitehead and the
I Ching." Cross reference: 11.7.5.

12. Aesthetics

CHAN, WING-TSIT, tr. and comp. <u>A Source Book in Chinese Philosophy</u>.
New Jersey: Princeton University Press, 1963. 856 pp.
   Note in particular pp. 5-6 (<u>Book of Odes</u>), 1: 12, 2: 5, 3: 3-4,
3: 17, 3: 19, 6: 25, and 8: 8 of the <u>Analects</u> of Confucius on ceremonies and music, pp. 87-88 and 91-92 (the <u>Great Learning</u>),
pp. 100, 102, 109-113 (the <u>Doctrine of the Mean</u>), and pp. 472-473
(Chou Tun-i).

PHELPS, D.L. "The Place of Music in the Platonic and Confucian Sys-
tems of Moral Education," in <u>Journal of the North China Branch of</u>
<u>the Royal Asiatic Society</u>, 59 (1928): 128-145.
   Stresses the parallel of the moral aspect of music in Plato and
Confucius. Indirectly related to the present topic.

ZAU, SINMAY. "Confucius on Poetry," in <u>T'ien Hsia Monthly</u>, 7 (1938):
137-150.
   Probably the best article on the subject in the English language.

<u>The Complete Works of Chuang Tzu</u>. Tr. by Burton Watson. New York:
Columbia University Press, 1968. 397 pp.
   Note in particular the famous passage about the debate between
Chuang Tzu and his friend Hui Shih on the happiness of the fish
(pp. 188-189)--the very passage showing Chuang Tzu's notion of
empathy.

FUNG YU-LAN. <u>A History of Chinese Philosophy</u>. Tr. by Derk Bodde.
Princeton, New Jersey: Princeton University Press, 1952-1953. 2
vols. Vol. 1, 455 pp. Vol. 2, 783 pp.
   Note in particular Vol. 1, sections 4 ("How to Attain Happiness")
and 5 ("Liberty and Equality") of chapter 10 on Chuang Tzu, where
Fung discusses Chuang Tzu's ideas of the fitness of the nature of
things, of happiness, etc. Chuang Tzu's notion of empathy should
be understood in connection with these ideas.

12.3 MUSIC OF HEAVEN, OF EARTH, AND OF MAN (CHUANG TZU)

Chuang Tzu, A New Selected Translation with an Exposition of the
  Philosophy of Kuo Hsiang. Tr. by Fung Yu-lan. Shanghai: Commercial
  Press, 1933. 164 pp. Reprinted in New York: Paragon.
    Note in particular the Neo-Taoist Kuo Hsiang's as well as Fung's
  commentaries on the opening passages of chapter 2 (pp. 43-45).

The Complete Works of Chuang Tzu. (See 12.2).
    Note in particular the opening passages of chapter 2 (pp. 37-38),
  in which Chuang Tzu beautifully describes three kinds of music,
  illustrative of his metaphysical doctrine of the equality of all
  things.

12.4 (UTILITARIAN) ATTACK ON WASTEFUL MUSICAL FESTIVALS AND CEREMONIES (MO TZU)

    Readers interested in this topic are referred to 10.16 where this
  subject is discussed in full.

12.5 "SOUND WITHOUT JOY OR SORROW" (HSI K'ANG)

See also 1.10.6.

HOLZMAN, DONALD. La vie et la pensée de Hi K'ang (223-262 AP. J-C).
  Leiden: Brill, 1957. 186 pp. Cross reference: 1.10.6.

12.6 THE RELATIONS BETWEEN METAPHYSICS OF TAO AND ART CREATION

CAHILL, JAMES F. "Confucian Elements in the Theory of Painting," in
  The Confucian Persuasion. Ed. by A. Wright. Stanford: Stanford
  University Press, 1960. Pp. 115-140.
    The author confines himself to "the exploration of possible
  instances of dependence upon Confucian ideas, not in the practice
  of painting but in the theory of it" and pays particular attention
  to "the Sung Dynasty wen-jen hua (paintings of the literati)
  theorists' treatment of two problems: the function of painting,
  and the nature of expression in painting" (p. 117), by means of
  which he "begins to work toward a definition of what is specifically Confucian in Chinese art theory and criticism" (p. 117).

CHANG, CHUNG-YUAN. Creativity and Taoism: A Study of Chinese Philosophy, Art, and Poetry. New York: Julian Press, 1963. 241 pp., in
  paperback in Harper Colophon Books, 1970.
    Tao interpreted as a mystical exercise in terms of modern psy-
  chology. The section on Taoist yoga describes its physiological
  and psychical operations, its goal of peace and tranquility, and
  its identification of reality and appearance. A very useful book
  on the subject.

The Complete Works of Chuang Tzu. (See 12.2).
   The whole book of Chuang Tzu is the best exemplar of the Taoist
philosophy unifying both metaphysics and art, that is, the Complete
Works of Chuang Tzu is an important book on Taoist metaphysics and
on art and literature as well. Chuang Tzu's influence on the subsequent creation of art and literature in China is indeed tremendous.

LIN YUTANG.   The Chinese Theory of Art.   New York: Putnam, 1967.
   244 pp.
   English translations from the masters of Chinese art reflecting
the strong Taoist philosophical influence on art creation in terms
of landscape painting, etc.

12.7 ANTI-CONVENTIONAL ROMANTICISM (LIGHT CONVERSATION)

   Readers interested in this topic are referred to 1.10.3 and 3.24,
where this subject is discussed in full.

13. Philosophy of Education

13.1 UNIVERSAL EDUCATION WITHOUT CLASS DISTINCTIONS (CONFUCIUS)

CHAN, WING-TSIT, tr. and comp. A Source Book in Chinese Philosophy.
New Jersey: Princeton University Press, 1963. 856 pp.
   Note in particular 7: 7 and 15: 38 of the Analects of Confucius
in chapter 2. Confucius said, "In education there should be no
class distinctions" (15: 38).

13.2 MORAL EMPHASIS ON EDUCATION

CHAN, WING-TSIT. A Source Book in Chinese Philosophy. (See 13.1).
   On the topic, note in particular 1: 1, 6, 8, 14; 2: 11, 15; 6:
25; 7: 2, 7, 24; 15: 38; 16: 9; 17: 8, and 19: 6 of the Analects
of Confucius in chapter 2, 2A: 2; 4A: 5, 11, 12, 19; 4B: 7, 12, 18,
28; 5A: 1, 2, 8; 5B: 1; 6A: 9, 11; 6B: 2; 7A: 4, 21; 7B: 5, 9, 32,
35 of the Book of Mencius (chapter 3), the Great Learning (chapter
4), and the Doctrine of the Mean.

CHU HSI, in collaboration with Lü Tsu-ch'ien. Reflections on Things
at Hand: The Neo-Confucian Anthology. Tr. by Wing-tsit Chan. New
York: Columbia University Press, 1967. 441 pp.
   On the topic, note in particular chapter 2 ("The Essentials of
Learning"), chapter 3 ("The Investigation of Things and the Investigation of Principle to the Utmost"), chapter 11 ("The Way to
Teach"), and chapter 14 ("On the Dispositions of Sages and
Worthies"). This does not mean that other chapters are less important, for, as a matter of fact, the Neo-Confucian moral emphasis
on education can be found throughout this anthology. The Index
at the end of the book is carefully done and should be consulted
often. Check, for example, entries such as "education," "learning,"
or "school system."

SAKAI, TADAO. "Confucianism and Popular Educational Works," in Self
and Society in Ming Thought. Ed. by Wm. Theodore de Bary. New
York: Columbia University Press, 1969. 775 pp. Pp. 331-336.
   On popular encyclopedias, morality books, and their influence on
the civil service examinations and popular morality.

WANG YANG-MING. Instructions for Practical Living and Other Neo-Confucian Writings by Wang Yang-ming. Tr. by Wing-tsit Chan. New York: Columbia University Press, 1963. 358 pp.
    On Wang Yang-ming's moral emphasis on education, check "education" (p. 351), "learning" (p. 354) and some other related entries in the Index. As a matter of fact, the whole work can be regarded as a great Neo-Confucian treatise on moral education leading towards sagehood.

13.3 (CONFUCIAN) GOAL OF (MORAL) EDUCATION

Readers interested in this topic are referred to 3.16 where this subject is discussed in full. For further reference, see also 3.15, 3.17, and 3.22.

13.4 METHODS OF SELF-CULTIVATION

Readers interested in this topic are referred to 3.17, 3.18, 3.19, 3.26, and especially 5.11 in which the various approaches to the cultivation of the mind, Confucian or non-Confucian, are mentioned.

13.5 ETHICO-SOCIAL RESTRAINTS (HSÜN TZU)

Readers interested in this topic are referred to 3.3 and 10.2 where this subject is discussed in full. For further reference, see also 1.3.3, 3.11, and 3.21.

13.6 "THREE ITEMS AND EIGHT STEPS" (*THE GREAT LEARNING*)

Readers interested in this topic are referred to 3.17 where this subject is discussed in full.

13.7 "HONORING THE MORAL NATURE" AND "FOLLOWING THE PATH OF STUDY AND INQUIRY" (*THE DOCTRINE OF THE MEAN*)

Readers interested in this topic are referred to 3.18 where this subject is discussed in full.

13.8 FIVE STEPS (*THE DOCTRINE OF THE MEAN*)

Readers interested in this topic are referred to 6.7 where this subject is discussed in full.

13.9 EQUAL EMPHASIS ON THE INTERNAL AND THE EXTERNAL

Readers interested in this topic are referred to 6.6 where this subject is discussed in full.

13.10 INVESTIGATION OF THINGS AND EXTENSION OF KNOWLEDGE

Readers interested in this topic are referred to 6.1 and 6.2 where this subject is discussed in full.

13.11 SYSTEM OF PRIVATE ACADEMY

CHANG, CARSUN. The Development of Neo-Confucian Thought. New York: Bookman Associates, Inc., 1962. Vol. 1, 376 pp.
   Chapter 3, entitled "Institutions according to the School of the Philosophy of Reason," discusses quite extensively the institutions which grew out of or were supported by the Sung school of philosophy. On pp. 65-69, Chang discusses specifically the nature, aims, and curricula of the Sung private academies, such as the famous White Deer Grotto Academy.

CREEL, HERRLEE G. Confucius, The Man and the Myth. New York: John Day, 1949. 363 pp. Also published as Confucius and the Chinese Way. New York: Harper Torchbooks.
   See chapter 7 on Confucius as a teacher and his educational doctrines.

FUNG YU-LAN. A History of Chinese Philosophy. Tr. by Derk Bodde. Princeton, New Jersey: Princeton University Press, 1952-1953. 2 vols. Vol. 1, 455 pp. Vol. 2, 783 pp.
   In section 1 of chapter 4 of Vol. 1 is some discussion of Confucius' method of teaching, the relations between him and his disciples, as well as the private education system Confucius initiated in the history of Chinese education.

13.12 EMPHASIS ON THE CULTIVATION OF THE MIND

Readers interested in this topic are referred to 2.10, 3.8, and 5.10.2 where this subject is discussed in full.

13.13 EMPHASIS ON PRACTICAL LEARNING (YEN YÜAN)

Readers interested in this topic are referred to 6.5 where this subject is discussed in full.

13.14 SOURCES OF CONFUCIAN EDUCATION SUCH AS THE FOUR BOOKS

CHAN, WING-TSIT. A Source Book in Chinese Philosophy. (See 13.1).
   Note footnote 5 on p. 85, where Chan points out the fact that Chu Hsi made the Four Books important for Confucian education and that since then the Four Books were honored as Classics and even served from 1313 until 1905 as the basis of civil service examinations in traditional China.

CHANG, CARSUN. The Development of Neo-Confucian Thought. (See 13.11).
    On pp. 62-65, Chang briefly discusses the importance of the canon-
    ical books, such as the Five Classics, the Four Books, or Reflections
    on Things at Hand, all of which are used as the basic primary
    sources of Confucian (moral) education in traditional China.

SAKAI, TADAO. "Confucianism and Popular Educational Works." Cross
    reference: 13.2.

14. Presuppositions and Methods

14.1 CONFUCIAN CLASSICS (ESPECIALLY FIVE CLASSICS AND FOUR BOOKS) PRESUPPOSED AS THE PHILOSOPHICAL FOUNDATIONS OF CONFUCIAN THOUGHT

See also 13.14.

CHAN, WING-TSIT. "Confucian Texts," in Encyclopaedia Britannica (Macropaedia). 1975. 15th ed. Vol. 4, pp. 1104-1108.
   A very extensive and careful discussion of the classical Confucian texts seldom touched upon in the English-speaking world.

de BARY, WM. THEODORE, WING-TSIT CHAN, and BURTON WATSON, comps. Sources of Chinese Tradition. New York: Columbia University Press, 1960. 976 pp.
   On the present topic in its historical perspective, note in particular chapter 1 (The Chinese tradition in antiquity).

FUNG YU-LAN. A History of Chinese Philosophy. Tr. by Derk Bodde. Princeton, New Jersey: Princeton University Press, 1952-1953. 2 vols. Vol. 1, 455 pp. Vol. 2, 783 pp.
   On the present topic in its historical perspective, note in particular Vol. 1, pp. 47-48, and 63-66 (Confucius), 336 (Confucians of Ch'in and Han Dynasties), 378-382 (the Book of Changes), 400-407 (Confucian discussions on the Six Disciplines, and the ultimate triumph of Confucianism), and Vol. 2, pp. 1-6 (general discussion of the period of Classical learning), 7-10, and 133-136 (the New Text school and the Old Text school), 673-683 (K'ang Yu-wei), and 705-721 (Liao P'ing, 1852-1932).

_____. A Short History of Chinese Philosophy. New York: Macmillan, 1948. 368 pp.
   Note Fung's brief discussion of the relation between Confucius as the first educator and the Six Classics (including the Spring and Autumn Annals), on pp. 38-41.

LIU, WU-CHI. A Short History of Confucian Philosophy. Baltimore: Penguin Books, 1955. 229 pp. Also in paperback in New York: Dell Publishing Co.

On the topic, note in particular chapter 8 on the <u>Classics</u> inscribed on stone tablets, under the headings of (a) the revival of
learning, (b) eruditi of the <u>Five Classics</u>, (c) the "Science of
Catastrophes and Anomalies," (d) two imperial conferences, (e) Old
Script versus the Modern, (e) the voice of rationalism, and (g) Confucius canonized.

NAKAMURA, HAJIME. <u>Ways of Thinking of Eastern Peoples: India, China,</u>
<u>Tibet, Japan</u>. Honolulu: East-West Center Press, 1964. 712 pp.
   In chapter 18 on "Conservatism Expressed in Exaltation of Antiquity," the author discusses, among other things, the continuity of
the classical way of thinking (pp. 206-208), non-development of free
thought (pp. 212-214), and the traditional character of scholarship
(pp. 214-216), all of which are very much related to the present
topic. But the author seems to have no clear understanding of the
significance of the Confucian classics as the philosophical
foundation.

14.2 <u>BASIC PHILOSOPHICAL PRESUPPOSITIONS IN CHINESE THOUGHT</u>

   14.2.1 <u>Harmonious Unity of Heaven and Man</u>

      Readers interested in this topic are referred to 2.15
   where this subject is discussed in full.

   14.2.2 <u>Mandate of Heaven</u>

      Readers interested in this topic are referred to 2.3,
   3.1.1, and 10.9 where this subject is discussed in full.
   For further reference, see also 7.1.

   14.2.3 <u>Yin and Yang</u>

      Readers interested in this topic are referred to 2.16
   where this subject is discussed in full.

   14.2.4 <u>Tao</u>

      Readers interested in this topic are referred to 7.3 where
   this subject is discussed in full.

   14.2.5 <u>Original Goodness of Human Nature (Confucianism)</u>

      Readers interested in this topic are referred to 2.5.1
   where this subject is discussed in full. For further reference, see also 2.9 and 2.12.

14.2.6 Moral Perfectibility of Man

Readers interested in this topic are referred to 2.8 where
this subject is discussed in full.

14.2.7 *Li* (Principle) and *Ch'i* (Material Force) (Neo-Confucianism)

Readers interested in this topic are referred to 7.8,
7.9.1, and 7.9.2 where this subject is discussed in full.
For further reference, see also 2.9.

14.2.8 *Wu-chi* (Ultimateness) and *T'ai-chi* (Supreme Ultimate)

Readers interested in this topic are referred to 7.2.1
and 7.2.2 where this subject is discussed in full.

14.3 METHOD OF SELF-CULTIVATION AND MEDITATIONAL PRACTICE

14.3.1 Full Development of One's Original Nature

Readers interested in this topic are referred to 2.2, 2.7,
2.10, 3.8, 3.17, and 5.10.1 where this subject is discussed
in full.

14.3.2 "Strong, Moving Power"

Readers interested in this topic are referred to 3.19
where this subject is discussed in full.

14.3.3 Sitting-In-Forgetfulness

Readers interested in this topic are referred to 5.11.2
where this subject is discussed in full.

14.3.4 Sitting-In-Meditation

Readers interested in this topic are referred to 5.11.7
where this subject is discussed in full.

14.3.5 Identity of Wisdom and Meditation (Hui-neng)

Readers interested in this topic are referred to 5.11.8
where this subject is discussed in full.

14.3.6 Transformation of Consciousness into Wisdom

Readers interested in this topic are referred to 5.11.13
where this subject is discussed in full.

14.3.7 "Three Thousand Worlds Immanent in a Single Instant of Thought"

Readers interested in this topic are referred to 5.10.6 where this subject is discussed in full.

14.3.8 Gradual Awakening Versus Sudden Awakening

Readers interested in this topic are referred to 1.11.7.1 and 1.11.7.2 since Hui-neng and Shen-hsiu are regarded as the originators of the School of Sudden Awakening (the Southern School) and the School of Gradual Awakening (the Northern School), respectively.

14.3.9 *Kung-an (Kōan)*, Traveling, Shock Therapy, etc.

Readers interested in this topic are referred to 8.8 where this subject is discussed in full.

14.3.10 *Ching* (Seriousness), *Ting* (Proper Abiding), Central Harmony

See also 5.2.1, 5.11.10.

CHAN, WING-TSIT, tr. and comp. A Source Book in Chinese Philosophy. New Jersey: Princeton University Press, 1963. 856 pp.
    See the texts of the Great Learning (pp. 86-87) and the Doctrine of the Mean (p. 98) for the first primary sources on the subject. Refer also to Chu Hsi's "First Letter to the Gentlemen of Hunan on Equilibrium and Harmony" (pp. 600-602).

14.4 METHODS OF LEARNING

14.4.1 Three Items and Eight Steps (*The Great Learning*)

Readers interested in this topic are referred to 3.17 where this subject is discussed in full.

14.4.2 Five Steps of Extensive Learning, etc. (*The Doctrine of the Mean*)

Readers interested in this topic are referred to 6.7 where this subject is discussed in full.

14.4.3 Emphasis on Investigation of Things and Extension of Knowledge

Readers interested in this topic are referred to 6.1 and 6.2 where this subject is discussed in full.

14.4.4 Emphasis on "Honoring the Moral Nature" (Lu-Wang Idealism)

Readers interested in this topic are referred to 2.6, 2.7, 2.10, 3.8, 3.18, and 5.10.1 where this subject is discussed in full.

14.4.5 Ways of Studying Confucian Classics

See also 11.1, 13.14, 14.1.

CHANG, CARSUN. The Development of Neo-Confucian Thought. New York: Bookman Associates, Inc., 1962. Vol. 1, 376 pp.
    In chapter 12 on Chu Hsi the great synthesizer, the author discusses quite extensively Chu Hsi's prolific writing, especially his compilation of and commentaries on the Confucian Classics, as well as his way of teaching and learning, all of which show Chu's emphasis on "following the path of study and inquiry."

HU SHIH. "The Scientific Spirit and Method in Chinese Philosophy," in Philosophy and Culture--East and West. Ed. by Charles A. Moore. Honolulu: University of Hawaii Press, 1962. Pp. 199-222. Reprinted in The Chinese Mind. Ed. by Moore. Honolulu: East-West Center Press, 1967. Pp. 104-131.
    The growth and strength of the tradition of skepticism in philosophers like Wang Ch'ung, the naturalistic view of the universe in Wang Ch'ung, Tung Chung-shu, and others, the scientific spirit of doubt and investigation in Chu Hsi and other thinkers like Tai Chen in the past eight centuries. It is interesting to note Hu's emphasis on the Ch'ing Neo-Confucianists' scientific (textual-critical) studies of the Confucian Classics.

14.4.6 Practice of Tao **versus** Increase of (Positive) Knowledge (Lao Tzu)

FUNG YU-LAN. The Spirit of Chinese Philosophy. Tr. by E.R. Hughes. London: Kegan Paul, 1947. 224 pp. Also in Beacon paperbacks.

In chapter 4 Fung discusses and evaluates the Taoist philosophy of Lao Tzu and Chuang Tzu, and emphasizes the trans-
cendental--"nameless"--aspect of Taoism, wherein is found a
philosophical significance of the "decrease" of (positive)
knowledge or learning.

The Way of Lao Tzu. Tr. by Wing-tsit Chan. Indianapolis:
Bobbs-Merrill, 1963.
    Note in particular Lao Tzu's words (in chapter 48: "The
pursuit of learning is to increase day after day. The pursuit of Tao is to decrease day after day. It is to decrease
and further decrease until one reaches the point of taking
no action" (p. 184). In this connection, refer also to
chapters 2, 3, 10, 37, 43, 48, 57, 63, and 64 (non-action),
48, 57, and 63 (non-affairs), 3, 10, 19, 20, 48, 65, and 81
(non-knowledge), 2, 5, 43, 56, 73, and 81 (no-word), and 18,
19, and 38 (non-morality or non-artifice).

14.5 LOGICAL METHODS AND SCIENTIFIC METHOD

14.5.1 "Three Standards" of Basis, Examination, and Application (Mo Tzu)

Readers interested in this topic are referred to 6.14
where this subject is discussed in full.

14.5.2 "Seven Methods of Argumentation" (Moism)

Readers interested in this topic are referred to 6.15
where this subject is discussed in full.

14.5.3 Names and Actualities

Readers interested in this topic are referred to 8.2 where
this subject is discussed in full.

14.5.4 Logical Paradox

Readers interested in this topic are referred to 8.3 where
this subject is discussed in full.

14.5.5 Naturalistic Sceptical Approach to Things in Nature
(Wang Ch'ung)

Readers interested in this topic are referred to 1.9.5
where this subject is discussed in full.

14.5.6 <u>Investigation of Principles in Nature (Ch'eng-Chu Rationalists)</u>

Readers interested in this topic are referred to 6.1 and 6.2 where this subject is discussed in full. For further reference, see also 6.21.

14.5.7 <u>Methods of Textual Criticism (Ch'ing Neo-Confucianism)</u>

CHAN, WING-TSIT. "Confucian Texts." Cross reference: 14.1.

CHANG, CARSUN. <u>The Development of Neo-Confucian Thought</u>. (<u>See</u> 14.4.5), Vol. 2.
  On the present topic, note in particular chapter 9 (Ku Yen-wu, 1613-1682, advocate of classical study), chapter 14 (school of philological and investigatory study), and chapter 15 (opposition to the school of investigatory study).

FUNG YU-LAN. <u>A History of Chinese Philosophy</u>. Cross reference: 14.1, Vol. 2.

HU SHIH. "The Scientific Spirit and Method in Chinese Philosophy." Cross reference: 14.4.5.

15. Comparisons

15.1 CONFUCIUS AND LAO-TZU

FUNG YU-LAN. The Spirit of Chinese Philosophy. Tr. by E.R. Hughes. London: Kegan Paul, 1947. 224 pp. Also published in Beacon paperbacks. Chapters 1 and 2.
  On Fung's unique, critical comparison of Confucius and Lao Tzu using "the criterion of 'attainment to the sublime and concern for the common'" (p. 5).

MUNRO, DONALD J. The Concept of Man in Early China. Stanford: Stanford University Press, 1968. 288 pp.
  Ancient Chinese view of man's possibilities and limitations, and his relations with other men and with the universe, with special emphasis on the natural equality of man and the contrasting Confucian and Taoist doctrines of moral training. Comparison of Confucius and Lao Tzu is made here and there throughout the book.

The Way of Lao Tzu. Tr. by Wing-tsit Chan. Indianapolis: Bobbs-Merrill, 1963. 285 pp.
  In the first of the three introductory essays on Lao Tzu, Chan discusses the historical background and the Taoist reaction, the meaning of Tao, and in particular makes a comparison of Lao Tzu and Confucius (pp. 17-19).

15.2 LAO TZU AND CHUANG TZU

CREEL, HERRLEE G. "On Two Aspects in Early Taoism," in his What Is Taoism? and Other Studies in Chinese Cultural History. Chicago: University of Chicago Press, 1970. 192 pp.
  A very interesting comparison of Lao Tzu as representing the "purposive aspect" and Chuang Tzu as representing the "contemplative aspect" in early Taoist philosophy.

de BARY, WM. THEODORE, WING-TSIT CHAN and BURTON WATSON, comps. Sources of Chinese Tradition. New York: Columbia University Press, 1960. 976 pp.
  On the topic, note in particular pp. 62-63 (chapter 4). Brief but clear.

FUNG YU-LAN. A History of Chinese Philosophy. Tr. by Derk Bodde.
  Princeton, New Jersey: Princeton University Press, 1952-1953. 2
  vols. Vol. 1, 455 pp. Vol. 2, 783 pp. Vol. 1, chapters 8 and 10.
  See especially pp. 172-175. A very good, philosophical discussion
  of the two early Taoist philosophers.

_____. The Spirit of Chinese Philosophy. (See 15.1).
  Note in particular chapter 2 where Fung gives a critical evaluation of the Taoist contributions by Lao Tzu and Chuang Tzu.

The Way of Lao Tzu. Tr. by Wing-tsit Chan. (See 15.1).
  For a comparison of Lao Tzu and Chuang Tzu, note in particular
  pp. 19-22.

15.3 MENCIUS AND HSÜN TZU

CHAN, WING-TSIT, tr. and comp. A Source Book in Chinese Philosophy.
  New Jersey: Princeton University Press, 1963. 856 pp.
  A brief comparison on pp. 115-116.

de BARY, WM. THEODORE, WING-TSIT CHAN, and BURTON WATSON, comps.
  Sources of Chinese Tradition. (See 15.2).
  On the topic, note in particular pp. 98-100. Short but clear.

DUBS, HOMER H. "Mencius and Sun-dz on Human Nature," in Philosophy
  East and West, 6 (1956): 213-222. Cross reference: 2.1.

FUNG YU-LAN. A History of Chinese Philosophy. (See 15.2), Vol. 1.
  Comparison of Mencius and Hsün Tzu is made here and there in
  chapter 12. Note in particular section 2 (pp. 280-281) on Hsün
  Tzu's attitude toward Confucius and Mencius.

GRAHAM, A.C. "The Background of the Mencian Theory of Human Nature,"
  in Tsing Hua Journal of Chinese Studies, 6, nos. 1-2 (1967):
  215-274. Cross reference: 2.1.

LAU, D.C. "Theories of Human Nature in Mencius and Shyuntzyy," in
  Bulletin of the School of Oriental and African Studies, 15 (1953):
  541-565. Cross reference: 2.1.

SARGENT, G.E. "Les Débats entre Meng-tseu et Siun-tseu sur la Nature
  Humaine," in Oriens Extremus, 3 (1956): 1-17. Cross reference: 2.1.

15.4 NEO-TAOISM AND CHINESE MĀDHYAMIKA

Chao Lun: The Treatises of Seng-chao. Tr. by Walter Liebenthal.
  Hong Kong: Hong Kong University Press, 1968. 152 pp.

On Taoist and Neo-Taoist influences on Seng-chao's philosophy, note in particular the translator's excellent introductory essay. A very scholarly and important treatise on the subject.

FUNG YU-LAN. A History of Chinese Philosophy. (See 15.2), Vol. 2.
Note in particular pp. 240-243 on "Buddhism and Taoism."

_____. A Short History of Chinese Philosophy. New York: Macmillan, 1948. 368 pp. Chapter 21.
On the foundation of Chinese Buddhism, with a short account of the ideological interplay between Chinese Mādhyamika and the Taoist tradition.

LINK, ARTHUR E. "The Taoist Antecedents of Tao'an's Prajñā Ontology," in History of Religions, 9, no. 2/3 (1969-1970): 181-219.
A fresh attempt at linking Neo-Taoist metaphysics and Tao'an's (312-385) prajñā (wisdom) ontology. Divided into three sections: introduction, the "six schools" and the "seven sects," and the concept of pen-wu (original non-being) and hsing-k'ung (emptiness of nature) in Tao'an's writings.

ZURCHER, E. The Buddhist Conquest of China. Leiden: Brill, 1959. 2 vols. 468 pp.
The most scholarly work on the spread and adaptation of Buddhism in early medieval China, and in particular its contact with Chinese thought, such as Neo-Taoism. On the subject, note in particular pp. 86-95, pp. 128-130, and chapter 6 on the early history of Buddho-Taoist conflict.

15.5 CH'ENG-CHU RATIONALISM AND LU-WANG IDEALISM

CHANG, CARSUN. The Development of Neo-Confucian Thought. New York: Bookman Associates, Inc., 1962. Vol. 1, 376 pp.
In chapter 7 the author gives a detailed analysis of Chou Tun-i's cosmological speculations in terms of wu-chi and t'ai-chi. And in chapter 13, he discusses in detail the debate between Chu Hsi and Lu Hsiang-shan, mainly with respect to the meaning of the first sentence in Chou Tun-i's "Explanation of the Diagram of the Great Ultimate," i.e., "The Ultimate of Non-being and also the Great Ultimate!" An extremely important debate regarding the ontological relation between the Ultimate of Non-being and the Great Ultimate in the history of Neo-Confucian metaphysics.

FUNG YU-LAN. A History of Chinese Philosophy. (See 15.2), Vol. 2.
Note in particular the author's comparison of Chu Hsi and Lu Hsiang-shan on pp. 585-592 and of Chu Hsi and Wang Yang-ming on pp. 605-610. A good, philosophical comparison.

FUNG YU-LAN. The Spirit of Chinese Philosophy. (See 15.1), chapter 9.
   A critical evaluation of Neo-Confucian philosophy by using the
criterion of "attainment to the sublime and concern for the common"
(p. 5). Some comparison of the two main schools of Neo-Confucianism
is also made.

15.6 CHU HSI AND LU HSIANG-SHAN

See also 15.5.

CHING, JULIA. "The Goose Lake Monastery Debate," in Journal of Chinese
   Philosophy, 1 (1973-1974): 161-178. Cross reference: 1.13.8.

HUANG, SIU-CHI. Lu Hsiang-shan. A Twelfth Century Chinese Idealist
   Philosopher. New Haven: American Oriental Society, 1944. Chapter
   4, 116 pp.
   The author compares Lu's cosmology with that of Chu Hsi under the
headings of (a) the authenticity of the "Explanation of the Diagram
of the Great Ultimate," and (b) the difference between Chu's and
Lu's cosmology.

15.7 CH'ENG HAO AND CH'ENG I

CHAN, WING-TSIT. A Source Book in Chinese Philosophy. (See 15.3).
   On the subject, note in particular Chan's introductory essays in
chapters 31 (Ch'eng Hao) and 32 (Ch'eng I). The primary sources
selected and rearranged in these two chapters should be carefully
read in order to have a clear understanding of the philosophical
similarities and differences between the Ch'eng brothers.

CHANG, CARSUN. The Development of Neo-Confucian Thought. (See 15.5),
   Vol. 1.
   On the subject, see chapters 9 (Ch'eng Hao) and 10 (Ch'eng I).
Note in particular pp. 207-211.

FUNG YU-LAN. A History of Chinese Philosophy. (See 15.2), Vol. 2.
   On the subject, see pp. 498-532. Note in particular pp. 520-527
on Ch'eng Hao's theory of spiritual cultivation and pp. 527-532 on
Ch'eng I's theory of spiritual cultivation.

GRAHAM, A.C. Two Chinese Philosophers: Ch'eng Ming-tao and Ch'eng
   Yi-ch'uan. London: Lund Humphries, 1958. 195 pp.
   The only English work in book form on the philosophical doctrines
of the Ch'eng brothers. A very good, philosophical clarification
of the major terms is given, whereby the similarities and differences between Ch'eng Hao and Ch'eng I are pointed out.

15.8 CHU HSI AND WANG YANG-MING. Cross reference: 15.5.

15.9 SUNG-MING NEO-CONFUCIANISTS AND CH'ING NEO-CONFUCIANISTS

Readers interested in this topic are referred to 14.5.7 and 14.4.5 where this subject is discussed in full.

15.10 PHILOSOPHICAL TAOISM AND RELIGIOUS TAOISM

KALTENMARK, MAX. Lao Tzu and Taoism. Tr. from the French by Roger Greaves. Stanford: Stanford University Press, 1969. 158 pp.
A very interesting account of both philosophical Taoism and religious Taoism under the headings of (a) Lao Tzu, (b) the teaching, (c) the holy man, (d) Chuang Tzu, (e) the Taoist religion, and conclusion. The author's discussion of philosophical Taoism is relatively weak.

SEIDEL, ANNA K. "The Image of the Perfect Ruler in Early Taoist Messianism: Lao Tzu and Li Hung," in History of Religions, 9, nos. 2 and 3 (1969-1970): 216-247.
A historical article on the mythologization of Lao Tzu in the movement of religious Taoism.

The Way of Lao Tzu. Tr. by Wing-tsit Chan. (See 15.1).
On the subject, note in particular pp. 26-29.

WELCH, HOLMES. Taoism: The Parting of the Way. Boston: Beacon Press, 1965. 194 pp.
Part 2 deals with Lao Tzu, and Part 3 discusses the movement of religious Taoism. The author's treatment of religious Taoism is interesting, but his account of Lao Tzu and philosophical Taoism is not satisfactory.

15.11 TRADITIONAL CHINESE PHILOSOPHY AND MAOIST IDEOLOGY

See also 1.19.

CHAN, WING-TSIT. Chinese Philosophy, 1949-1963: An Annotated Bibliography of Mainland Chinese Publications. Honolulu: East-West Center Press, 1967. 441 pp.
Presenting the summaries, outline, nature, important points, or conclusions of 213 books and 756 articles published in the People's Republic of China during 1949-1963. A bird's-eye view of how Marxist philosophers in today's China re-examine and criticize traditional Chinese philosophy from the Maoist point of view.

_____. "Chinese Philosophy in Communist China," in Philosophy East and West, 11 (1961): 115-123.
A short discussion followed by selections from Fung Yu-lan and others on the nature of the history of Chinese philosophy, how to

continue the philosophical heritage, and guidance for future development. Same as chapter 44 of Chan's A Source Book in Chinese
Philosophy. (See 15.3).

Chinese Studies in Philosophy. New York: International Arts and
Sciences Press, Inc.
   This is one of the journals in the Asian Translation Series, and
includes in each issue English translations of the important publications in China on Chinese Marxist philosophy and the Marxist-Maoist
examination and criticism of traditional Chinese philosophy. A very
useful journal for references concerning the present topic. Prior
to Fall, 1969, the journal was called Chinese Studies in History
and Philosophy, out of which are now the two separated journals of
Chinese Studies in Philosophy and Chinese Studies in History.

DOW, TSUNG-I. "Some Affinities between Confucius and Marxian Philosophical Systems," in Asian Profile, 1 (1973): 247-259.
   An interesting discussion of the philosophical similarity between
traditional Confucianism and the dialectical system of Marxism-
Leninism, though the similarity in question is somewhat exaggerated.

FEUERWERKER, ALBERT, ed. History in Communist China. Cambridge:
   the M.I.T. Press, 1968. 382 pp.
   This anthology includes some articles on the present topic, such
as Munro's "Chinese Communist Treatment of the Thinkers of the
Hundred Schools Period," Levenson's "The Place of Confucius in Communist China," and Wilhelm's "The Reappraisal of Neo-Confucianism."

FU, CHARLES WEI-HSUN. "Confucianism, Marxism-Leninism and Mao: A
   Critical Study," in Journal of Chinese Philosophy, 1 (1974):
   339-372.
   This article exposes the underlying structure of Marxism-Leninism-
Maoism as fundamentally a moralistic working ideology, and analyzes
the peculiar ideological relation between Mao and Confucianism,
thereby shedding some light on the political-ideological implications of the present anti-Confucianism campaign in China.

_____. "Rejoinder to Professor Howard Parsons' Critical Remarks,"
in Journal of Chinese Philosophy, 1 (1975): 114-121.
   As against Parsons' defense of the orthodoxy of Marxism-Leninism,
Fu counter-argues that the ultimate meaning of dialectical and
historical materialism consists in its functioning as a moralistic
working ideology, and that Mao's Cultural Revolution finally disclosed Mao's persistent determination to carry out the dictatorship of the proletariat in terms of day-to-day moral transformation
of man in the proletarian way.

HOU WAI-LU. A Short History of Chinese Philosophy. Peking: Foreign
Language Press, 1959. 177 pp.
  Mostly a story of how Maoism has overcome its ideological opposi-
tions in traditional Chinese philosophy.

MUNRO, DONALD J. "Chinese Communist Treatment of the Thinkers of the
Hundred Schools Period," in The China Quarterly, 24 (1965): 119-141.
Also in History in Communist China. Ed. by Albert Feuerwerker.
(See above).
  Confucius as an idealist, Mencius as subjective, Hsün Tzu as a
major materialist, uncertain qualities in the Taoists and Legalists.

WANG HSUEH-WEN. "The Maoists' Criticism of Mencius," in Issues and
Studies, 10, no. 10 (July, 1974): pp. 29-45.
  Critically reviews the Maoist attack upon Mencius' theory of
human nature as well as his moral and political teachings. In the
concluding part of the article, Wang vindicates Mencian Thought
against Mao Tsetung Thought.

_____. "The Maoist Criticism of Chu Hsi," in Issues and Studies, 10,
no. 12 (September, 1974): pp. 62-72.
  Wang observes that in a similar fashion to what they have done to
Confucius, Mencius, and Tung Chung-shu, the Maoists criticize
Chu Hsi as another evil "idealistic" apriorist and invariably asso-
ciate this "struggle to criticize" with the criticism of Lin Piao.

_____. "The Development of the Maoists' Criticism of Confucius
Movement," in Issues and Studies, 10, no. 6 (March, 1974): pp. 32-54.
  Wang launches a strong Nationalist attack upon the anti-Confucius
campaign the Maoists initiated in the winter of 1973.

15.12 THE EARLY FUNG YU-LAN AND FUNG YU-LAN THE MARXIST

See also 1.18.5.

FUNG YU-LAN. "Contemporary Chinese Philosophy: The Development of
Marxism-Leninism in China," in Philosophy in the Mid-Century. Ed.
by Raymond Klibansky. Firenze: La Nuova Italia Editrice, 1959.
Vol. 4, pp. 252-262.
  Discusses Mao Tse-tung's "On Practice," in which he explains the
origin of knowledge and the criteria of truth, and his "On Contradiction," in which he explains the two opposing metaphysical and
materialistic-dialectic outlooks.

_____. "Criticism and Self-Criticism on Discussions about Confucius,"
in Chinese Studies in History and Philosophy, 1, no. 4 (Summer,
1968): 70-91.

Fung confesses that as a result of many discussions of Confucius,
he has changed his evaluation of the Confucian concept of jen
(humanity) in his new version of the history of Chinese philosophy.
He now realizes that jen was originally an illusion for the common
benefit of the people but was eventually used by the feudal class
as an instrument to resolve class conflicts.

FUNG YU-LAN. "More on Some Problems Relating to Research in History
of Chinese Philosophy," in Selections from China Mainland Magazines,
no. 541 (1966): 13-20.
Fung criticizes himself for using a wrong method in a 1965
article and argues that "materialistic" Wang Ch'ung, Wang Fu-chih,
etc. turned "poisonous weeds" of superstition and idealism into
"good fertilizer."

_____. "Problems in the Study of Confucius," in People's China, 1957,
no. 1 (January): 21-22 and 27-31.
Insists that contemporary conflicting views on Confucius are all
conjectural. He himself considers Confucius to be an idealist and
not a materialist, a progressive and not a reactionary. Quite a
daring statement under the Communists.

LEE, CYRUS. "The Intellectual Conversion of Fung Yu-lan from Confucianism to Communism," in Chinese Culture, 9, no. 2 (June, 1958):
107-119.
The article is divided into two parts, Part 1 deals with Fung as
an orthodox scholar, his educational background, his educational
activities, and his work in the field of philosophy. Part 2 is on
Fung as a student of Marxism and Maoism, as a fighter within and
without, and as a "surrendered follower" of Maoism. While the
account is factual, the interpretation is chiefly political. A
careful analysis of Fung's works would show that he has many
reservations.

15.13   HUA-YEN, CH'AN, AND NEO-CONFUCIAN PHILOSOPHY

CHAN, WING-TSIT. "How Buddhistic is Wang Yang-ming?" in Philosophy
East and West, 12 (1962): 203-216. Reprinted in Chan's Neo-
Confucianism, Etc. Essays by Wing-tsit Chan. Ed. by Charles K.H.
Chen. Hanover, N.H.: Oriental Society, 1969: 516 pp. (the English
section) and 129 pp. (the Chinese section).
On Wang's criticism of Buddhism.

CHAN, WING-TSIT. A Source Book in Chinese Philosophy. (See 15.3).
On the Neo-Confucian examination and criticism of Buddhism,
especially Zen, see pp. 454-459 (Han Yü and Li Ao), 500-517 (Chang
Tsai), sections 21, 32, 46, 76, and 77 of chapter 31 (Ch'eng Hao),

sections 23, 25, 50-55 of chapter 32 (Ch'eng I), section 4 of
chapter 33 (Lu Hsiang-shan), sections 134-147 of chapter 34 (Chu
Hsi), and p. 429, 662, and 677 of chapter 35 (Wang Yang-ming). The
best comprehensive primary source on the subject, well translated
and arranged.

CHU HSI, in collaboration with Lü Tsu-ch'ien. Reflections on Things
at Hand: The Neo-Confucian Anthology. Tr. by Wing-tsit Chan. New
York: Columbia University Press, 1967. 441 pp.
    On the topic, note in particular chapter 13 on "sifting the hetero-
doxical doctrines."

FU, CHARLES WEI-HSUN. "Morality or Beyond: The Neo-Confucian Confrontation with Mahāyāna Buddhism," in Philosophy East and West,
23, no. 3 (July, 1973): 375-396.
    Concentrates on the ideological "love and hate" between Neo-
Confucianism and Mahāyāna Buddhism.

HUANG, SIU-CHI. Lu Hsiang-shan. A Twelfth Century Chinese Idealist
Philosopher. (See 15.6).
    Note in particular pp. 67-74 on "Buddhism in Lu Hsiang-shan's
Methodology," under the three headings of (a) the teaching of quiet
sitting, (b) the comparative negligence of written texts, (c) the
doctrine of mind culture, and (d) Lu's criticism of Buddhism. A
very useful reference for a clear understanding of Lu's "affili-
ation" with and criticism of Buddhism, especially Ch'an.

SARGENT, GALEN EUGENE. Tchou Hi contre le Bouddhism. Paris:
Imprimerie Nationale, 1955. 156 pp.
    An examination, well supported by standard works and original
sources, of Chu Hsi's criticisms of Buddhism on social, practical,
theoretical, and historical grounds, and a translation of many,
though not all, of Chu Hsi's sayings and short essays on the
subject.

15.14 COMPARISON WITH WESTERN PHILOSOPHY

CHANG, CHUNG-YUAN. "Tao: A New Way of Thinking," in Journal of
Chinese Philosophy, 1 (1973-1974): 137-152.
    A comparison of Taoist thinking with the thinking of Plato, the
Buddhists, Hegel, and Heidegger, particularly the latter. Refer-
ences are made to European thinkers' reactions to the Tao-te ching.

COHEN, MAURICE. "Confucius and Socrates," in Journal of Chinese
Philosophy, 3 (1976): 159-168.
    Holds that Confucius and Socrates, as philosophers, share a
devotion to the clarification of concepts. What sets them apart

from many others are their choice of concepts, their preferred
methods, and the social roles they constructed for themselves.

DUBS, HOMER H. "A Comparison of Ancient Chinese Philosophy with that
of Greece," in China Journal, 10 (1929): 116-122 and 166-170.
    Confucius, Lao Tzu, and Mo Tzu are compared with Greek philos-
ophers on a general level, noting especially similarities.

FORKE, ALFRED. "Chinesische und indische Philosophie," in Zeitschrift
der deutschen morgenlandischen Gesellschaft, 98 (1944): 195-237.
    In equating Tao with Brahman, the Five Agents with gunas
(attributes), etc., Forke fails to distinguish the essential difference between Chinese philosophy of immanence and Indian philosophy
of transcendence.

FU, CHARLES WEI-HSUN. "Creative Hermeneutics: Taoist Metaphysics and
Heidegger," in Journal of Chinese Philosophy, 3 (1976): 115-143.
    Fu's objective is to employ his method of creative hermeneutics
in a fresh attempt to divulge the secret of Lao Tzu's Tao by way
of examining the metaphysical sayings of Chuang Tzu, Wang Pi, and
Kuo Hsiang, as well as by contrasting Taoism with Heidegger.

_____. "Beyond Aesthetics: Heidegger and Taoism on Poetry and Art,"
in East-West Dialogue in Aesthetics. Ed. by Kenneth K. Inada.
New York: The Council for International Studies, SUNY at Buffalo,
1978.
    A philosophical examination of the Heideggerian and Taoist trans-
aesthetic approaches to poetry and art.

_____. "Heidegger and Zen on Being and Nothingness: A Critical Essay
in Transmetaphysical Dialectics," in Buddhism and Western Philosophy: A Critical Comparative Study. Ed. by Nathan Katz. New
Delhi: Sterling Publishers, 1978.
    A critical evaluation of Heidegger's thinking on Being and
Nothingness, as well as a creative construction of what Fu himself
calls "the transmetaphysical dialectics of Being and Nothingness"
from the Zen point of view.

_____. "The Trans-Onto-Theo-Logical Foundations of Language in
Heidegger and Taoism," in Journal of Chinese Philosophy, 5 (1978).
    A critical examination of Heidegger's thinking on language as
the house of Being from the Taoist point of view. Highly sophisticated and creative.

_____. "The Underlying Structure of Metaphysical Language: A Case
Examination of Chinese Philosophy and Whitehead," in Journal of
Chinese Philosophy, 5 (1978).

A critical uncovering of the essential nature of Chinese metaphysics and Whitehead's speculative philosophy, as well as of the
underlying structure of metaphysical language.

HUGHES, E.R. The Individual in East and West. London: Oxford University Press, 1937. 197 pp.
     Argues strongly that Chinese philosophy emphasizes the individual,
that Confucius discovered the individual, and that the individual
is no less strong in Taoism and Buddhism.

MAHOOD, GEORGE H. "Socrates and Confucius: Moral Agents or Moral
Philosophers?" in Philosophy East and West, 21 (1971): 177-188.
     After comparing Socrates and Confucius in their sense of mission,
in their ways of expressing themselves, in their understanding of
virtue and knowledge, and in the way they modified the moral term-
inology of their societies, the author concludes that what they
learned of moral experience as moral philosophers, through reflec-
tion on language and the concepts it expresses, committed them
finally to being moral agents.

MORTON, W. SCOTT. "The Confucian Concept of Man: the Original Formulation," in Philosophy East and West, 21 (1971): 69-77.
     According to the original formulation by Confucius, who gave the
term chün-tzu (gentleman) a new meaning, the gentleman is (a) im-
perturbable and resolute, (b) conciliatory, modest, humble, and
even mild, (c) has a well-balanced character, (d) is faithful, a
man in whom one can place trust, (e) is conscious of faults, and
(f) has independence. In both Confucius' and Aristotle's concept
of man, the mean is regarded as the criterion of virtue and the
following of the middle way as one of the chief marks of the good
man.

NEEDHAM, JOSEPH. Science and Civilisation in China. Cambridge,
England: Cambridge University Press, 1954-1962. 4 vols. Vol. 2,
History of Scientific Thought (1956): 696 pp. Pp. 287-304, 342-
345, and 678-582.
     For comparisons of Chinese and Western philosophers, especially
Chu Hsi and Whitehead, and for Chinese parallel with, influence on,
and anticipation of Western thinkers.

NIVISON, DAVID S. "Moral Decision in Wang Yang-ming: The Problem of
Chinese 'Existentialism,'" in Philosophy East and West, 23 (1973):
121-138.
     A very interesting comparison between Wang Yang-ming's doctrine
and existentialism, pointing out both similarities and differences,
with frequent references to Sartre, Husserl, and Kierkegaard,
especially the latter. Wang's moral decision is analyzed. All
this is discussed on the basis of Wang's doctrines of the innate

knowledge of the good, the unity of knowledge and action, and the
famous "Four Propositions." A fresh attempt at interpreting Wang
Yang-ming as a Confucian "existentialist" in terms of moral decision.

NORTHROP, FILMER S.C. "The Complimentary Emphasis of Eastern Intui-
tive and Western Scientific Philosophy," in Philosophy East and West.
Ed. by Charles A. Moore. Princeton: Princeton University Press,
1944. Pp. 168-190. Reprinted with some modification in Northrop's
The Logic of the Sciences and the Humanities. New York: Macmillan,
1947. Pp. 77-100.
   Sharply contrasts Eastern thinking as an aesthetic continuum and
Western thinking as postulational.

SUN, GEORGE CHIN-HSIN. Chinese Metaphysics and Whitehead. Southern
Illinois University Ph.D. thesis, 1971. 241 pp.
   Affirms that Chinese philosophy, Buddhist philosophy, and the
philosophy of Whitehead share a common view of the world as a
process of configuration of events. The author says that five concepts of Confucianism and three of Taoism can be treated with
reference to Whitehead's philosophy of organism, as can three
Buddhist schools, the Mādyamika, the T'ien-t'ai, and Hua-yen, especially the last.

TONG, LIK KUEN. "Confucian Jen and Platonic Eros: A Comparative
Study," in Chinese Culture, Vol. 14, no. 3 (September, 1973): 1-8.
   Both the Confucian jen and Platonic eros are understood as
rational, but the accent of Confucius is on the subject whereas
the accent of Plato is on the object.

WIENPAHL, PAUL. "Spinoza and Wang Yang-ming," in Religious Studies,
3 (1969): 19-27.
   Points out some similarities between the two: (1) Both were pragmatists. (2) Both identified knowledge with action. (3) Both
taught extending innate knowledge. Essentially the article is on
Spinoza.

WU, JOSEPH. "Whitehead and the Philosophical Meeting of East and
West," in Chinese Culture, 12, no. 4 (December, 1971): 84-91.
   Mostly on Whitehead, with some references to Needham's Science
and Civilisation in China. (See above), Vol. 2, History of Scien-
tific Thought. With quotations from the Lao Tzu to show where the
East and West can meet.

16. Authoritative Texts and Their Philosophical Significances

For English references, see 13.14, 14.1, 14.4.5, and 14.5.7. There are very few comprehensive works in English dealing with this subject peculiar to the Confucian tradition, and there is little English material on the formation and classification of Seven Classics, Nine Classics, etc. More research and investigation on the present topic should be done in the English-speaking world. The first best step, of course, is to undertake the task of systematic translation of the Chinese works on the present topic by the Chinese scholars themselves, such as Hsiung Shih-li's Tu-ching shih-yao (essential key to the way of learning Confucian Classics), Ch'ien Mu's Kuo-hsüeh kai-lun (introduction to Sinological learning), P'i Hsi-jui's (1850-1908) Ching-hsüeh t'ung-lun (general introduction to the learning of Classics) and his Ching-hsüeh li-shih (history of classical learning), as well as Ma Tsung-huo's Chung-kuo ching-hsüeh shih (history of classical learning in China).

CHAN, WING-TSIT. "Confucian Texts," in Encyclopaedia Britannica (Macropaedia). 15th ed. 1975. Vol. 4. Pp. 1104-1108. Cross reference: 14.1.

CH'EN, KENNETH. Buddhism in China: A Historical Survey. New Jersey: Princeton University Press, 1964. 560 pp.
On the subject, note in particular pp. 297-300, 305-311. A very useful secondary source on the classification of the sūtras and teachings made by the T'ien-t'ai School.

HURVITZ, LEON. Chih-i (538-595). An Introduction to the Life
and Ideas of a Chinese Buddhist Monk. Bruges: Imprimerie
Sainte-Catherine, 1963. 372 pp.
   The best comprehensive treatment of Chih-i, the real
founder of the T'ien-t'ai School. On the subject, note in
particular Part 3 ("Chih-i's ideas").

NAKAMURA, HAJIME. Ways of Thinking of Eastern Peoples: India,
China, Tibet, Japan. Honolulu: East-West Center Press,
1964. 712 pp.
   On the present topic, note in particular pp. 226-230. The
author observes that the Chinese Buddhist "critical classification of doctrines" shows the traditional Chinese fondness
for formal conformity.

TAKAKUSU, J. The Essentials of Buddhist Philosophy. 3rd ed.
Honolulu: Office Appliance Co., 1956. 221 pp.
   On the subject, note in particular pp. 131-134. See also
1.11.5.

16.2.2 The Hua-yen Approach

CHAN, WING-TSIT, tr. and comp. A Source Book in Chinese
Philosophy. New Jersey: Princeton University Press, 1963.
856 pp.
   See pp. 410-411 for Fa-tsang's "Discussing the Five
Doctrines."

CH'EN, KENNETH. Buddhism in China. (See 16.2.1).
   Note in particular pp. 318-320.

FUNG YU-LAN. A History of Chinese Philosophy. Tr. by Derk
Bodde. Princeton, New Jersey: Princeton University Press,
1952-1953. 2 vols. Vol. 1, 455 pp. Vol. 2, 783 pp.
   On the present topic, note in particular Fa-tsang's "Discussing the Five Teachings" dealt with in Vol. 2,
pp. 346-349.

NAKAMURA, HAJIME. Ways of Thinking of Eastern Peoples: India,
China, Tibet, Japan. Cross reference: 16.2.1.

TAKAKUSU, J. The Essentials of Buddhist Philosophy. (See
16.2.1).
   On the subject, note in particular pp. 114-122. See also
1.11.1.

16.3 THE FORMATION OF THE *FOUR BOOKS*

See also 13.14.

CHAN, WING-TSIT. "Confucian Texts." Cross reference: 14.1.

16.4 THE PHILOSOPHICAL SIGNIFICANCE OF THE *FOUR BOOKS* AND THE *FIVE CLASSICS* IN (MORAL) EDUCATION, CIVIL SERVICE EXAMINATION, TEXTUAL CRITICISM, LITERATURE, AND OTHER CULTURAL ASPECTS

See also 13.14, 14.1, 16.1.

ROBERTS, MOSS PENSAK. The Metaphysical Context of the Analects and the Metaphysical Theme in Later Chou Confucianism. Columbia University Ph.D. thesis, 1966. 150 pp.
Not on metaphysical theories, but on a contextual study of the philosophical relation of the Analects to the Doctrine of the Mean, the Book of Mencius, and the Book of Changes.

16.5 THE PROBLEM OF TEXTUAL CRITICISM: DATING, AUTHENTICITY, COMPARISON OF DIFFERENT EDITIONS, ETC.

BODDE, DERK. "Lieh-tzu and the Dove: A Problem of Dating," in Asia Minor, n.s., 7 (1959): 25-31.
Thinks that the work was written in the first century A.D. or later.

CHAN, WING-TSIT. "Confucian Texts." Cross reference: 16.1.

DUBS, HOMER H. "The Date and Circumstances of the Philosopher Laodz," in Journal of the American Oriental Society, 61 (1941): 215-221. Further discussions with Bodde, ibid., 62 (1942): 8-13 and 300-304, 64 (1944): 24-27. Cross reference: 1.4.2.

GRAHAM, A.C. "The Composition of Gongsuen Long Tzyy," in Asia Major, n.s., 2 (1957): 147-183.
On the basis of the usage of certain terms, concludes that the last three chapters of the Kung-sun Lung Tzu were written between 300 and 600 A.D.

_____. "The Date and Composition of Liehtzyy," in Asia Major, n.s., 8 (1961): 139-198. Cross reference: 1.10.2.

_____. "Two Dialogues in the Kung-sun Lung Tzu: 'White Horse' and 'Left and Right,'" in Asia Major, 11 (1965): 128-152.
On the assumption that the texts are dislocated, the author rearranged them. Like most rearrangements of ancient texts, it raises as many questions as it answers.

HU SHIH. "A Criticism of Some Recent Methods Used in Dating Lao Tzu,"
in Harvard Journal of Asiatic Studies, 2 (1937): 373-397.
     A very careful, well-documented, and cogently argued treatise on
the date of Lao Tzu, demolishing many popular theories of the time,
which held Lao Tzu to be either legendary or a thinker of the 4th
century B.C.

_____. "The Scientific Spirit and Method in Chinese Philosophy," in
Philosophy and Culture--East and West. Ed. by Charles A. Moore.
Honolulu: University of Hawaii Press, 1962. Pp. 199-222. Reprinted
in Moore's The Chinese Mind. Honolulu: East-West Center Press,
1967. Pp. 104-131.
     See 6.1. It is interesting to note Hu's emphasis on the Ch'ing
Neo-Confucianists' scientific (textual-critical) studies of the
Confucian Classics.

The Way of Lao Tzu. Tr. by Wing-tsit Chan. Indianapolis: Bobbs-
Merrill, 1963.
     In the second introductory essay on "Lao Tzu the Man" and the
third on "Lao Tzu the Book," Chan gives a comprehensive account of
the various answers given by the specialists on Lao Tzu with regard
to the problem of dating, authenticity, different editions, etc.

16.6 PHILOSOPHICAL COMMENTARIES ON AUTHORITATIVE CLASSICS AND THEIR
      UNIQUE CONTRIBUTIONS

CHAN, WING-TSIT. A Source Book in Chinese Philosophy. (See 16.2.2).
     For some very important examples of the philosophical commen-
taries on authoritative classics, see Chu Hsi's remarks on the
Great Learning in chapter 4, Wang Pi's Commentary on the Book of
Changes (pp. 320-321), and Commentary on the Lao Tzu (pp. 321-324),
Kuo Hsiang's Commentary on the Chuang Tzu (pp. 326-335), Wang Yang-
ming's "Inquiry on the Great Learning" (pp. 659-667), and Tai
Chen's Commentary on the Meanings of Terms in the Book of Mencius
(pp. 711-722).

CHANG, CARSUN. The Development of Neo-Confucian Thought. New York:
Bookman Associates, Inc., 1962. Vol. 1, 376 pp.
     On Chang's extensive discussion of Chu Hsi's great contributions
in his editing of and philosophical commentary work on the ancient
Classics, see pp. 243-248 and 251-253.

The Complete Works of Han Fei Tzu. Tr. by W.K. Liao. London:
Probsthain. 2 vols. Vol. 1 (1939): 310 pp. Vol. 2 (1959):
338 pp.
     The chapters on "Commentaries on Lao Tzu's Teaching" and on
"Illustrations of Lao Tzu's Teachings" are the oldest philosophical
commentaries on the Lao Tzu, chiefly from the Legalist point of
view.

16.7 HERMENEUTIC PROBLEMS: E.G., WHICH INTERPRETATIVE VERSION IS
      MORE RELIABLE AND JUSTIFIABLE?

CHAN, WING-TSIT. A Source Book in Chinese Philosophy. (See 16.2.2).
    See chapter 4 and pp. 659-667 for a clear understanding of the
    two hermeneutic approaches to the Great Learning by Chu Hsi the
    Rationalist and Wang Yang-ming the Idealist. The very controversy
    here concerning the original meaning of the Great Learning is not
    simply hermeneutic, but it involves in a deeper sense the basic
    philosophical positions Chu and Wang hold respectively. It is
    probably the most interesting example for the case study of hermen-
    eutic controversies in the history of Chinese philosophy.

FU, CHARLES WEI-HSUN. "Lao Tzu's Conception of Tao," in Inquiry, 16
    (July, 1973): 367-394.
    Note in particular Fu's discussion of Tao as Origin and his judg-
    ment on the two possible hermeneutic versions in the nature of Tao
    as Origin.

FUNG YU-LAN. "Some Characteristics of the Philosophy of Kuo Hsiang,"
    in the Appendix of his Chuang Tzu. A New Selected Translation with
    an Exposition of the Philosophy of Kuo Hsiang. Shanghai: Commercial
    Press, 1933. 164 pp. Reprinted in New York: Paragon.
    Shows Fung's own evaluation of Kuo Hsiang as a commentator on the
    Chuang Tzu and as a philosopher in his own right, as well as his
    clarification of where Kuo's contributed lies in terms of his in-
    terpretation of Chuang Tzu and where Kuo Hsiang's philosophical
    creativity lies beyond his commentary work.

T'ANG, YUNG-T'UNG. "Wang Pi's New Interpretation of the I Ching and
    Lun-yü." Cross reference: 7.19.2.

16.8 HISTORY OF THE FORMATION AND COMPILATION OF AUTHORITATIVE
      TEXTS

See also 14.1, 14.5.7, 16.1, 16.5.

CHAN, WING-TSIT. "Confucian Texts." Cross reference: 16.1.

Author/Title Index

Fu, Charles Wei-hsun (continued)
"The Trans-Onto-Theo-Logical
Foundations of Language in
Heidegger and Taoism"
15.14
"The Underlying Structure of
Metaphysical Language: A Case
Examination of Chinese Philosophy and Whitehead"
15.14
Fung Yu-lan
"Contemporary Chinese
Philosophy"
1.19, 15.12
"Criticism and Self-Criticism"
15.12
A History of Chinese Philosophy
1.2.1, 1.2.2, 1.3.1, 1.3.2,
1.3.3, 1.3.4, 1.3.5, 1.4.1,
1.4.2, 1.4.3, 1.5.1, 1.5.2,
1.6.1, 1.6.3, 1.7, 1.8, 1.9,
1.9.2, 1.9.3, 1.9.4, 1.9.5,
1.10.1, 1.10.8, 1.11.2.2,
1.11.3, 1.11.4, 1.11.5,
1.13.1, 1.13.3, 1.13.4,
1.13.5, 1.13.6, 1.13.7,
1.13.8, 1.13.9, 1.15.3,
1.16.4, 1.17.1, 1.17.2,
2.5.2, 2.5.3, 2.6, 2.9, 2.10,
2.11, 2.12, 2.16, 3.1.1, 3.3,
3.5, 3.6, 3.7, 3.9, 3.12,
3.14, 3.17, 3.20, 3.21, 3.25,
5.4, 5.6, 5.8, 5.9, 5.10.2,
5.11.3, 5.11.4, 6.6, 6.7,
6.10, 6.15, 7.1, 7.2.1, 7.2.2,
7.3, 7.5, 7.6, 7.7.2, 7.7.4,
7.8, 7.9.2, 7.19.2, 10.4,
10.9, 10.11, 10.12, 10.12.1,
10.15, 10.16, 10.17, 11.1,
11.2, 11.3, 12.2, 13.11, 14.1,
14.5.7, 15.2, 15.3, 15.4,
15.5, 15.7, 15.12, 16.2.2,
"I Discovered Marxism-
Leninism"
1.18.5
"The Legacy of Chinese
Philosophy"
1.19, 2.7
"More on Some Problems Relating to Research in the History
of Chinese Philosophy"
15.12

"Philosophy in New China According to Fung Yu-lan"
1.18.5
"Problems in the Study of
Confucius"
15.12
A Short History of Chinese
Philosophy
1.3.1, 1.3.2, 1.3.3, 1.4.1,
1.4.2, 1.4.3, 1.4.4, 1.5.1,
1.5.2, 1.7, 1.8, 1.9.2,
1.10.2, 1.10.3, 1.10.7,
1.10.8, 1.13.7, 1.13.8,
1.15.3, 1.18.5, 6.17, 8.4,
10.14, 14.1, 15.4
"Some Characteristics of the
Philosophy of Kuo Hsiang"
16.7
The Spirit of Chinese Philosophy
1.4.3, 1.4.4, 1.6.3, 1.9,
1.10.8, 3.6, 3.16, 5.9,
14.4.6, 15.1, 15.2, 15.5
"The Struggle between Materialism and Idealism"
1.19, 3.1.1, 3.3, 7.1
"Two Problems in the Study of
the History of Chinese
Philosophy"
1.19

G

Gedalecia, David
"Excursion Into Substance and
Function:..."
1.13.8, 7.9.5
Wu Ch'eng: A Neo-Confucian of
the Yüan
1.14
Gimello, Robert M.
"The Civil Status of Li..."
3.3
Goto, Toshimidzu
"The Ontology of the 'Li'..."
3.4, 7.9.1
Graf, Olaf
Tao und Jen...
1.13.2, 3.2, 7.3
Graham, A.C.
"The Background of the Mencian
Theory of Human Nature"
1.3.2, 2.1, 15.3